PG-DVR-965

PRAISE FOR *THE SEDONA METHOD*

"*The Sedona Method* is a wonderful contribution to the field of self-acceptance and transformation. This is like an accessible, western form of Buddhist teachings that can free our hearts and minds from our self-made limitations and the old stories we tell ourselves."

—Lama Surya Das, author of *Awakening The Buddha Within*
and *Letting Go Of The Person You Used To Be*

"The Sedona Method is an effective tool for getting rid of the 'victim' mentality. Instead of giving away our power to others, Hale Dwoskin encourages us to look inside and take control of our own experiences of life. That's powerful!"

—Susan Jeffers, Ph.D., author of *Feel the Fear and
Do It Anyway* and *Embracing Uncertainty*

"Hale Dwoskin has succeeded in presenting a masterful healing system with a treasure of practical examples for bringing it to life. *The Sedona Method* contains many jewels of illumination that can take your life to the next level. Practicing these principles can bring you home. Here is a rare and useful manual for awakening."

—Alan Cohen, author of *Why Your Life Sucks:
And What You Can Do about It*

"There is no pilgrimage more important than the one we undertake to explore ourselves. *The Sedona Method* is a valuable tool to help make our journey of self-discovery one that leads to powerful personal breakthroughs and new beginnings. Designed with wisdom, simplicity, and compassion, it will offer you ways to live the life you've always dreamed of."

—Barbara De Angelis, Ph.D., author of *Real Moments*
and *What Women Want Men To Know*

"This is a powerful and profound way of achieving immediate and lasting improvements and breakthroughs in your personal and business life. Incredibly effective!"

—Brian Tracy, author of *Deals!*

"*The Sedona Method* is an extremely powerful tool for emotional freedom and wellness."

—Mark Victor Hansen, co-creator of the New York Times
#1 best-selling series *Chicken Soup for the Soul* and
co-author of *The One-Minute Millionaire*

"Just as Kabbalah teaches us the basic spiritual laws of our existence, Hale Dwoskin looks far beyond the mere symptoms of emotional negativity to emotional freedom and mastery. If you want to fundamentally change your life for the better in the shortest possible time, start using the Sedona Method today."

—Yehuda Berg, Author of *The 72 Names of God*

"A breakthrough book in terms of realizing your goals and dreams and living a life that is richer, more meaningful and much more enjoyable. And all without having to work so damn hard at it!"

—Robert Kriegel, Ph.D., New York Times best-selling author of
If It Ain't Broke—Break It! and *How to Succeed in Business
Without Having to Work so Damn Hard*

"*The Sedona Method* is an easy-to-use, practical guide to releasing emotional tension, one of the key steps I recommend in my medical practice for achieving resilience, vitality, and long-term health. This book is a valuable adjunct to every healthcare program."

—Frank Lipman, M.D., author of *Total Renewal*

"The Sedona Method taught us to work from our strengths rather than our fears. After learning to release, we have become best-selling authors, lecturers, and spiritual counselors. These were things we could only dream about until the Sedona Method taught us to let go of the blocks we had erected to keep us from our 'greatness.' Releasing moved us along our spiritual path faster than any other work we have done. We were fumbling around and the Sedona Method opened the doors to our spiritual work. We believe with all our hearts that if you learn to release ANYTHING is possible."

—Barbara Mark, and Trudy Griswold, co-authors of *The Angelspeake
Trilogy* and *Heaven and Beyond: Conversations with Souls in Transition*

"As an author, international speaker, and widow of Earl Nightingale, I have given many years to the pursuit of a method that I might teach, which would enable others to 'let go' and live their lives without limitations. While the timeless truth that we become what we think about has revolutionized the lives of millions of people around the world, the majority of people find that old habits die hard. Changing a lifetime of restrictive thinking, more often than not, requires something more. Recently, I discovered a tried-and-true method that can and will work for everyone: the Sedona Method. Now, you can discover it, too!"

—Diana Nightingale, owner, Keys Publishing, international speaker,
and author of *Learning to Fly as a Nightingale*

THE
SEDONA
METHOD®

Your Key to Lasting
Happiness, Success, Peace
and Emotional Well-being

By HALE DWOSKIN

Printed in the U.S.A. by Malloy Inc. on acid free 85% recycled paper.

Publisher:

Sedona Press

2000 Plymouth Road

Minnetonka, MN 55305-2335

Phone: (928) 282-3522

Fax: (928) 203-0602

E-mail: info@sedona.com

Web: www.sedona.com

Cover design and interior book design by Lightbourne, Inc. © 2010

SECOND EDITION

Library of Congress Control Number: 2003102949

ISBN-13: 978-0-9719334-1-5

ISBN-10: 0-9719334-1-3

10 9 8 7 6 5

Dedicated to Lester Levenson

Contents

Acknowledgments

This book could not have been published without the assistance and encouragement of many individuals to whom I would like to extend my most sincere gratitude.

First and foremost, many thanks to my wife Amy for all her love and support.

I offer my deep appreciation to Jack Canfield for his friendship and generosity.

My thanks to Stephanie Gunning, my brilliant editor, for her integrity, skill, intelligence, and humor.

Thanks to the book designers, Shannon Bodie and Bob Swingle at Lightbourne, LLC, for their creativity, diligence and professionalism.

I would like to thank our staff for their dedication and hard work.

Heartfelt thanks to the numerous people who so kindly and willingly shared their personal stories so that readers could glimpse what is possible from the Sedona Method.

Finally, to all Sedona Method graduates everywhere for their courageousness of spirit in using this glorious technique and sharing it with the world: Thank you!

Foreword
By Jack Canfield

I have been hearing wonderful things about the Sedona Method® from clients and friends for about 20 years. Recently, I finally took the course with my wife and my 12-year-old son. I've been amazed at the simplicity of the Method and the powerful impact it has had on my life. Through my work with *Chicken Soup for the Soul* and through my Self-Esteem Seminars, I have been exposed to many self-improvement techniques and processes. This one stands head and shoulders above the rest for the ease of its use, its profound impact, and the speed with which it produces results. The Sedona Method is a vastly accelerated way of letting go of feelings like anger, frustration, jealousy, anxiety, stress, and fear, as well as many other problems—even physical pain—with which almost everybody struggles at one time or another.

One of the wonderful byproducts of taking the seminar is that I have become friends with Hale Dwoskin. He is one of the calmest, clearest, most joy-filled people I have ever met, living proof that the Sedona Method works wonders. I am ecstatic about our friendship. During the seminar, I found myself constantly in awe of Hale's brilliant teaching style. I experienced one breakthrough after another. As a result, I've already referred many family members, friends, and business associates to the Sedona Method seminars, and I've also had the entire staff at Chicken Soup for the Soul Enterprises learn the Method through the audio programs that Hale put together.

Now I am thoroughly delighted to be able to recommend *The Sedona Method: Your Key to Lasting Happiness, Success, Peace and Well-being*. Reading this book is the equivalent of taking the Sedona Method Basic Course and several Advanced Courses rolled together. Filled with practical techniques and enlightening true stories, Hale clearly and generously explains everything we need to know to master the releasing process and to continue using the Method day by day, moment by moment in real life situations, such as having more fulfilling and harmonious relationships, building financial security, developing satisfying careers, breaking nasty habits, losing weight, and enjoying good health. He reveals the Sedona Method's powerful secret for manifesting what you want in your life, while showing you how to be at ease and comfortable with what you already have. The Method also enables you to have greater ease, enjoyment, and peace of mind with all that you experience on a daily basis.

So I highly encourage you to read *The Sedona Method* with an open mind and heart. Please allow the simplicity of its message and the power of this process to open you to all the wonders that life has to offer. It is one of those rare things in today's world that delivers more than it promises . . . way more. I urge you to pay close attention to Hale's message in this book. If you do, it will change your life.

THE
SEDONA
METHOD®

Author's Note

The stories in this book are true. However, in an effort to safe-guard the privacy of certain individuals who have been Sedona Method students or whose lives have touched mine, some of the names and identifying details of the people mentioned in this book have been changed.

Introduction

What Is the Sedona Method?

You feel like your heart is warm and open, your spine is pleasantly tingling, and your body is floating on air. As you look around the room, the colors seem brighter and the sounds clearer, like you are truly experiencing your surroundings for the first time. Your mind feels profoundly quieter, yet there are many new and wonderful possibilities floating into your awareness about how you can improve your life and live happily now. You feel relaxed and at ease, knowing that all is well and everything is unfolding as it should be.

Your eyes are a little teary, because it is hard for you to believe that such simple exercises could make such a profound and immediate difference in how you feel. You are excited about the future, knowing that you can face whatever happens with a new feeling of inner strength, ease, and confidence, no matter what curves life throws your way.

Best of all, you know this is just the beginning.

You can easily have this type of experience for yourself, just like the tens of thousands of others who have been living and using the simple, yet powerful techniques that Sedona Training Associates have taught for years in our live seminars and audio programs. Now these techniques are available to you in this book!

Are you open to being truly happy? Are you willing to achieve everything that you have been wanting in your life? Are you ready to find what your heart has always been seeking? If you answered "no" to all three of these questions, then please don't bother reading this book. If you answered "yes," to any of them, *The Sedona Method* will show you a practical way to tap an inner source of boundless happiness, to achieve your wildest dreams and highest potential, and to become a spiritual "finder" instead of a seeker.

We live in a world that's in a state of rapid change—and not all of it is positive. Most of us crave a certainty, security, and solidity that we cannot find outside of ourselves no matter how hard we try. But these qualities already exist within each of us, waiting to be revealed. It is as though we possess an inner wishing well or a fountain of joy and vitality that's disconnected from the water supply. Yet, secretly, everyone has a tool to reconnect.

Intrigued? I hope so. Because I would love to share a simple process with you that can deliver on this promise: the Sedona Method. The technique has already helped many thousands of people to tap their natural ability to let go of uncomfortable or unwanted emotions on the spot. It is our limiting emotions that prevent us from creating and maintaining the lives that we choose. We abdicate our decision-making ability to them. We even imagine that our emotions can dictate to us who we are supposed to be. This is made apparent in our use of language. Have you ever said to someone, "I am angry," or, "I am sad"? When we speak like this, we are saying to those around us and to ourselves, without realizing it, that we *are* our anger, or we *are* our grief. We relate to others and ourselves as though we are our feelings. In fact, we even invent whole stories of why we feel the way we feel in order to justify or explain this misperception of our identity.

It is not that feelings don't occasionally appear to be justified. It's just that feelings are only feelings, feelings are not who we are—and we can easily let them go. Choosing to let them go frees us to perceive what is actually here, and to act, or refrain from acting, accordingly. This translates into an ability to handle life—to make stronger, clearer choices. It allows you and me to act in ways that support us in achieving our goals and aspirations as opposed to sabotaging them. I have seen the process of letting go of the emotions grow into an ability to have more money, better relationships, more radiant health and physical well-being, and an ability to be happy, calm, and focused, no matter what is going on around us.

Sounds good, doesn't it? I thought it did back in 1976 when I met Lester Levenson, the man who inspired the creation of the Sedona Method and would also become my mentor. Back then, I was an ardent, although confused, seeker who had gone to numerous seminars led by teachers from both the East and the West. I had studied various body-centered disciplines, including yoga, tai chi, and shiatsu. I had actively participated in numerous personal growth courses, including EST, Actualism, Theta Seminars, and Rebirthing. At these seminars, I had many nice experiences and heard and understood—at least intellectually—many useful concepts. Still, I felt incomplete. I longed for a simple and powerful answer to some important yet vexing questions like: "What is my life's purpose?" "What is truth?" "Who am I?" and "How can I feel at home and at peace with my life?" Much of what I heard and experienced only added to my questioning. No one seemed to have truly satisfying answers or to have truly satisfied themselves about their true nature. There was also a strong, almost universal belief that growing was hard work that required baring your soul and reliving painful, unresolved issues. That all changed during my very fortunate encounter with this remarkable man.

Meeting Lester Levenson

I met Lester at a seminar led by a well-known speaker that Lester was attending as the leader's guest. That day, a group of us went out to lunch together. Lester's presence immediately struck me as unique. He was in total peace and equal-mindedness, very comfortable with himself. He was unassuming and easy to talk to and treated everyone as his friend—even me, a complete stranger. It was obvious that he'd ended his search by discovering the answers I'd been seeking. I knew I had to find out more.

When I asked Lester what he did, he invited me to a seminar that was being held the next weekend. All he would tell me was that "a group of people is going to sit around a table and release." I wasn't sure what *releasing* meant, but I knew if it could even point me in the direction of the qualities of which Lester was the living embodiment, I definitely wanted it. I took a leap of faith and signed up on the spot.

That weekend I was in essentially the same position you're in right now. I was about to embark on a journey for which I felt a little bit of trepidation. I wasn't sure exactly with what I was getting involved, and, since I had done so many seminars, I also had a healthy degree of skepticism. I found myself wondering, "Oh my God, is this going to be another one of those disappointments along the way?" As the course unfolded, however, I watched myself and other people in the class shedding long-held beliefs and limitations with amazing ease and speed, yet without having to relive or explain their life stories.

Almost overnight, I knew that I'd found what I was looking for. In fact, deep inside, I knew that this process of releasing was what I had been born to do and share with the world—and to this day I have never wavered. In the past 26 years, I've watched thousands of other people change their lives, radically yet gently, for the better just by learning one elegantly simple, yet powerful technique.

Origins of the Sedona Method

As my friendship with Lester developed, I discovered more about him that confirmed my initial impressions. He was a man who had mastered life's greatest challenge. In 1952, at age 42, Lester, a physicist and successful entrepreneur, was at the pinnacle of worldly success, yet he was an unhappy, very unhealthy man. He had many health problems, including depression, an enlarged liver, kidney stones, spleen trouble, hyperacidity, and ulcers that had perforated his stomach and formed lesions. He was so unhealthy, in fact, that after having his second coronary, his doctors sent him home to his Central Park South penthouse apartment in New York City to die.

Lester was a man who loved challenges. So, instead of giving up, he decided to go back to the lab within himself and find some answers. Because of his determination and concentration, he was able to cut through his conscious mind to find what he needed. What he found was the ultimate tool for personal growth—a way of letting go of all inner limitations. He was so excited by his discovery that he used it intensively for a period of three months. By the end of that period, his body became totally healthy again. Furthermore, he entered a state of profound peace that never left him through the day he died on January 18, 1994.

What Lester discovered firsthand is that we are all unlimited beings, limited only by the concepts of limitation that we hold in our minds. These concepts of limitation are not true; furthermore, because they're not really true, they can easily be released or discharged. Lester's experience made him understand that not only could he practice this technique himself, he could teach others how to do it as well. As a result, he began working with people, both in small groups and individually.

Lester believed strongly that personal growth was not dependent on any external source, including a teacher, and he did not want to be anyone's guru. But, because of how elevated people felt around him, despite his protestations and attempts to avoid it happening, many of Lester's students insisted on seeing him as a guru. So, in 1973, Lester realized that his teachings needed to be formalized into a system that he could allow others to teach—leaving him out of the equation. A way to transform his powerful techniques for personal growth into a do-it-yourself system was devised, which is now called the Sedona Method: the topic of this book.

How Releasing Has Influenced My Life

From the beginning, my relationship with Lester felt like being with a good friend. I was immediately so drawn by him and his teaching that I rapidly took all three of the courses he offered: the Basic Course in November, the Advanced Course in January, and the Instructors Training in February. I was in a rush to learn everything I could. I also started working with Lester on sharing his teachings with the world.

Working with Lester afforded me the opportunity to spend more time with him, observe him in action, and see how he dealt with life's inevitable challenges. I was very impressed. One of the ways we related was by sitting in coffee shops and speaking at length. He consistently enjoyed sitting and chatting over a cup of coffee, right up until shortly before his death. He frequently stated, "My office is my brief case, and the nearest place to get a good cup of coffee." Our meetings were always a little comical, and sometimes frustrating to me, because I always thought it was important to discuss the truth, whereas Lester would invariably steer the conversation to as mundane a topic as possible. Nonetheless, every time we were together, my understanding and direct experience of truth would deepen—even if we never spoke about it. He was a living example rather than a pontificator. This helped me discover the opportunity to release and experience greater freedom in every moment, a practice that stays with me to this day.

I was so engaged that I even started holding support groups for people using the Sedona Method in the living room of my Upper West Side apartment. But it wasn't long before I realized that I needed to mature and grow personally before I could be of much use to Lester and his budding organization.

I decided to support him as a volunteer and active participant instead of as an employee while continuing to explore in different ways how releasing would affect my everyday life.

Soon after that, I started my own business selling jewelry. The success of this venture afforded me the opportunity to work part-time while exploring life and my releasing full-time. I continued this venture and my more casual involvement with Lester until around 1981. As I worked with the Method in my business and personal life, I became ever more convinced that I'd found a technique that could help anyone. In the late '70's Lester moved out to Arizona. Except through his teachings, my contact with Lester during this period was occasional, but it continued to influence me profoundly.

Then, in 1981, I was invited to fly to Phoenix to participate again in an Instructors Training. This seminar began a new phase of our relationship. It also rekindled my desire to work closely with Lester on sharing the Method with the world. I started leading workshops for Sedona Method graduates on a regular basis in New York City and flew to Arizona several times a year for more training and to participate in weeklong or longer retreats called Intensives. Leading the workshops and participating in the Trainings and Intensives greatly accelerated my personal use of the Method. I noticed profound results in myself and in friends who were also participating.

During this same period, I decided to participate more actively, full-time, in the world of business. I briefly worked for my father selling industrial real estate in and around New York City, but I didn't feel the job suited me. Then I joined a firm in Manhattan that sold co-ops and condominiums. I was quickly able to use the Method to support my sales ability and became one of their top salespeople. For a while I enjoyed doing this, but then an opportunity presented itself to join my brother in establishing an investment division back in my father's real estate firm. I happily made the transition to selling office buildings, shopping centers, and other real estate investments.

For the first time in our lives, my brother and I became friends. I was able to release the old baggage that I had been carrying around about our earlier relationship, and we became a terrific business team. We were having a recurring problem, however, of starting many more deals than we were actually closing. Then, one day out of the blue, Lester called me up to see how I was doing. I explained what was happening. He said one sentence that totally turned around our closing ratio and the rest of my business career. He simply said, "Bank in the bank, not in your head." Without me saying anything about it, he had picked up on a tendency that I and most other people in the sales profession have, which is "head banking." I was so busy imagining how great it was going to be when I closed each deal that I was neglecting actually closing them. As soon as I started releasing instead of fantasizing, we started to close a lot more deals.

Another important lesson about letting go was learned when I received a listing for nine shopping centers from what was affectionately known in the industry then as a Xerox broker. A Xerox broker is someone who gets written listings on properties from other brokers, then copies and sends them to other brokers and principals without ever bothering to check the facts or get in contact with the actual owner or listing agent.

I sent a copy of the listing to one of my better customers, and he shot me back an immediate, almost full-priced offer. Of course I was excited, so I picked up the phone to call the man I thought was the principal, only to discover that the listing had come from a Xerox broker with no way of contacting the true owner.

Distraught, I realized that there was nothing I could do but let go. So I did. I cleared my mind and released all my feelings about the situation until I reached the point where it was okay whether or not I ever made the deal. The very next phone call in our office was from the actual principal of the shopping centers, responding to an ad looking for properties that we just happened to have running in the *Wall Street Journal*. When he offered us the listing on the very same property, I nearly fell over.

This is only one of many events that have led me to understand that a statement I'd heard repeatedly from Lester is absolutely true: "Even the impossible becomes completely possible when you are fully released on it."

I also got to practice using the Method right while closing deals, sometimes when people were renegotiating multi-million dollar contracts and trying to cheat me or each other by making up a whole new story of what we'd agreed on, instead of simply signing the papers and exchanging checks. These were tense occasions, as a lot of money was at stake. Nonetheless, because I was releasing, I knew when to be quiet—which is very difficult for a broker. I also knew when to stand up for what was correct. The financial rewards were beyond my expectations.

By early 1987, I'd saved enough money to move to Arizona to rejoin Lester and support him in sharing his wonderful technique with the world. Much to the consternation of my brother and father, I relocated to Phoenix and became a full-time volunteer for his non-profit organization, the Sedona Institute, doing whatever was needed to get the word out. I spent most of the remaining years of Lester's life working closely with him on his mission, almost entirely without monetary compensation. The reason I didn't mind working for free was that I could see how much good I was doing, and how much I was personally changing for the better.

In 1989, Lester asked me to move to Sedona to help him sell some of the organization's real estate holdings to graduates in order to raise money. It was there that I met my wife Amy. I saw her in a karate class and immediately recognized who she was to me, so the next day I asked her out. She was dating another man at the time, however, and asked for my card in case her situation changed. A few months later, I got a call from her and we went out on a date. That was a Wednesday. By that Saturday she was taking the Sedona Method Course.

Today, Amy and I have a beautiful, loving relationship, but it wasn't always that way. It was tough in the beginning. Honestly, Amy was interested in other men at the time we met, so I had to do a lot of releasing for her finally to pick me. Once we married, we still had our disagreements—which of course still happens, that's only natural. But because we both use the Sedona Method, when something happens that causes an upset, we let it go. From my perspective, our relationship is very unusual in that it just keeps getting better and more loving.

By the early '90's, my relationship with Lester had grown to a place of such mutual trust and respect that he decided to turn over the copyrights of his teachings to me and asked me to continue his work. I maintained the organization that he'd established toward this end until two years after his death. Then, in

1996, I decided it would be much more effective for Amy and me to start a new company, Sedona Training Associates, to convey the Method to the world in an even bigger way.

One of the things that impresses me most about the process of releasing is that it has resulted in a sense of unshakable peace, happiness, joy, and calmness that is always with me, no matter what's going on around me. Not that there still aren't ups and downs, but, as Lester used to say, this is really the "bottoms-up method." I know from my own direct experience that what I used to think was a peak experience, or something really terrific, is now normal, and my peaks just keeping getting higher and higher. I have no idea how far "up" is, and I'm looking forward to finding out.

The good news is that the good I have experienced using the Method isn't unique. People around the world have been able to produce the same kind of phenomenal results in their lives. Years ago, a study of the effectiveness of the Sedona Method was done with an insurance company called Mutual of New York. A group of field underwriters were trained in the Method, and their sales results were compared with as close a control group as possible over six months. Over the study period, the group that learned the Method outperformed the control group by 33 percent. The study was also broken down into two three-month segments, and the results in the second three months were better than the first three months. The Method's efficacy increased over time.

How to Use this Book

In this book, you'll be learning the Sedona Method, a technique that you can use every day for the rest of your life. As you begin letting go of all the emotional baggage that has been getting in the way of you doing what you already know you should be doing, and want to be doing, you'll find yourself becoming increasingly successful at everything you do. This book will not give you a whole new list of "shoulds" and "shouldn'ts," or new behaviors you "must" try to implement in your life. We are already "shoulding" on ourselves enough. Instead, you'll be learning how to change yourself from the inside out. When you change yourself from the inside out, the changes are permanent.

In addition, as you experiment with this simple system in your life, you'll keep discovering more ways that you can apply it. Whatever initial insights you gain from reading this book and working with the Method are only the tip of the iceberg. This single technique can affect every part of your life, because it is built on the fact that we are *already* unlimited beings. If you think back over your life, you've probably had glimpses of this unlimited state, which is natural to us all. You've probably also had glimpses or periods where you felt like you were in a state of flow, moments in which everything seemed to "click" and work effortlessly. Through using the Sedona Method, it is possible for you to experience the flow as part of your everyday life from now on.

I don't know what kind of a reader you are. You may be the type who participates fully in what you read, or you may just collect useful ideas that you can call on later as you choose. I recommend you participate fully and do all the exercises presented in this book. In my experience, the only way that you can effectively learn how to let go is by doing it yourself. Direct experience. Additional benefits will be gained from reading this book repeatedly, as that's how you'll learn and integrate the practical skill of tapping your natural ability to let go of limitation.

This book is divided into two parts. In Part One, we'll explore the basics of the letting go process and the underlying motivations for inner limitation. You'll be introduced to various techniques that can accelerate you on the path to freedom, such as ways for coping with resistance, being "present," resolving your feelings about past conflicts, achieving your goals, and balancing the positive and negative sides of emotional equations. In Part Two, we'll explore some of the specific areas of your life where the Sedona Method can have a strong, positive impact. These include finding freedom from guilt, shame, fear, and anxiety; breaking habits; building wealth; operating a business; improving relationships; developing radiant health; and contributing to the creation of a harmonious and peaceful world.

Please work with the material in order. Each chapter builds a solid foundation for the ones that follow. You will not have learned all that you can from this book until you've worked with the chapters in order and done your best to apply what you're learning in your daily life. Each chapter contains at least a few gems that can enrich your life. Allow yourself to be as open as you can to what is being communicated in this book and look at it as an opportunity to change your consciousness and your life.

If you want to go still further after you complete this book, Sedona Training Associates offers an audiotape version of this course, as well as live seminars in many major cities throughout the United States and the rest of the world.

Don't Believe Anything I Say

Please don't believe anything in this book unless you can prove it for yourself. Just because something is said in writing does not make it so. Especially with authorities of any kind, there is a tendency simply to accept what is said on hearsay or belief. Lester strongly believed that we should avoid doing this with our teachers. Instead, we should allow ourselves to stay open to a teacher's message as an experiment in growing. We should only accept what he or she teaches once we can verify it through our own direct experience. He called this "taking it for checking."

I suggest that you take for checking everything you're exposed to in this book. Give yourself permission to be as open to the message as you can be without accepting it on blind faith. The material will have much more value for you once you've explored and applied it, or checked it, under real life conditions.

The ideas in *The Sedona Method* may appear to contradict what you've learned from other methods and modalities. But there's no need to throw out the other material that you've learned. Merely set it aside, as best you can, while you explore this book. I highly recommend that you suspend comparison and judgment, if only for the moment. Once you've had time to draw your own conclusions, you can then go back and compare this material to everything else you've learned and see where it fits. People usually find releasing a wonderful adjunct to the other techniques and therapies they already use.

Contradiction is inevitable when you compare different paths or traditions of growth. This does not necessarily invalidate the different points of view. When it comes to self-discovery, if you can embrace multiple possibilities, you'll find yourself understanding and applying the insights you gain on a deeper, more heartfelt, and much more useful level. There are many rays that lead to the one sun.

It's a Matter of Resonance

From my perspective, everything in the world has its own vibration, or resonance, including you and everyone you meet. Have you ever noticed that some people tend to pull you up when you're with them while others seem to pull you down, and that they often don't need to say or do anything to have this effect on you? As we let go and grow in understanding, our resonance, or frequency, tends to go up. But it's not just a matter of "higher" or "lower." We all relate better to some people than others, even if they're on the same level of vibration as us. Of course, the same thing is true for teachers and ideas.

As you read *The Sedona Method*, you may find that you resonate intensely with certain chapters while others leave you feeling a little confused or unmoved. Sections of this book will have more value to you on different occasions. Over time, as you work with releasing, other sections will stand out more than they did initially. That is because you'll have changed and become ready to see things from a new perspective. When this happens, allow yourself to honor the change and shift your focus accordingly.

Adopt a Gentle, Playful Attitude

Above all, nurture yourself as you engage in the processes in this book. Be your best friend and supporter, rather than a drill sergeant or taskmaster. Transform yourself through the experience of joy. Soon you'll be making many interesting and inspiring discoveries about ways that you've been limiting yourself. Then, as these limitations drop away one by one, you'll be lighter, happier, more relaxed, and at ease.

The Sedona Method reminds us of what our spirits already recognize intuitively. We can have freedom and happiness now. We don't have to wait for it to arrive some far off day in the future when we've worked hard enough to deserve it, or when we've succeeded somehow in making ourselves ready. We have reason for joy, and to delight, now!

THE
SEDONA
METHOD
COURSE

Part One covers most of the material that's usually covered in both the live and audio versions of the Sedona Method Basic Course. It also covers material from the Advanced Courses, and some altogether new material, so that you can take all these tools, turn your life around, and keep it on track from here on. Although these techniques are extremely simple—as you'll soon discover—they are also much more powerful than you can probably imagine at this stage. As you continue to apply these techniques and principles in your life, however, their ease and power will grow on you exponentially.

Over a quarter of a century after first learning these processes myself, I am still seeing them each day through newly-amazed eyes. When I watch how easily people can make positive changes in their lives, I am always filled with wonder and gratitude at being given the chance to share this elegantly powerful process with the world.

Chapter 1

Beyond the Suppression-Expression Cycle

The rapid and positive changes that took place in Joe's life as soon as he began using the Sedona Method are an ideal model of what can happen for us all. Persistent difficulties clear up, exciting new possibilities emerge, and serendipity smoothes the flow of events. When Joe learned the Method, he was at a low point both personally and professionally. A year and half earlier, he'd been in a plane crash that had left him wheelchair bound for seven months, his company was forcing him out of his job, and his estranged wife and he had been tied up in legal knots for three years hammering out their divorce agreement. Within a few weeks, everything turned around 180 degrees. First, Joe's ex-wife agreed to go to mediation where they reached an amicable settlement. Then, he happened to run into the chairman of the company he was suing for wrongful termination at a charity ball. The chairman hadn't known about Joe's severance until then, and the next Monday Joe's lawyer called with news of a favorable settlement that was more than the original offer.

Even better, Joe decided to take a long weekend trip to a warm island paradise to celebrate his good fortune. Sitting and reading a book on the beach in Nassau, he pursued an idle conversation with a woman who turned out to be the love of his life. He wasn't looking for a date because he had to catch the plane home in a couple of hours. But Jean seemed familiar, and after she told him that she also lived in Toronto, he asked, "Look, this isn't a line, but do you live at such and such a corner?"

"Yes, I do," she answered.

"That's funny," said Joe. "I go to physiotherapy there. I must have seen you on the subway. Do you also go to the theater downtown?"

"Yes, once or twice a week," Jean replied.

"I work in downtown Toronto," Joe then mentioned, "in Scotia Plaza on the 53rd floor."

"That's strange . . . I work on the 30th floor!"

An hour went by. When Joe got up to leave, they traded phone numbers, and he didn't give her another thought for a couple of weeks until that same slip of paper fell out of his notebook and reminded him. When he called, they connected amazingly well. They soon fell in love, and Joe asked Jean to marry him.

The more Joe applied the Sedona Method, the faster his career as an executive in the investment banking industry took off, and the higher it flew. His income grew at an exponential rate. In terms of wealth and money, the Method has been absolutely incredible for him. In addition, Joe continued using the Method to let go of his worries about his physical condition. In the plane crash, he was crippled from breaking 32 bones, including bones in his left leg, his right kneecap, his hand, and his skull. Although his doctors told him he would never walk well again, today he walks perfectly with virtually no pain. Joe uses the same Sedona Method techniques that you'll be learning in this book—morning and night and all through the day. As a result, he is happy and successful, life is fun, and he is peacefully flowing from event to event. In his words: "I feel blessed. The Sedona Method turns big issues into small issues."

Life as We Know It

Harmony and unqualified happiness are natural to each and every one of us, yet here's how a typical workday looks and feels for too many people. We wake up, drag ourselves out of bed, and, even before we get to the bathroom, we begin worrying or planning what will happen during the day ahead. We are already spending what little energy we have stored up from our night's sleep—if we were lucky enough to have had one. Many of us then commute to our jobs, which puts additional stress on us due to traffic, or mass transit crowds, or just the frustration of "wasted" time. Once we arrive, we're not excited to be there and we are dreading the things we must get done. As we push ourselves through the day, we look ahead to lunch or the end of business. We have various interactions with coworkers—some satisfactory, many not. Since we believe there is nothing much we can do about anything that happens or how we feel about it, usually we simply stuff down our emotions and barrel on forward.

By the time we're done for the day, we're exhausted from bottling up our feelings. Maybe we drag ourselves to the local bar to hang out with some friends and eat, drink, and watch the news on TV—which adds its own layer of stress—hoping our feelings will just disappear. Even though we may feel a little better afterwards, in truth, the feelings have only gone underground. We are now like human pressure cookers with plugged stopcocks, and it takes us tremendous energy to keep the lid on. When we finally get home to our husbands or wives and children, and they want to talk about their days with us, we have no energy left to listen. We might try to put on a happy face only to lose our tempers over the smallest things. The family eventually zones out in front of the TV until it is time to go to bed. And the next morning we get up and start the whole scenario over again.

Kind of bleak, isn't it? But isn't it also kind of familiar?

Your story may be a little different; hopefully it's brighter than this picture. Perhaps you're a stay-at-home parent with young kids. Maybe you're an independent contractor and handle most of your daily affairs over the telephone and/or internet. Perhaps you're an artist. Still, the trend is probably quite similar. The ruts that we tend to find ourselves in seem to get deeper over time, until we can feel like there is no way out.

Well, it doesn't have to be that way. There is a way out.

Letting Go

One of the main ways that we ourselves create disappointments, unhappiness, and misjudgments is by holding on to limiting thoughts and feelings. It is not that "holding on," in and of itself, is inappropriate. Holding on is perfectly appropriate in many situations. I wouldn't suggest, for instance, that you *not* hold on to the steering wheel of a car that you were driving, or *not* hold on to a ladder that you were climbing.

Obviously, the results of such choices could be unfortunate. But have you ever held on to a point of view even when it didn't serve you? Have you ever held on to an emotion even though there was nothing you could do to satisfy it, make it right, or change the situation that appeared to cause it? Have you ever held on to tension or anxiety even after the initial event that triggered it was long over? This is the form of holding on that we will explore throughout this book.

What is the opposite of holding on? Well, "letting go," of course. Both letting go and holding on are part of the natural process of life. This fundamental understanding is the basis of the Sedona Method. No matter who you are, if you're reading these words, I can guarantee that you've already frequently experienced letting go, often without being aware that it was happening—and even without being taught the Method. Letting go, or *releasing*, is a natural ability that we're all born with, but which we get conditioned against using as we mature into adulthood. Where so many of us frequently get stuck is that we don't know when it is appropriate to let go and when it is appropriate to hold on. And most of us err on the side of holding on—often to our detriment.

There are a few synonyms for holding on and letting go that will probably make this point much clearer: closing and opening, for example. When you are throwing a ball, you need to hold your hand closed around the ball through much of your arm motion. But if you don't open your hand and release the ball at the appropriate time, the ball will not go where you want it to. You could even get hurt. Other synonyms are contraction and expansion. In order for us to breathe, we contract our lungs to force the used air out, and then we expand them, filling them with air. We can't only inhale; to complete the breathing process we must also exhale. Tensing and relaxing our muscles is another example. If we could not do both, our muscles literally would not function properly, as most muscles work in pairs of opposing partners.

It is interesting to note the emotional component of holding on and releasing, and the degree to which our bodies are impacted by our feelings. Have you noticed that, when people are upset, they often hold their breath? In the process of breathing, both inhalation and exhalation can be inhibited by holding on to unresolved emotions. Most of us also hold residual tension in our muscles, which never allows us to relax fully. Again, it's the unresolved or suppressed emotions that are the basis for these forms of constriction.

But why do we get stuck? When we suppress our emotions, rather than allowing ourselves to experience our feelings fully in the moment they arise, they linger and make us uncomfortable. Through avoidance, we are preventing our emotions from flowing through us, either transforming or dissolving, and it doesn't feel good.

"One of my big gains so far is my experience of not having to involve myself in so much unnecessary 'thinking' about certain destructive emotions. I can release them. The energy previously spent on anger, fear, and envy can be used very well in my already demanding projects as a professional, and for my family."

Suppression and Expression

Have you ever watched a very young child fall down and then look around to see if there is any reason to be upset? When children think no one is watching them, in an instant they just let go, brush themselves off, and act like nothing has happened. The same child in a similar situation, on seeing the opportunity to get attention, may burst into tears and run to the arms of a parent. Or have you ever watched a young child get furious with a playmate or a parent, and even say something like, "I hate you and will never speak to you again," and then, just a few minutes later, the child feels and acts as though nothing at all has happened?

This natural ability to release our emotions was lost to most of us because, even though we did it automatically as young children, without conscious control, our parents, teachers, friends, and society as a whole trained us out of it as we got older. In fact, it is because we were unconscious of our ability to release that it was possible to train us to hold on. Every time we were told "no," told to behave, to sit still and be quiet, to stop squirming, that "big boys don't cry" or "big girls don't get angry," and to grow up and be responsible, we learned to suppress our emotions. Furthermore, we were often seen as an adult when we got to the point where we were good at suppressing our natural exuberance for life and all the feelings that others convinced us to believe were unacceptable. We became more responsible to others' expectations of us than to the needs of our own emotional well-being.

There is a joke that aptly illustrates this point: for the first two years of a child's life, everyone around them is trying to get them to walk and talk, and for the next eighteen years everyone's trying to get them to sit down and shut up.

By the way, there is nothing wrong with disciplining children. Children need to learn boundaries in order to function in life, and they need to be protected at times from obvious danger. It is just that adults can unintentionally go overboard.

What we are referring to here as "suppression" is keeping a lid on our emotions, pushing them back down, denying them, repressing them, and pretending they don't exist. Any emotion that comes into awareness that is not let go of is automatically stored in a part of our mind called the subconscious. A big part of how we suppress our emotions is by escaping them. We take our attention off them long enough so we can push them back down. You have probably heard the expression "Time heals all wounds." It's debatable. For most of us, what that really means is, "Give me enough time, and I can suppress anything."

Granted, there are some times when suppression can be a better choice than expression—for instance, when you are at work, and your boss or a coworker says something that you don't agree with, but it is not the appropriate time to give them feedback. It is habitual suppression that is unhealthy and unproductive.

We escape our emotions by watching television, going to movies, reading books, drinking, using prescription and non-prescription drugs, exercising, and a whole host of other activities designed to help us take our attention off our emotional pain long enough so we can push it back down. I'm sure you would agree that most of the items on this list are not inappropriate in and of themselves. It is just that we tend to pursue these activities or use these substances to excess, and we lose control. We use them as a compensation for our inability to deal with our inner emotional conflicts. Excessive escape is so prevalent in our culture that it has spawned many thriving industries.

By the time we are labeled adults, we are so good at suppressing that most of the time it is totally second nature. We become as good or better at suppressing as we originally were at letting go. In fact, we have suppressed so much of our emotional energy that we are all a little like walking time bombs. Often, we don't even know that we have suppressed our true emotional reactions until it is too late: our body shows signs of stress-related illnesses, our shoulders are stuck in our ears, our stomach is in knots, or we have exploded and said or done something that we now regret.

Suppression is one side of the pendulum swing of what we are usually doing with our emotions. The other side of the pendulum swing is expression. If we are angry, we yell; if we are sad, we cry. We put our emotion into action. We have let off a little steam from the inner emotional pressure cooker, but we have not put out the fire. This often feels better than suppression, particularly if we have blocked our ability to express. We often feel better afterwards; nonetheless, expression also has its drawbacks.

Good therapy is generally based on helping us get in touch with and express our emotions. And healthy, lasting relationships certainly could not survive without us clearly expressing how we feel. But what about when we express ourselves inappropriately outside of a therapeutic situation? What about the feelings of the person to whom we have just expressed? Inappropriate expression can often lead to greater disagreement and conflict and a mutual escalation of emotion that can get out of control.

Neither suppression nor expression is a problem in and of itself. They are merely two different ends of the same spectrum of how we usually handle our emotions. A problem arises when we don't feel in control over which one is happening, and many times we find ourselves doing the opposite of what we intended. Very often we get stuck on one side of the spectrum or the other. These are the moments when we need to find the freedom to let go.

The Third Alternative: Releasing

The balancing point and natural alternative to inappropriate suppression and expression is releasing, or letting go—what we call the Sedona Method. It is the equivalent of turning down the heat and safely beginning to empty the contents of your inner pressure cooker. Because every feeling that has been suppressed is trying to vent itself, releasing is merely a momentary stopping of the inner action of holding these feelings in so you can allow them to leave, which you will find they do easily under their own steam. As you use the Sedona Method, you will discover that you will be able to be free to both suppress and express when it is appropriate, and you will find that you will more often opt for the point of balance, the third choice of *letting go*. This is something you already know how to do.

Though you have probably become an expert at suppression and/or expression, even so, you are still letting go. True laughter, for instance, is one of the ways that you let go spontaneously, and the benefits of laughter in the area of health and stress elimination are well documented. Think of the last time you had a really good belly laugh. You may have been watching a funny program on TV or having a conversation with a friend and, all of a sudden, something struck you as funny. You felt a tickle inside, heard a guffaw come up from deep in your middle, and your whole body started to bounce up and down. As you laughed, you probably felt lighter and lighter inside and progressively happier and more relaxed, almost warm and euphoric. This is also a good description of what you may experience at times as you use the process described in this book. Although most of the time you won't laugh out loud as you let go, you will often smile and feel the same sense of inner relief that comes from true laughter.

Have you ever lost your keys or your glasses and turned the whole house upside down only to find them in your pocket? Think back to the last time that happened. You probably felt more and more tense as you turned over the contents of your house, maybe even emptying garbage cans if you were desperate enough. You kept going over and over in your mind where you could possibly have put the keys. And then, almost as an afterthought, you reached into your pocket and let out a sigh of relief—*Aahhh*—as your tension and anxiety melted away when you discovered you already had the keys, or the glasses, all along. After calling yourself a couple of names, your mind probably got quiet, your shoulders relaxed, and you may have felt a wave of relief pass through your body. This is another example of how you release right now.

As you perfect your use of the Method, you will find yourself able to go right to this point of realization and relaxation, even on longstanding issues that you were tearing your life

33

apart trying to resolve. You will discover that the answers have been right inside you all along.

Sometimes a spontaneous release takes place in the middle of an argument. Picture a time that you were in a heated discussion with someone that you care about when the following happened: You were really into it, absolutely sure you were right and justified in your position, when all of a sudden you caught the other person's eyes and, without trying looked deeply into their being, you connected with them at the level that makes them as special to you as they are. In that instant, something relaxed inside and your position no longer felt as justified. You may even have glimpsed the conflict from their point of view. Perhaps you paused for a moment and reconsidered the situation, and then found an easy, mutually beneficial solution.

As you master the ideas in this book, you will learn how to see more than just your own point of view, which will free you from all sorts of conflicts, some that you may even have forgotten you have.

> "At work, I am more energetic, proactive, and positive. I am in sales, and rejection does not have the same effect on me. In fact, I am now finding I get much less rejection."
> —David Fordham,
> London, England

The Continuum of Letting Go

If you review your life, you will probably recall many instances that you have let go. We generally let go either by accident or when our backs are against the wall, and we have no other choice. As you focus on reawakening and strengthening this natural ability within yourself by practicing the

Sedona Method, you will be able to bring releasing under your conscious control and to make it a viable option throughout your everyday life—even when you have days like the one described earlier.

The chart below will give you a better understanding of the process of releasing, whether it's the spontaneous releasing you already do or the conscious releasing you will be doing as you explore this book. It will also help you to better distinguish between letting go, suppressing, and expressing. Each category represents a continuum that everyone is moving through in all moments.

The Releasing Flow Chart

APATHY GRIEF FEAR LUST ANGER PRIDE	RELEASE	COURAGEOUSNESS ACCEPTANCE PEACE
Tense	RELEASE	Relaxed
Unhappy	RELEASE	Happy
Confused	RELEASE	Clear
Dead	RELEASE	Alive
Heavy	RELEASE	Light
Closed	RELEASE	Open
Contracted	RELEASE	Expanded
Unproductive	RELEASE	Productive
Ineffective	RELEASE	Effective

As you practice releasing, you'll see that you tend to move from the left-hand side to the right-hand side of this chart. Sometimes you may find a difference in only a single category as you let go, and other times you will see a difference in many.

You can, and probably already do, force yourself at times to move to the right-hand side. For instance, you may force yourself to make a decision in order to stop thinking about a particular problem. But that's not real releasing. If you do force a decision, you may grow uncomfortable inside and increase your tension. When you are forcing yourself to change a behavior without changing how you feel, you will find some categories moving to the right while others move to the left. When you have consciously released, the whole continuum moves to the right.

But what do we mean by *consciously* releasing, letting go? How can we put releasing into practice?

The Five Ways of Letting Go

There are five ways to approach the process of releasing and all lead to the same result: liberating your natural ability to let go of any unwanted emotion on the spot and allowing some of the suppressed energy in your subconscious to dissipate.

The first way is by choosing to let go of the unwanted feeling. The second way is to welcome the feeling—to allow the emotion just to be. The third way is to dive into the core of the emotion. The fourth way is by holistically embracing both sides of any issue or belief. And the last way of releasing—called The 5th Way—helps you to discover the Beingness that you already are here and now. Included at the back of this book are two entire chapters on the fourth and fifth ways of releasing.

Deciding to Drop It

Let me explain by asking you to participate in a simple release. Pick up a pen, a pencil, or some small object that you would be willing to drop without giving it a second thought. Now, hold the object in front of you and really grip it tightly. Pretend this is one of your limiting feelings and that your hand represents your gut or your consciousness. If you held the object long enough, this would start to feel uncomfortable yet familiar.

Now, open your hand and roll the object around in it. Notice that you are the one holding on to it; it is not attached to your hand. The same is true with your feelings. Your feelings are as attached to you as this object is attached to your hand.

We hold on to our feelings and forget that we are holding on to them. It's even in our language. When we feel angry or sad, we don't usually say, "I feel angry," or "I feel sad." We say, "I am angry," or "I am sad." Without realizing it, we are misidentifying that we *are* the feeling. Often, we believe a feeling is holding on to us. This is not true . . . we are always holding on and just don't know it.

Now, let the object go.

What happened? You let go of the object, and it dropped to the floor. Was that hard? Of course not. That's what we mean when we say, "Let go or 'release.'"

You can do the same thing with any emotion: choose to let it go.

Welcoming or Allowing the Emotion

Sticking with this same analogy: If you walked around with your hand open, wouldn't it be very difficult to hold on to the pen or other object you're holding? Likewise, when you allow or welcome a feeling, you are opening your consciousness, and this enables the feeling to drop away all by itself like clouds passing in the sky or smoke passing up an open chimney flue.

Because we spend so much time resisting and suppressing our emotions, rather than letting them flow freely through us, welcoming or allowing an emotion to be is often all that is necessary to allow it to release.

My student Natalie learned to release effortlessly by acknowledging her feelings in the moment. As a daily commuter, she often used to have trouble passing trucks on the highway because she was anxious. Noisy thoughts and gruesome images of accidents would rush into her mind and she'd panic. Then, she began listening to a guided releasing recording from one of our audio programs while traveling to and from work on the interstate. She would dialogue with herself.

"So, you're anxious?"

"Yes, I'm anxious."

"Could you allow yourself to feel as anxious as you do?"

"Yes."

She discovered that, in a short time, she'd be over it. Just by allowing her panic rather than resisting it, her physical sensations of rapid breathing and shakiness would evaporate, and her mind would become quiet.

Diving into the Core of the Emotion

Now, if you took the same object—a pencil, pen, or pebble—and magnified it large enough, it would appear more and more like empty space. You would be looking into the gaps between the molecules and atoms. When you dive into the very core of a feeling, you will observe a comparable phenomenon: Nothing is really there.

As you master the process of releasing, you will discover that even your deepest feelings are just on the surface. At the core you are empty, silent, and at peace—not in the pain and darkness that most of us would assume. In fact, even our most extreme feelings have only as much substance as a soap bubble. And you know what happens when you poke your finger into a soap bubble. It pops. That's exactly what happens when you dive into the core of a feeling.

Please note: It is not recommended that you try diving in to a feeling while doing anything else. It works much better when you take time out, by yourself, to focus inside. It also works best when you are in touch with a stronger feeling.

Here is what you may experience: You receive some news that gets you upset. You start to feel a strong feeling of fear or grief, and you have the time to take a few minutes to release. You sit down, close your eyes, and relax into the feeling as best you can. Then you ask yourself questions like:

What is at the core of this feeling?

Could I allow myself to go in consciousness to the core of this feeling?

Could I allow myself to dive into this feeling?

You will probably come up with your own versions of these questions as you work with them over time. You may picture yourself actually diving into the center of the feeling and/or you may find yourself merely feeling what is at the core. Once you start to go deeper, you may experience various pictures and sensations. You may also notice a temporary intensification of the emotion. So, keep asking yourself: Could *I go even deeper?* Cajole yourself to go even deeper beyond whatever picture, feeling, or story you may be telling yourself about the emotion.

39

As you persist in this direction, you will reach a point where something pops inside, or you may find that you can go no deeper. You will know you have reached the core when your mind is calm and you feel peaceful inside.

Remember, if the feeling still feels strong or has even intensified, you are not at the core. *All* feelings except peace are on the surface. This may be very different from what you have been told before about going deeply into a feeling. Many of us avoid diving into a feeling, because we are afraid we will get lost or it will get worse. However, if you really let yourself go past the surface and get to the actual core, you'll discover that this could not be further from the truth, as my student Margie found out.

Margie came to class with a deep sense of grief that she had been carrying around for over ten years, ever since she had felt betrayed by the staff of another self-help organization. Without getting involved in the elements of her story, we mutually decided that diving in to the grief would be the best way for her to let go of it. I asked her the questions from above, and at first her grief intensified. As she began to cry, I simply encouraged her to go even deeper than the sensations and the story, and we kept going. To Margie's surprise, in just a few minutes, she entered a state of profound peace. She said afterwards that she'd avoided the grief because she felt like she was drowning in an ocean of it. After she released, she realized that the grief was always just on the surface. What she'd actually been avoiding inside, without knowing it, was an ocean of love.

Holistic Releasing

Lastly, as you focus on the object in your hand you will notice that it is defined by opposites. In other words, the reason you can perceive the object is because of the space around it. Without space there can be no contents. When it comes to emotionally-based problems and feelings, they are defined or held together by opposites as well. We have good and bad, right and wrong, happy and sad, and love and hate to just name a few. When you welcome both sides of any of these pairs, as opposed to clinging to one and resisting the other, you find that they both dissolve, leaving you with the empty space that allows for all experiencing. An entire bonus chapter on Holistic Releasing can be found at the back of this book, as well as another bonus chapter on a transformational new way to release called The 5th Way.

You will get the most out of the process of releasing the more you allow yourself to see, hear, and feel it working, rather than by thinking about how and why it works. Lead, as best you can, with your heart, not your head. If you find yourself getting a little stuck in trying to figure it out, you can use the identical process to let go of "wanting to figure it out."

The Basic Releasing Questions

What is your NOW feeling?
Could you welcome/allow that feeling?
Could you let it go?
Would you let it go?
When?

These are the five basic releasing questions that serve as the foundation of The Sedona Method. Here is how to apply them on your own. Experiment with asking the questions both in the first person and in the third person and find which one works best for you.

Step 1: Focus on an issue that you would like to feel better about, and then allow yourself to feel whatever you are feeling in this moment.

Ask yourself: *What is my NOW feeling about this topic?*

This doesn't have to be a strong feeling. In fact, you can even check on how you feel about this book and what you want to get from it.

Step 2: Welcome the feeling, as well as any sensations, sounds, thoughts, and pictures that arise with the feeling, and allow whatever you are experiencing to be here as fully or as best you can.

Ask yourself: *Could I allow myself to welcome this feeling?*

This instruction may seem simplistic, but it needs to be. Most of us live in our thoughts, pictures, and stories about the past and the future, rather than being aware of how we actually feel in this moment. The only time that we can actually do anything about the way we feel (and, for that matter, about our businesses or our lives) is NOW. You don't need to wait for a feeling to be strong or to have a label before you let it go. In fact, if you are feeling numb, flat, blank, cut off, or empty inside, those are feelings that can be let go just as easily as more recognizable ones. Simply do the best you can.

Step 3: Ask yourself: *Could I let this feeling go?*

This question is merely asking you if it is possible to take this action. "Yes" or "no" are both acceptable answers. You will often let go even if you answer "no." As best you can, answer the question that you choose with a minimum of thought, staying away from second-guessing yourself or getting into an internal debate about the merits of that action or its consequences.

All the questions used in this process are deliberately simple. They are not important in and of themselves but are designed to point you to the experience of letting go, to the experience of stopping holding on. Go on to Step 4 no matter how you answer this question.

Step 4: No matter which question you started with, ask yourself this simple question: *Would I?* In other words: Am I willing to let go?

Again, stay away from debate as best you can. Also remember that you are always doing this process for yourself, for the purpose of gaining your own freedom and clarity. It doesn't matter whether the feeling is justified, longstanding, or right.

If the answer is "no," or if you are not sure, ask yourself: *"Would I rather have this feeling, or would I rather be free?"* Even if the answer is still "no," go on to Step 5.

Step 5: Ask yourself a simpler question: *When?*

This is an invitation to just let it go now. You may find yourself easily letting go. Remember that letting go is a decision you can make any time you choose.

Step 6: Repeat the preceding five steps as often as needed until you feel free of the particular feeling with which you started the process.

Note: If you are having a hard time deciding to let go or simply feeling a difference, then you can also give yourself permission to hold on for a moment. If you give yourself permission to do what you are already doing, you will find that it becomes much easier to make a new decision. This will usually make getting to a genuine "yes" and the corresponding letting go much easier.

You will probably find yourself letting go a little more on

each step of the process. The results at first may be quite subtle. Very quickly, if you are persistent, the results will get more and more noticeable. You may find that you have layers of feelings about a particular topic. However, what you let go of is gone for good.

Feelings Only Lie

When you catch yourself rationalizing a specific emotion, telling yourself what a useful function it serves and justifying why you're absolutely right to hold on to it, it is a signal that you're being handed a pack of lies. As you move further into the exploration of letting go, one of the things that you'll notice is that the feelings you're releasing tend to argue for their own preservation. Feelings lie and make empty promises, such as: "Fear keeps you safe," "If I feel guilty, I won't do it again," "If I hold on to my anger, I'm getting back at another person (rather than only hurting myself)." All that's happening is that a particular feeling is perpetuating the problem it appears to be preventing. It's a lie.

Two simple sentences that I use in my classes sum this up. You may find them a little like a Zen Buddhist koan that cannot be understood unless you just let go. So, here we go: "Feelings only lie. They tell us we are going to get from letting go of them what we already have from holding on to them."

The Mind Is Like a Computer

To put the Sedona Method in perspective, let's take a look at the many ways in which the human mind functions similarly to a computer. Computer functioning, of course, is partly based on the model of the human mind, so this shouldn't seem like too much of a stretch. You are probably aware that a computer needs both hardware and software to operate. For the sake of this analogy, consider the hardware the equivalent to the brain and nervous system, and consider the software the equivalent of our thoughts, feelings, memories, and beliefs, as well as our basic, inborn intelligence.

What does the human operating system consist of? Software programs that run the body and the mind are the underlying intelligence that allows the system to function and accumulate knowledge. Almost everything we need in order to function well in life is innate. The only exceptions are the specific skills we acquire, which can vary widely. These range from playing a musical instrument to performing brain surgery.

In the same way that a computer functions faster and more efficiently the more memory, or space, it has available, so do we. As we go through life, we have experiences and accumulate data until our resident memory fills up and our processing capabilities become burdened and slow down. In computers, you can free up space by deleting or compressing files. Likewise, experiences that have a neutral emotional content and feel complete are highly compressed. Conversely, emotionally charged or incomplete experiences are like programs and files that have been left open and are running in the background of our lives. They use too much of our available memory and processing capability.

Open programs are not a big problem for most of us when we are younger, but as we age, there is less memory available even for bodily functions like respiration and digestion. As a result, the entire system gets overloaded and starts to break down. Then open programs and files take a toll on our basic ability to function effectively in life and to learn new, useful skills. They create mental confusion and conflict, because they're often sending us messages that contradict and interfere with each other and with our conscious intentions.

As we apply the Sedona Method, we let go of the emotional charges that are keeping old programs and files running in the background of our lives. We therefore increase our available memory and speed up our processing capability. Releasing enables us to retain the wisdom gained from experience without having our energy and memory drained by an emotional sense of incompletion. In other words, the more we use the Method, the better the human system functions.

Written Releasing: What Do You Want in Your Life?

Upon occasion, throughout *The Sedona Method* you'll be invited to explore your feelings on paper in self-created worksheets. At Sedona Training Associates, we call this type of process "written releasing." I recommend that you purchase a spiral-bound notebook or a simple journal to devote to this purpose for the duration of your reading. Once you've finished the book, for privacy, shred the parts you used for written releasing. There is no reason to save your releasing notes.

So, before you read on, please get out your new releasing journal, and make a list of anything and everything you would like to change or improve in your life. This list will serve as a declaration of your intentions for this self-study course on the Sedona Method. We will refer back to it as we move through the process together, so take as much time as you need and be as complete as possible.

As you write down your intentions, remember not to limit yourself to what you think is "possible" to achieve from reading a book. You are learning a tool that will be with you for the rest of your life. Have fun. This book is designed to help you begin a process that can lead to you having, being, and doing it *all*. The process is so powerful, in fact, and works at such a basic level, that many of the intentions on your list will come to fruition even without you working on them directly.

> "My gains include freedom from disabling sensations of anxiety at my job, increased success and enjoyment in my work, and much less fear of the future."
> —Bonnie Jones,
> Olympia, WA

Write Down Your Gains

As you let go, I highly recommend that you write down your gains, as they occur, to spur you on to even greater self-discovery. Keep track of these positive outcomes in your releasing journal, or purchase a second notebook small enough to carry around in your breast pocket or handbag in which to jot down your thoughts.

Here is what you can expect:

- Positive changes in behavior and/or attitude
- Greater ease, effectiveness, and joy in daily activities
- More open and effective communications
- Increased problem-solving ability
- Greater flexibility

- Being more relaxed and confident in action
- Accomplishments, completions, new beginnings
- New abilities or skills
- An increase in positive feelings and a decrease in negative ones
- More love toward others

In addition to gains, as you explore the material in this book, you'll discover your patterns of limitation and the specific ways that you could change your life for the better. I highly recommend that you write these realizations down whenever they occur.

Coming Back to Life

In these pages, it's my goal to help you learn everything you need in order to have, be, and do whatever you will or desire. I promise that if you work faithfully with the Sedona Method, it will transform every part of your life for the better. You will feel as though you are coming back to life. You'll catch yourself with a smile on your face and laughing out loud as your inner stress and tension easily melt away.

Between now and when you read the next chapter, play around a little bit with what we just did together and see what you can discover for yourself. Practice releasing throughout the day and also notice ways you already release on your own. The more you focus on this way of dealing with your emotions, the more the benefits and ease of letting go will grow on you. Be persistent. The more you explore letting go, the more natural it will become as an alternative to suppression and expression—and it will set you free.

Chapter 2

Your Formula for Success

Throughout this book, my purpose is to guide you, in an experiential way, in learning how to let go of the reactions or feelings that are holding you back from performing at your best, achieving your full potential, and living a life filled with happiness, joy, and well-being. Since you've now had the opportunity to explore the releasing questions at least a little bit, this chapter will provide you with some more detailed guidelines for using the Sedona Method effectively. These suggestions are based on over a quarter of a century's experience in facilitating seminars and retreats about the Method, as well as training other Sedona Method instructors and exploring the most supportive ways to gain the maximum value from releasing.

As you move forward, please be aware that the releasing process is completely internal. That is, it has nothing to do with anything or anyone else except you yourself. It only pertains to your internal reactions or feelings toward the people and circumstances in your life. When you let go of these, the process is so simple and so enjoyable that it may even make you laugh. People do tend to laugh a lot in my workshops. Because the releasing process works on a very basic, internal level, even when you practice the Method with a partner—as you'll learn how to do presently—you'll find that you never need to share details of a personal nature in order to get the maximum results from this work. You can release with a partner and still maintain your privacy.

While participating in the explorations within this book, simply allow yourself to let go of your feelings as best you can. "As best you can" means "to the extent of your ability at that exact moment." You never have to push for a feeling or a release that isn't honestly there. You are also letting go only of what you are feeling in this moment. If you are working on anger, for instance, the releasing questions are not referring to all anger for all time. They are merely an invitation to let go of the anger you are feeling NOW. Please note that because of the relaxing nature of this process, as well as human nature in general, you may not always experience your feelings strongly. This doesn't mean that you are not doing great work. In general, letting go is just as effective for light or strong feelings. In fact, if you make it a habit to let go as you go about your daily life—even of the "small stuff"—eventually everything will feel like small stuff. As you begin to let go of your internal tension and other stressful feelings, you'll notice that you experience a sense of relief and heightened alertness. This is only one of the many benefits you can achieve through the Sedona Method.

I guarantee that you'll make tremendous—and rapid—progress and experience many powerful, positive effects from releasing when you apply what you've learned. As we have already mentioned, at Sedona Training Associates we call these changes "gains." Be aware, however, that there are sometimes surprises. These are pleasant ones, to be sure, but nonetheless unexpected outcomes. For instance, the specific area of your life that you would like to change by applying the Sedona Method may not transform as quickly as you would like, while another area begins to shift right away. Your target area may actually be one of the last areas of your life to turn around. But it is more likely that changes will happen much faster than you'd ever have dreamed possible.

To explain another way, let's imagine that a particular individual turns to the Sedona Method specifically to open herself to greater financial success. She reads the book attentively, dutifully works with the material it contains, and yet finds no immediate financial gain. Instead, she may initially find herself gaining superior health, and then perhaps discover improvements in her personal relationships. After that, she might develop heightened abilities in the workplace. And only then she may finally allow herself to achieve the financial success that she was originally seeking.

Please don't misunderstand me. The Sedona Method will

"As a Toastmaster, I had succeeded in giving prepared speeches but was never good at speaking impromptu. I felt tense and nervous whenever I was called up to speak without preparation. Since I started using the Sedona techniques, I've become much more relaxed and at ease when I speak impromptu. As a result, I've become a much more effective speaker. I have managed to let go of my stage fright."
—Charles Stark,
New York, NY

definitely bring about important changes in your life. It is only that on occasion those changes may not arrive in exactly the order you hoped for, or predicted. Change may also be gradual. Your friends, co-workers, and employees might notice the changes in you before you do.

As you incorporate releasing into your life on a regular basis, you'll soon notice that you are becoming more sensitized to your feelings. This is a sign of progress. It means that you are ready to become aware of, and let go of, many of the emotions that you have either been suppressing or avoiding. In my experience, people usually don't experience feelings they're not ready to face—although I've had a few students who experienced a restless night or two of sleep as their resistance to certain feelings began to dissipate. But they kept releasing and quickly let go of everything that was troubling them. Most people absolutely do not have their sleep affected, except in a positive way. The good news is that the more you use the releasing process, the easier you'll find it to let go. And this is what creates the safety for you to experience all your feelings—both the painful and pleasurable ones—more deeply. By feeling all your feelings more fully, you'll gain even more enjoyment and aliveness out of everything you do.

> "I'm able to have a good night's sleep after many years of having difficulty sleeping all night. It feels great."
> —Rosella Schroeder

The following analogy is a little like using the Sedona Method. Have you ever eaten from a salad bar or at a cafeteria where they had plate or tray dispensers? If so, you probably noticed that after you took your plate or tray out of the dispenser another one popped up to take its place. The same is true of our emotions as we let them go. If there are more feelings related to a topic than the ones we began releasing, more will keep coming up until they are all gone about that particular topic, until the "dispenser" is empty. Unlike a plate dispenser, however, every feeling that you take out and release is gone for good. When exploring the processes in this book, most likely you will start by letting go of one feeling at a time, then groups of feelings, until you become so good at releasing that you are ultimately working at the deepest levels—on whole "stacks" of feelings at the same time about any given issue.

Often, it is when we are not looking for, or trying to accomplish, anything that the mind relaxes enough to allow for releases and realizations. While you'll definitely experience releases, realizations, and gains as you consciously work with the Method, you may find that they come when you least expect them. So make room throughout your day for the possibility of gains, and stay open to the unexpected. As best you can, relax and accept that the timing of your greatest breakthroughs and realizations, including the ultimate realization of your true nature, may be totally out of your control.

Frequently Asked Questions

When people attend Sedona Method courses, they often ask the following questions. Review the answers as often as you need to as you work with the releasing process.

- *How often should I release?* Releasing is one good thing you can't overdo. The more often you apply the Method throughout your day, the more benefits you'll receive from it. Releasing can be done anywhere and at any time to immediately feel better, clearer, more confident, and alive. Simply allow yourself to remain open inside, while your feelings come up and move through you. Look at each upset in your life as an opportunity for greater freedom. Also remember to have fun. Avoid turning releasing into another "should." As you get into the habit of letting go in the moment as feelings arise, you'll develop a wonderful momentum that will support you when deeper feelings surface. You will find it easier to let them go as well.

- *How long does it take to learn how to let go?* That's up to you. In Chapter 1, you learned some of the basics of the releasing technique. How quickly you'll see results you can measure depends on how much you apply what you learned in your everyday life. Letting go gets easier to do the more you do it. Also, you may or may not feel big shifts right away. The results may start out subtly, or they may be extremely profound.

- *How could something so simple be so powerful?* The most powerful and useable tools in life are often the simplest. When processes are allowed to remain simple, they are easy to remember and duplicate. No one has to convince you how critical breathing is, for instance. Still, if I wanted to give you instructions about the procedure to follow for breathing, it would be: "Breathe in, breathe out . . . and repeat as needed." What could be simpler? Yet there is little of more central importance to your life.

  As you use the Method over time, you'll discover that it

is easy and can become second nature, requiring as little thought from you as the act of breathing does now. Do you recall how suppressed feelings were likened in Chapter 1 to an emotional pressure cooker? When you release often, you'll also discover that keeping the lid off your feelings and allowing them to release is more natural than trying to keep them crammed inside.

- *What does it feel like to let go?* The experience of letting go is highly individual. Most people feel an immediate sense of lightness or relaxation as they use the process. Others feel energy moving through their bodies as though they are coming back to life. Changes can become more pronounced over time. In addition to physical sensations, you'll notice that your mind is getting progressively quieter and your remaining thoughts are clearer. You will start to perceive more solutions rather than problems. Over time, your experience of releasing may even feel positively blissful.

- *How do I know that I'm doing it right?* If you notice any positive shifts in feeling, attitude, or behavior when you're releasing, then you are doing it right. However, each issue that you work on could require different amounts of letting go. If at first it doesn't shift completely, let go and then let go again. Continue releasing until you have achieved your desired result.

- *What should I do if I find myself getting caught up again in old patterns of behavior, or if I just plain forget to release?* First, it's important to understand that this is to be

55

expected—and it's okay. Your ability to release spontaneously and in the moment that it's necessary will increase over time. Soon, you'll be able to release in "real time." Meanwhile, you can always release once you do recognize that there has been a problem. Soon, when you catch yourself in the middle of an old behavior pattern, you'll be able to release as the pattern is happening and interrupt it. By doing so, you'll find that you're able to change the pattern. After a while, you'll learn to catch yourself before you get caught up in the old pattern, and then you'll release and not do it. Ultimately, you won't need to release about that particular tendency anymore, because you'll have let it go entirely. If you allow yourself to be persistent, your attitude and effectiveness will eventually change for the better, even with longstanding problems. You may even get to the point where the only time you'll remember that you even had a particular problem is when someone else reminds you of it.

It can also be helpful to schedule short releasing breaks throughout the day to remind yourself to release.

• *Do I have to change my beliefs or believe something new to do the Sedona Method?* Absolutely not. As I mentioned in the Introduction, please don't believe anything in this book unless you can prove it for yourself. Just because something is said in writing does not make it so. Knowledge is not useful unless or until you can verify it for yourself experientially. Simply be as available as you can to what is being communicated in this book and look at it as an opportunity to change your consciousness and your life. Remain open to discovery and prove or disprove it for yourself. Whatever your religious beliefs or affiliations, they will only be supported by the process of letting go. People who have used the Sedona Method report that it helps them to be more in tune with and open to uncovering their true spiritual experience and conviction.

- *What should I do if I am already involved in therapy or some other system for personal growth?* Since letting go is the essence of any good therapy and every effective tool for personal growth, you'll find that using the Sedona Method is an ideal support for other systems. This includes those you are already doing and those you may do in the future. As you combine releasing with other forms of self-exploration, results will come more quickly and easily. The Method will make it easier to stick with whatever process is working in your life, because you'll be able to understand and apply the concepts that you're learning on a more consistent basis. People who learn the Method frequently comment that it is the missing piece they've been looking for in everything else they've done to help themselves.

    Note: If you are presently involved in any form of psychological or medical treatment, please do not change your treatment regimen without first consulting your healthcare professional.

Harness the Strength of Your Different Modes of Sensing

Most of us have a predominant form of physical sensing: visual (sight), kinesthetic (physical feeling), or auditory (sound). If you're not sure which one is your leading mode of sensing, then, in addition to asking yourself the releasing questions, try incorporating all three of these modes into the process. Later, use the one that works best for you.

Visual Sensing

If you lead with your visual sense, or you simply like working with it, allow yourself to come up with visual images while you go through the releasing questions. Here are a few suggestions to get you started:

- Visualize a knot where you feel tension or another sensation in your body, and see it unraveling as you let it go.

- Picture that there's a lid with hinges on your internal pressure cooker, and accept that all you need to do is open the lid and the feeling will leave. See yourself opening the lid and the hinge becoming looser. If you use this image frequently, after a while, you'll be able to keep this lid open and easily allow your feelings to come up and out.

- Picture yourself tightly gripping a feeling in your hand, and then see your hand opening and the feeling leaving. As you'll see in the kinesthetic sensing section, you can reinforce this image physically by making an actual fist as you hold on to a feeling and then opening it as you let go.

- Imagine that your feelings are pockets of unwanted energy trapped in your body. See yourself poking holes in these pockets and watch negative energy drain out.

- You may also experience your limiting feelings as a sense of darkness. As you use this process, picture the darkness being washed away, illuminated by the light.

Kinesthetic Sensing

If you are predominantly kinesthetic, you lead with your physical sensations. Therefore, allow yourself to experience a feeling as fully as you can in your body first, and then relax, open, and feel the feeling leaving as you let go. You may especially enjoy reinforcing the experience of releasing with touch and movement. Try the following:

- Place both hands face down touching each other on your solar plexus. As you let go a feeling, simply tilt your hands up, creating an imaginary space through which it can pass up and out.

- Make a fist with one hand, holding it to your solar plexus, and then open your hand as you let go of a feeling.

- Combine the physical action of opening your arms with the same inner sense that you have when you're about to hug someone whom you care about deeply. First, place your hands together in front of you in a prayerful position and simply allow yourself to become aware of whatever you're feeling in the moment. Then, slowly open your arms wide and, at the same time, let yourself feel welcoming. Keep opening inwardly as best you can while moving your hands slowly outward until they are as far apart as they can go without straining. Afterwards, notice how you feel. If you did this with as little thought as possible, you would probably feel lighter.

- Here is another simple way to reinforce your releasing process physically and help yourself lead more with your heart than your head. Simply place your hand on the spot in your body where you are feeling a feeling— often this place is around the solar plexus or gut. Use this action as a reminder to focus on the feeling itself rather than your thoughts about the feeling.

Auditory Sensing

If you lead with your auditory sense, the basic releasing questions outlined in Chapter 1 and explored throughout this book may be more than enough to induce you to release. You might also engage in a positive, encouraging internal conversation to reassure yourself that it's okay to let go as you ask the questions. However, if you use conversation, please keep it to a minimum and avoid debate. It is always better just to say "yes" or "no" to the releasing questions, rather than debating the merits of letting go or anticipating the potential consequences. As you become more experienced in releasing, you may be surprised at what you hear, such as my student who was welcoming a feeling of judgment and heard the words "bad, bad, bad" repeated in her own voice in her mind as though she were a naughty dog. This made her giggle, and so she released.

People who lead with any one of the three modes of sensing can benefit from using any of the suggestions above at different times. Think back to the brief exercise in the last chapter in which you held on to and then dropped a pen, pencil, or other small object. Why not use that technique if it helps? Just hold on to an object as you ask yourself the releasing questions. When you are ready to release, let the object go as a tangible reinforcement of your internal experience.

In order to bring your natural ability to release into focus, allow yourself to play a little game as you go about your day. The goal is to practice both holding on to your feelings and letting them go. But keep the pressure low by playing only with your petty annoyances and casual feelings. Notice when you're holding on and when you're letting go. Whenever you're holding on, give yourself permission to continue. Then check in with yourself to determine if you're willing to give the releasing process a try. If you are, ask the releasing questions: "What am I feeling? Could I allow myself to have this feeling? Could I let it go? Would I let it go? When? Now how am I feeling? Could I let this feeling go? Would I? When?" and so on. This game enhances emotional fluidity.

When Two or More Are Focused on a Goal

You may have heard the following story told many different ways. This one is my favorite. A man goes to heaven and meets God at the Pearly Gates. God welcomes him and then asks, "Is there any last wish, my son, before you spend the rest of eternity in heaven?" "Yes," the man replies. "I would like to see what hell is like so I can more thoroughly appreciate my good fortune." God says, "Fine," snaps his fingers, and instantly they enter hell. Before them, as far as the eye can see, is a table piled high with the most wonderful delicacies that anyone's heart could desire, and on both sides of the table, also as far as the eye can see, are millions of unhappy people starving to death.

The man asks God, "Why are these people starving?" God replies, "Everyone must eat from the table with 11-foot long chopsticks." "That's terribly harsh," the man says compassionately. God snaps his fingers again, and they're transported to heaven.

On entering heaven, the man is surprised to see an almost identical scene—a bountiful table stretching as far as the eye can see—except that everyone is happy and well-fed. He turns and asks God, "What do the people eat with here? They must have different utensils." "No, my son," says God, "everyone here eats with 11-foot long chopsticks, too." The man is confused. "I don't understand. How is this possible?"

God replies, "In heaven, we feed each other."

The processes explored throughout this book are taken from the Sedona Method audio programs, as well as from the Basic and Advanced Courses we teach at Sedona Training Associates. They are purposefully designed so that you can do them on your own or share them with a friend, relative, or loved one. An awesome power is unleashed when people gather together to focus on freedom. That is why Sedona Training Associates host live seminars to explore the topic, and why you can benefit from sharing this material with others. On earth, as in heaven, when we take care of each other's needs, no one goes "unfed."

If you choose to do the exercises throughout this book with someone else, you can ask each other the questions or lead each other through the explorations. All you need to do is be as present as you can with your partner and read from the book. Grant your partner the authority of his or her self-knowledge by allowing your partner to have his/her own experience.

When you are facilitating your partner in letting go, do your best to let go, too. This will happen naturally if you are open to it. Allow your partner to go as deeply into the process as he or she chooses. Refrain from leading, judging your partner's responses, or giving him/her advice. It is not your job to "fix" your partner.

Refrain from discussing the explorations until you and your partner have both completed them during that sitting and you mutually agree to discuss them. Be sure to validate your partner's point of view, even if it does not agree with your own. Your partner may say, "I'm sad," when you believe he/she actually feels angry, for instance. Therefore, help them release on sadness. Honor your partner by accepting what he/she tells you at face value. A common disagreement between partners is whether there has or has not been a full release. You may believe your partner needs to continue releasing on a topic, even though he/she is telling you, "I feel good. I'm done." Again, as tempting as it may be, it is inappropriate to impose your feelings and interpretations on a partner.

Please refrain from playing the role of counselor or therapist unless you're a trained counselor or therapist and your partner has specifically asked you to play this role with him or her. Also, if your partner brings up a medical condition that would ordinarily require treatment from a trained health care professional, suggest that he/she gets whatever support is needed in this area. If you're not sure whether or not your partner truly needs medical support, you can suggest it anyhow, just to be sure.

Kenneth: Letting Go of His Attachment to a Story

Kenneth was a direct witness of the World Trade Center attacks in New York City on September 11, 2001. In spite of daily releasing ever since, he'd been in a continuous state of high anxiety for almost a month when he arrived for a Seven-day Retreat in Sedona that October. He told our group this dramatic story: "I was running late for a 9 A.M. appointment with a client across the street from Ground Zero. Coming out of the subway, the escalator was clogged up with people who were New York-style aggravated. When I reached street level, I turned to the right and saw a number of bystanders looking up at the North Tower, which was burning then. At that moment, none of us knew what had happened. It just looked like there was a fire on two floors. My only thought, as I continued hurrying along, was, 'Wow! The Fire Department had better show up soon.'

"When I entered my client's building, I took the elevator to the 14th floor. But no one was there, and the office was locked. It was now a few minutes after the hour and they had already evacuated the building. I went back downstairs and exited and stood on the sidewalk for a while and watched the fire. After 5 or 10 minutes, I don't recall exactly how long, there was a tremendous explosion at the other tower—the sound approximated the clicking of an igniter on a gas stove. First, there was a *whooshing* noise, but magnified a million times over. Oddly, I didn't even learn that it was a plane crash until I got home later and spoke on the phone to my girlfriend, who was watching the scene on CNN in Illinois. Right then, it looked like a bomb blast. That's when it became apparent to us, the people in the street, that this event was something besides a simple fire.

"When the explosion occurred, a tremendous amount of paper began raining down on us. People panicked and rushed up Day Street. In their haste to get as far away as possible, I almost got run over. I wasn't consciously releasing at the time. I felt curious instead of panicked. I tried to call out on my cell phone, because I wanted to tell my girlfriend what I was witnessing, but it wasn't working down there since the transmitters had actually been on top of the towers. After a couple more minutes, there was also the cacophony of fire engines and police sirens coming towards us. Paper was still falling, not dust yet. It was surreal. I remember that one paper dropped right at my foot, and I noticed it had the name of a German bank on it. It struck a chord in me, as I'm German.

"The next dramatic thing, which has been haunting me, is that people began jumping from the top floors of the North Tower. It happened to be a beautiful, clear morning, so it looked almost unreal to me. It was a Panavision perfect picture, and I felt like I was watching a movie. Perfect colors and wide-open shots. One image in particular stuck in my mind: a businessman jumping out, holding on to his briefcase. Such a clear day, legs up in the air, hands down, and the tie up in the air and waving as he was flying down. Because the towers were high, it took quite a while for him to come down. Gratefully, I didn't see the impacts of the bodies because other buildings obscured them.

"That's when I knew that something extremely serious was going on. People were crying in the streets, and whenever someone jumped, everyone went *Haaaaaaaah*, sucking in their breath. I felt compelled to watch, even though it was horrific. But I told myself, 'You have GOT to get out of here—NOW!

There's a possibility that something else might happen. We don't know what caused the impact. There might be more bombs. LEAVE THE AREA AND GO HOME!' So I worked myself against the flow of the crowd to get to the subway station at Brooklyn Bridge a few blocks north of where I'd been. To get there, I passed by a park near the mayor's office. There were crowds of people outside in the park, throngs watching the drama unfold. Once or twice I almost turned back and looked over my shoulder. But I had made up my mind to go. Luckily the subway was still running then, but I was almost the only person on it and it soon stopped.

"I got home and immediately called my girlfriend on the landline. She explained what I had seen. I shared my feelings with her and the impact it had on me. Then I went into shock. I couldn't turn on the TV right away because it was stored in a closet. So I got it out and turned it on. The reception was terrible because the antennas had been blown away. There was a powerful sense that the attack wasn't true somehow, tremendous disbelief even though I'd been a witness. I urgently needed to see the drama unfolding."

As Kenneth was recounting the story, I walked him through a release on pieces of the experience: the sounds, sights, feelings, thoughts, and sensations. He released some fear and anxiety. But Kenneth had a lot of resistance, and often he answered "no" when I asked him, "Could you let this go?" I knew that everyone in the group would benefit from his releasing process, since we had all been deeply affected by the scale of the tragedy. It wasn't until he was able to recognize how he was subtly proud of having been in such a unique situation, and developing such a great story about it, that he was able to let go completely. Once he did see the pride and released it, the anxiety that he'd been experiencing vanished and did not reoccur.

As Kenneth says, "Pride is a powerful emotion, but I was finally able to let go. Persistence paid off. In the end, I was oblivious of the group. It was me dealing with this particular event. It wasn't about pleasing Hale, or about seeking anyone's approval, not even my own. After the release I felt good. September 11th was still very much on people's minds and there was constant talk about it, but I never brought it up again the whole time I was in Sedona. Even better, I was actually sick of it."

Common Pitfalls to Avoid

Many people stumble into common pitfalls when they embark on the path of personal development, no matter what road they take. Here are some tips on avoiding them.

- *"I suffer, therefore I am."* Strange as it may seem, this statement reflects the way that most of us live our lives. We identify with our problems, believing that we are the one having them. It is almost as though we feel that we justify our existence by having obstacles to overcome, problems to fix, and how much suffering we can bear. We also identify with our self-created suffering. We become so versed in being the person with a particular problem that we're often afraid we won't know who we are without it. When we take a moment to reflect on "our" problems, we may even discover that we've grown so attached to these patterns of thought and behavior that it's hard to imagine ourselves without them. Rather than being open to the uncertainty that comes from letting go, we are clinging to the artificial sense of security that comes from knowing what to expect, even if that expectation is not beneficial.

It doesn't have to be this way. Think of a problem that you believe belongs to you, and ask yourself: "Would I rather have the false sense of security that comes from knowing all about this problem, or would I rather be free?" If you'd rather be free, you'll spontaneously let go of your attachment to the problem, and you'll begin discovering natural solutions to it, as opposed to justifying having, or being stuck with, the problem.

- *"But what will I talk about?"* Most of us base a significant amount of our interpersonal communications on seeking sympathy for our problems or commiserating with others about theirs. Often we become such experts at describing our problems to others that we do not want to give up our expertise. It is not that sharing our problems is detrimental. In fact, the freedom to share what's bothering you with others is often the first step in letting go and moving on. Also, being able to be there for our friends and partners when they are in emotional need is a sign of being a good friend. Where we get stuck is in continually sharing the same problem repeatedly, with no relief.

  If you find yourself telling the same story more than once, check to see if you are seeking agreement or approval for the problem. If you are, ask yourself:

- *Could I let go of wanting others to agree with me about my having this problem?*
- *Could I let go of wanting approval for this problem?*

- *"It's mine, that's why."* Pride is a shifty emotion. For we don't only feel proud of our accomplishments, we also get really hooked into being subtly proud of our problems. We feel so special for having them. This pitfall on the path to freedom may take the form of feeling proud of having prevailed even with the problem, proud of having borne it for so long, or proud of having a problem that is unique to us alone.

  Keep an eye open for pride. Look at your problems as you release on them, and check to see if you feel that they make you "special." If you find any pride and you can honestly admit it and let it go, then you'll find yourself free to let go of the problem, too.

- *It is not wise to ask, "Why?"* Wanting to understand or figure out why, or from where, problems arise can also be a major obstacle to letting them go. For we have to hold on to our problems in order to figure them out. Interestingly, if there is something that's important for you to understand, letting go of wanting to understand often brings the understanding that you've been seeking with a lot less effort. Ask yourself a question: Would I rather understand my problems or just be free of them? If you would rather be free, I highly recommend letting go of wanting to figure them out.

The reason this is so important is that, in order to figure out a problem, we must leave the present moment, which is the only place we can truly solve anything. In addition, we only truly need to understand a problem if we are planning to have it occur again or are planning in some way to maintain it.

Years ago, during a Sedona Method course that I was teaching, I suggested to my class that if they let go of wanting to figure out their problems, the answers would come. There was one man in particular who had a hard time embracing the concept. He was an electrical engineer, and he "knew" beyond any shadow of a doubt that he needed to want to figure things out in his profession or he would not be able to do his job. I didn't fight with him about his point of view; I merely suggested that he remain open at least to the possibility that letting go of wanting to figure it out might be of service to him.

In between the two weekends of the course, the engineer had an experience that totally changed

"Coming from a background of poverty and excessive physical discipline, I've been working on myself for umpteen years. But a number of issues have persisted, despite my efforts to shift them. Having completed the Course, I'm relieved of much of my old anger, and I am better able to deal with the deep-rooted fears that come up. I'm not sure I recognize me, but I'm prepared to be surprised. The Method easily comes to mind when faced with daily challenges, so I have gained some highly effective tools and a calmer, happier way of living."

—Yvonne Wigman,
Kingston, Australia

his perception. He was working to create a sample circuit and needed a particular part to complete it. But when he went to find it in the parts room—a room consisting of rows upon rows of bins stacked on floor-to-ceiling shelves and filled with small electronics parts that were sorted according to their specifications—the bin where the part was supposed to be was empty. He thought, I am sure that this letting go of wanting to figure out stuff can't possibly work with this kind of problem, but I'm going to give it a try anyhow. So, he just stood there for a few minutes and let go of wanting to figure out where the part might be. Then he found himself walking around the corner to a new row of bins, where he reached into one that was labeled for something else, and, lo and behold, there was the part he was seeking. He was dumbfounded because he had just done this on a lark, certain it wouldn't work—and it did anyway!

I highly encourage you to be open to the possibility that you can get the answers you crave in your life through this process of letting go of wanting to figure it out. Like the electrical engineer, you may be surprised!

- *Stop rushing past life.* Begin to approach your life as though you have all the time in the world. We live in an incredibly fast-paced world where we're constantly forcing ourselves to move more rapidly in order just to keep up. In our rush to attain our goals, even in the realm of self-improvement, we often rush past the very moment that offers the greatest opportunity for self-discovery and self-recognition—now.

Exploration: Look for the Freedom that Is Here and Now

No matter where your consciousness has gotten hooked in the past, in addition to releasing on that issue directly, develop the habit of looking for its opposite. Most of us have become very good at finding problems and limitations. We are experts at the quest for limitation because of our habit of looking for our problems when they are not here.

The freedom that we inherently are is always closer than our next thought. The reason we miss our freedom is that we jump from thought to thought, from familiar perception to familiar perception, missing what's really happening *here* and *now*.

Even when you are working on a particular problem, allow yourself to look for where the problem *isn't*. Notice how even your worst problem is not always with you in the current moment (NOW). When you start becoming aware of your basic nature of unbound freedom, you'll find that this awareness puts all of your supposed problems into perspective and allows you to live your natural state of freedom now.

The following process will help you start to move in this direction. It is a way to experience what's beyond your apparent problems and get more in touch with the second form of releasing—welcoming.

Easily allow yourself to become aware of your sensory perceptions, beginning with your sense of hearing. *Could you allow yourself just to hear, listen, or welcome whatever is being heard in this moment?*

Then, while allowing yourself to continue to focus on hearing: *Could you also allow yourself to welcome the silence that surrounds and interpenetrates whatever is being heard?*

For a few moments, switch back and forth between listening to what is being heard and not heard, including your thoughts.

When you feel ready, allow yourself to focus on what is being seen. *Could you allow yourself to welcome whatever is being seen, as best you can?*

Then, could you allow yourself also to welcome or notice the space, or emptiness, that surrounds every picture or object, including the white space between the writing on this page?

Again, alternate between the two perceptions for a few moments.

Next, focus on whatever sensations are arising in the moment. *Could you allow yourself to welcome whatever sensation is being perceived in this moment?*

Then, could you allow yourself to welcome the space, or the absence of sensation, that surrounds every sensation?

Easily switch back and forth between the two ways of perceiving.

Then, could you allow yourself to focus on a particular problem, and welcome that memory with all the pictures, sounds, sensations, thoughts, and feelings that are associated with it?

Could you then allow yourself to notice how most of your experience happens apart from this particular problem?

And, could you allow yourself to welcome at least the possibility that this problem is not as all consuming as it has seemed?

Switch back and forth between welcoming the problem and all its associated perceptions, and then noticing and welcoming what is actually here now.

As you do the above, you'll find yourself gradually gaining a new sense of clarity about your supposed problems and also noticing the exquisiteness of what is already here now.

Growth Can Be Fun

Please be an active participant in the releasing process. The more you put into it, the more you will get out of it. But set aside any unpleasant notions you have about work. Many people believe in the adage "no pain, no gain." As you practice letting go, I'm sure you'll discover that this simply doesn't have to be true. Rather than *working* with this process, allow yourself to engage in it as a game of exploration of everything that is truly possible for you. Yes, personal growth and healing—becoming *whole*—can be playful and fun.

Have the courage to make wonderful changes for the better in your life. Give yourself the happiness, success, and well-being you deserve. I want you to have it, and this process was developed to help you get it. As you allow the ease, simplicity, and amazing power of the Sedona Method to reveal itself to you in the pages of this book and through your personal explorations, you'll be gaining a tool that will be with you from now on. For nearly 30 years, people just like you have been using this incredible technique to radically improve every aspect of their lives.

Chapter 3

Your Roadmap to Emotional Freedom

Please read this chapter with an open heart and mind. It is designed to help you explore and release through the nine basic emotional states that everyone experiences throughout the day: apathy, grief, fear, lust, anger, pride, courage, acceptance, and peace. Not only will this information help you to gain greater clarity about your emotions, and those of others, it will also aid you in incorporating the process of conscious releasing into your life.

Freedom/Imperturbability

Freedom, or imperturbability, is the ultimate goal of the Sedona Method—the freedom to choose to have, be, or do or to *not* have, be, or do anything and everything. This is the natural state of being when we cannot be disturbed any longer by what happens in our lives. Your freedom is already here and now, resting just beneath the surface of your emotions, and, as you master releasing, you'll eventually uncover it within. Then nothing and no one can perturb you. Although you'll be aware of everything that's happening, and you'll enjoy it, you won't be attached to, or bothered by, any particular outcomes. You will remain at rest, at peace.

Right now you may be wondering, "I don't know if I want to let go of all my emotions. They give color to life. They make me feel alive." I assure you that releasing in no way leads to emotional deadness. The exact opposite is true. Because we typically keep so much suppressed, we don't really let ourselves feel enough. That numbness cuts us off from the natural goodness and richness of life even more than it cuts us off from the so-called negative emotions. Once you understand that you can let your emotions go, and you start letting them go, you'll be able to feel everything to a greater degree and in a very positive way. You will rest safely in the knowledge that no feeling has power over you unless you choose to allow it.

Uncover Your Intuition

Another reason many people are hesitant when they begin letting go of feelings is the belief that feelings give them important information and intuition. In my experience, the opposite is true. Although limiting feelings may seem to arise from the same place below conscious awareness as intuition does, intuition is actually the natural knowing of our true nature that gets obstructed by emotions. When we release, we uncover intuition.

Lester Levenson used to say, "Intuition is only right 100 percent of the time." Until you can tell the difference between your intuition and your emotional reactions, you may find this hard to accept. So, use the process of letting go to distinguish more easily between them. Simply release in the moment and pay attention. You'll soon discover that as you let go of a limiting feeling, it diminishes or disappears, whereas intuition simply gets clearer and quieter when you release. You cannot release intuition. In fact, the more you release, the more intuitive you'll be—without even needing to let go in the moment.

The Nine Emotional States

Inherent in all of us are nine emotional states: apathy, grief, fear, lust, anger, pride, courageousness, acceptance, and peace. These emotional states are listed on a two-page graph at the end of this chapter (see page 106). These fall along a gradient scale of energy and action. In apathy, we have almost no energy available to us and take little or no external action. We have more energy and take more external action when we move up to grief. Each successive emotion in this scale, all the way up to peace, has more energy and affords us a greater capability for outward action.

Here's an analogy you may find useful. Imagine that your emotions are how you would experience an ocean of energy being channeled through a garden hose that represents your body and your mind. When you're in apathy, the hose is almost totally crimped, letting very little energy through. In grief, it is a little more open. By the time you get to courageousness, it's mostly open, so you can focus your energy on creating what you choose. In peace, there is no longer any constriction: you are one with the ocean. Among other things, if you look at your emotions this way, it can help you to stop judging yourself for those emotions you do or do not have. After all, emotions are just energy.

Please use the remainder of this chapter to help you identify which emotional state you're experiencing in a given moment.

Refer to the lists of words and phrases that describe each of the nine emotional states whenever you're having a hard time getting in touch with what you're feeling. For instance, if you find that you often give up, feel negative about yourself or others, or just have a hard time getting started, you're probably experiencing a state of *apathy*. Perhaps you find yourself thinking, "I'm not like them. I'm right. I'm smarter than everyone," or feeling smug or better than . . . . Thoughts and feeling of this nature indicate that you're probably experiencing a state of *pride*.

As you work through this material, you'll probably find that you can relate more easily to certain emotions than others, and that you tend to spend more time experiencing certain emotional states than others. It is important, however, to work on releasing your emotions while experiencing all nine emotional states in order to attain true imperturbability and freedom in life.

The nine emotional categories are a way to make sense of the large part of our mind that is below our conscious awareness. This part of our mind is like a junk drawer—you know, the place where you throw everything that you don't know what else to do with. Some of us have a junk room or a junk attic or garage that looks that way. Over time, we've tossed everything into this part of our minds that we didn't know how to handle or that remains unresolved in any way. As I mentioned earlier, any feeling that's not let go of gets stored in the subconscious mind, which is filled with buried emotional baggage and limiting thoughts and feelings. Because of the accumulation of unresolved issues that most of us develop, it is often hard to remember what we consider important and far too easy to remember what we wish we could forget.

I don't know about you, but when I used to keep a junk

drawer, I could get very frustrated trying to find anything there. Finally, I cleared it out and organized its contents. Using the Sedona Method, you can do this with the mind as well. As you spend time working through and releasing the nine emotional states, you'll see that all the emotions relate to each other in a very organized way. This will help you to sift through your accumulation, discard what you no longer need, and uncover what is important to you. As you release, you'll find your mind getting progressively sharper and your memory progressively clearer. Not only will you get clearer about what you're feeling in the moment, you'll also begin to understand other people's emotions better.

When you visualize the scale of energy and action, or look at the chart at the end of this chapter, imagine that courageousness, acceptance, and peace are buried under the other emotions. As you let go of your apathy, grief, fear, lust, anger, and pride, you'll be uncovering these higher energy emotions, which are the real you that has always been here. Your whole life will turn around as a result. Everything will get easier for you.

"Understanding my feelings gives me a more peaceful life with better focus. I feel more in present time. The Sedona Method Course gave me what no other course ever did: a clear-cut system to support my goal of letting go of the barriers. I can also decide for myself where to go and how fast to develop."
—B.V., Gent, Belgium

Please be aware that the turnaround might not happen suddenly. It might be a gradual process. However, every time you work through the process of releasing, no matter where you start out—whether in apathy, grief, fear, lust, anger, or pride—you will find that you tend to gravitate naturally towards courageousness, acceptance, and peace. Recognizing your underlying strengths in this way can make a tremendous difference in how you feel and act and your whole outlook on life.

As you read through the nine sections that follow, permit yourself to be as open as you can to whatever feelings, thoughts, or pictures arise. Please pause any time you'd like to release whatever has come up. Definitely pause at the end of each section and spend some time releasing everything that is in your awareness.

Apathy

When we experience apathy, we feel as though desire is dead and it's no use. We can't do anything, and no one else can help. We feel dense and heavy and see no way out. We withdraw and play weak so we won't get hurt. Our minds can get so noisy that we may go numb. The pictures we have are limited and destructive. We only see failure and how we can't do it and how no one else can, either. We have little or no energy to act on our pictures and thoughts, because inwardly we are being pulled in so many conflicting directions.

Cheryl was retired and had been living in the same house for over 30 years, a period she'd spent collecting all kinds of objects and detritus. Her house, in fact, looked like the junk drawer I described a few pages ago in reference to the subconscious mind. By the time she decided to attend the Sedona Method Basic Course, she reported feeling quite heavy and apathetic about the condition of her environment. Interestingly, during the course she never directly released on the issues of her accumulation or her apathy. She merely listed procrastination as one of her goals. But when she arrived for the second weekend of the course—looking much more alive—she excitedly told the story of how, as she released throughout the week, she found herself cleaning and throwing things out. As her surroundings became less cluttered, her energy and self-confidence grew steadily higher. Cheryl said that she'd been trying to force herself to clean her home for many years, but to no avail. When she lightened up by releasing, she found herself doing just that.

Words and phrases that describe apathy:

- Bored
- Can't win
- Careless
- Cold
- Cut-off
- Dead
- Defeated
- Depressed
- Demoralized
- Desolate
- Despair
- Discouraged
- Disillusioned
- Doomed
- Drained
- Failure
- Forgetful
- Futile
- Giving up
- Hardened
- Hopeless
- Humorless
- I can't
- I don't care
- I don't count
- Inattentive
- Indecisive
- Indifferent
- Invisible
- It's too late
- Lazy
- Let it wait
- Listless
- Loser
- Lost
- Negative

- Numb
- Overwhelmed
- Powerless
- Resigned
- Shock
- Spaced out
- Stoned
- Stuck
- Too tired

- Unfeeling
- Unfocused
- Useless
- Vague
- Wasted
- What's the use?
- Why try?
- Worthless

Allow yourself to take a few moments and remember the last time that you or someone you know experienced apathy. Then give yourself a few moments just to be with whatever feeling this memory brings up in this moment.

Could you allow yourself to welcome this feeling as best you can?

Could you allow yourself to let it go?

Would you let it go?

When?

Repeat the releasing process a few more times until you feel as though you're able to let go of some or all of what you are feeling. Then move on to the next emotion.

Grief

When we experience grief, we want someone else to help us because we feel that we can't do anything on our own. We hope maybe someone else can. We cry out in pain for someone to do it for us. Our bodies have a little more energy than in apathy, but the energy is so contracted that it is painful. Our minds are a little less cluttered than in apathy, but they are still very noisy and opaque. We picture our pain and loss, often getting lost in these pictures. Our thoughts revolve around how much we hurt, what we have lost, and whether we can get anyone else to help us.

When Sarah's aging mother had a stroke, she realized they had turned a corner. She felt extremely sad to be losing the relationship they used to enjoy when her mom was vital and capable. Because of how much help her mom now required, it was as though Sarah were taking on the role of being the parent while her mom was becoming the child, at least part of the time. Making a decision one day, Sarah dove into her grief and found a measure of peace. She understood that, as long as she used the Sedona Method, she could allow herself to grieve appropriately instead of being stuck in a constant state of sorrow. Although there was sadness, and the unknown, there was also a feeling of great relief and movement. Releasing made it easier to welcome the changes in her mother.

Words and phrases that describe grief:

- Abandoned
- Abused
- Accused
- Anguished
- Ashamed
- Betrayed
- Blue
- Cheated
- Despair
- Disappointed
- Distraught
- Embarrassed
- Forgotten
- Guilty
- Heartbroken
- Heartache
- Heartsick
- Helpless
- Hurt
- If only
- Ignored
- Inadequate

- Inconsolable
- It's not fair
- Left out
- Longing
- Loss
- Melancholy
- Misunderstood
- Mourning
- Neglected
- Nobody cares
- Nobody loves me
- Nostalgia
- Passed over
- Pity
- Poor me

- Regret
- Rejected
- Remorse
- Sadness
- Sorrow
- Tearful
- Tormented
- Torn
- Tortured
- Unhappy
- Unloved
- Unwanted
- Vulnerable
- Why me
- Wounded

Allow yourself to take a few moments and remember the last time that you or someone you know experienced grief. Then give yourself a few moments just to be with whatever feeling this memory brings up in this moment.

Could you allow yourself to welcome this feeling as best you can?

Could you allow yourself to let it go?

Would you let it go?

When?

Before you go on, repeat the releasing process a few more times. Keep at it until you feel as though you are able to let go of some or all of what you are feeling, and then continue with the next emotion.

Fear

When we experience fear, we want to strike out, but we don't, because we think the risk is too great. We believe we'll probably get hit harder. We want to reach out, but do not because we think we'll get hurt. Our bodies have a little more energy than in grief, but the energy is still so contracted that it is mostly painful. Feelings can rise and fall very rapidly, like cool water on a hot skillet. Our minds are a little less cluttered than in grief, but still very noisy and opaque. Our pictures and thoughts are about doom and destruction. All we can think of and see is how we will get hurt, what we may lose, and how we must protect ourselves and those around us.

Releasing is an excellent tool for coping with fear, as Judy discovered on a six-week camping trip through Morocco and Kenya. On an isolated and precarious road atop the Atlas Mountains, the four-wheel drive jeep that she and eleven others were riding in suddenly turned over. For a few moments, everyone thought they were going to die, until the jeep stopped partway over the cliff. Hearts pounding, they scrambled carefully out onto the slope where they remained stranded overnight under challenging conditions. It was windy and chilly. They had few supplies or provisions, several people had diarrhea, and one injured man went into shock. Yet, throughout it all, Judy kept releasing her fear. As a result, she was calm, even fascinated, wondering if they would ever get out of their predicament and thinking it was an incredible adventure, however it wound up. Best of all, she lived to tell the tale without carrying around any sense of trauma from what had happened.

Words and phrases that describe fear:

- Anxious
- Apprehensive
- Cautious
- Clammy
- Cowardice
- Defensive
- Distrust
- Doubt
- Dread
- Embarrassed
- Evasive
- Foreboding
- Frantic
- Hesitant
- Horrified
- Hysterical
- Inhibited
- Insecure
- Irrational
- Nausea
- Nervous
- Panic
- Paralyzed
- Paranoid
- Scared
- Secretive
- Shaky
- Shy
- Skeptical
- Stage fright
- Superstitious
- Suspicious
- Tense
- Terrified
- Threatened
- Timid
- Trapped
- Uncertain
- Uneasy
- Vulnerable
- Want to escape
- Wary
- Worry

Allow yourself to take a few moments and remember the last time that you or someone you know experienced fear. Then give yourself a few moments just to be with whatever feeling this memory brings up in this moment.

Could you allow yourself to welcome this feeling as best you can?

Could you allow yourself to let it go?
Would you let it go?
When?

Now do this a few more times until you feel as though you are able to release some or all of what you are feeling before you move on to the next emotion.

Lust

When we experience lust, we desire possession. We are WANTING. We hunger for money, power, sex, people, places, and things, but with hesitation. We may or may not reach out. We have an underlying feeling that we cannot, or should not, have. Our bodies have a little more energy than in fear. It is still quite contracted, but the sensations now are sometimes quite pleasurable, especially compared to the previous three lower energy emotions. Feelings can be very intense. Our minds are a little less cluttered than in fear, but still very noisy and obsessive. We may try and medicate our pictures with positive fantasies, but underneath our pictures are really about what we don't have. Our thoughts are about what we need to get and what we don't have. No matter how much we do get, we never feel satisfied and rarely enjoy what we have.

Ron is a basketball fan who lives in Seattle and roots ardently for the Sonics. The year that the team was in the play-offs against the Chicago Bulls, he found himself in an intense state of lust. He remembered how nerve-wracking it had been for him as a kid when he cared about a game—he'd literally tremble with the effort of wanting his team to win. So, the few times he was able to attend a Sonics-Bulls playoff game, he spent the entire time in the stands releasing on how much he wanted to control the outcome. It made him feel a lot better. He enjoyed watching the game a lot more, and, in a funny way, he felt that he was releasing for 10,000 people. Ron wasn't mindlessly cheering the team on, and he was just as euphoric at the end of the game without the jitters. Now his wife jokes that he's got to go to all the games, because the Sonics won every time he saw them in person.

Words and phrases that describe lust:

- Abandon
- Anticipation
- Callous
- Can't wait
- Compulsive
- Craving
- Demanding
- Devious
- Driven
- Envy
- Exploitive
- Fixated
- Frenzy
- Frustrated
- Gluttonous
- Greedy
- Hoarding
- Hunger
- I want
- Impatient
- Lascivious
- Lecherous
- Manipulative
- Miserly
- Must have it
- Never enough
- Never satisfied
- Oblivious
- Obsessed
- Overindulgent
- Possessive
- Predatory
- Pushy
- Reckless
- Ruthless
- Scheming
- Selfish
- Voracious
- Wanton
- Wicked

Allow yourself to take a few moments and remember the last time that you or someone you know experienced lust. Then give yourself a few moments just to be with whatever feeling this memory brings up in this moment.

*Could you allow yourself to welcome
this feeling as best you can?*

Could you allow yourself to let it go?

Would you let it go?

When?

Before you move onto the next emotion, repeat this process a few more times until you feel as though you are able to release some or all of what you are feeling.

Anger

When we experience anger, we desire to strike out to hurt and stop others, but with hesitation. We may or may not strike out. Our bodies have a little more energy than in lust. It is less contracted, and the sensations can often be very intense and explosive. Our minds are a little less cluttered than in lust, but they are still noisy, stubborn, and obsessive. Our pictures are about destruction, and what we are going to do to others. Our thoughts are about getting even, about how we are going to make others pay. This energy can frighten us, and can cause us to force ourselves back into experiencing lower energy levels, even to hurt ourselves. The actions we take are mostly destructive to us and to those around us.

Paige harbored resentment against an ex-boyfriend whom she felt had betrayed her. Although their relationship had ended two years earlier, whenever she thought about him, she found herself bubbling over with an anger that virtually paralyzed her.

When this would happen, she indulged in revenge fantasies. Because she kept reliving her memory of having been hurt, the pain of the experience remained fresh. Even more important, her anger was getting in the way of developing a new, satisfying relationship.

When Paige took the Sedona Method Course, one of her goals was to release her longstanding anger and forgive her former boyfriend. In class, she was astonished to discover how easy it was to let go of the residual hurt and disappointment, which remarkably disappeared after only a few rounds of questioning. Almost immediately, she began opening to the possibility of relationship again. Then, whenever negative feelings arose, she simply released them and felt lighter, happier, and more hopeful about life.

Words and phrases that describe anger:

- Abrasive
- Aggressive
- Annoyed
- Argumentative
- Belligerent
- Boiling
- Brooding
- Caustic
- Defiant
- Demanding
- Destructive
- Disgust
- Explosive
- Fierce
- Frustrated
- Fuming
- Furious
- Harsh
- Hatred
- Hostility
- Impatience
- Indignant
- Irate
- Jealous
- Livid
- Mad
- Mean
- Merciless

- Murderous
- Outraged
- Petulant
- Pushy
- Rebellious
- Resentment
- Resistant
- Revolted
- Rude
- Savage
- Simmering
- Sizzling
- Smoldering
- Spiteful
- Steely
- Stern
- Stewing
- Stubborn
- Sullen
- Vengeful
- Vicious
- Violent
- Volcanic
- Wicked
- Willful

Allow yourself to take a few moments and remember the last time that you or someone you know experienced anger. Then give yourself a few moments just to be with whatever feeling this memory brings up in this moment.

Could you allow yourself to welcome
this feeling as best you can?

Could you allow yourself to let it go?

Would you let it go?

When?

As with the previous emotions, do this a few more times until you feel as though you are able to release some or all of what you are feeling. Then continue.

Pride

When we experience pride, we want to maintain the status quo. We are unwilling to change or move; therefore, we stop others from movement so they won't pass us up. Our bodies have a little more energy than in anger, but it often becomes unavailable. Even though it is less contracted, it is often muted and less visible. Our minds are a little less cluttered than in anger, but still noisy, rigid, and self-involved. Our pictures and thoughts are about what we have done and what we know. If we are even aware of others, we hope they will notice how great we are to cover over our nagging doubts.

Martin was what most people would consider a high-powered executive. Earlier in his career, he'd quickly moved up the corporate ladder without much concern for whom he stepped on along the way. By the time he'd bought the Sedona Method audiotapes, however, he'd hit a career wall. Although he thought he was still doing the right things, they had stopped producing the results he wanted. He had been passed over for a few promotions, and he couldn't understand why his managers didn't see how much better he was than the people who were getting promoted.

As he listened to the tapes, Martin discovered that he'd slipped into pride, which blinded him to his shortcomings and also to the support that would have been readily available all around him had he been open to receive it. As he let go, he started to appreciate his peers and his staff more spontaneously, and he felt more willing to work with the whole team without trying to maintain the distance from them that he had in the past. After he made this shift, he got promoted. Now Martin knows that he can continue his rise to the top without the need to step on or over anyone else along the way.

Words and phrases that describe pride:

- Above reproach
- Aloof
- Arrogant
- Bigoted
- Boastful
- Bored
- Clever
- Closed
- Complacent
- Conceited
- Contemptuous
- Cool
- Critical
- Disdain
- Dogmatic
- False dignity
- False humility
- False virtue
- Gloating
- Haughty
- Holier than thou
- Hypocritical
- Icy
- Isolated
- Judgmental
- Know-it-all
- Narrow-minded
- Never wrong
- Opinionated
- Overbearing
- Patronizing
- Pious
- Prejudiced
- Presumptuous
- Righteous
- Rigid
- Self-absorbed
- Self-satisfied
- Selfish
- Smug
- Snobbish
- Special
- Spoiled
- Stoic
- Stubborn
- Stuck-up
- Superior
- Uncompromising
- Unfeeling
- Unforgiving
- Unyielding
- Vain

Allow yourself to take a few moments and remember the last time that you or someone you know experienced pride.

Then give yourself a few moments just to be with whatever feeling this memory brings up in this moment.

Could you allow yourself to welcome this feeling as best you can?

Could you allow yourself to let it go?

Would you let it go?

When?

Now do this a few more times until you feel as though you are able to release some or all of what you are feeling before you move on to the next emotion.

Remember, the first six emotional states actually form a thin crust over the next three emotions of courageousness, acceptance, and peace. Where the first six mostly include feelings of "I can't," as we allow ourselves to uncover the next three emotional states within ourselves, we begin more and more to feel "I can."

Courageousness

When we experience courageousness, we have the willingness to act without hesitation. We can do. We can correct. We can change whatever, whenever needed. We have the willingness to let go and move on. Our bodies have a lot more energy than in pride, and it is available for constructive outward action. Our energy is high, available and clear. Our minds are much less cluttered than in pride, and a lot less noisy. We are flexible, resilient, and open. Our pictures and thoughts are about what we can do and learn, and of how we can support others in the same way. We are self-motivated and self-reliant while still being willing for others to succeed. We can laugh out loud, even at our own mistakes. Life is fun.

We tap the energy of courageousness every time we say "yes" to the releasing questions. Because courageousness is our natural state, we can access it no matter how covered over it appears to be at the moment due to the prevalence of any of the other emotions.

In addition to being a Sedona Method instructor, David is a professional mime and performs a 40-minute show for inner city public school students in New York City on the dangers of drugs. Each year, at least 20,000 young people from kindergarten through the eighth grade see him, and, these days, he approaches the students from a steady core of courage and acceptance. But it wasn't always so. For five or six years, he often experienced fear of losing control and not being able to make it through or knowing how to handle the students. On several occasions, there had been as many as 500 rebellious kids in the room where he was performing. He had an abstract fear that something would go wrong, that they would fight or be loud, and he couldn't be successful.

Now, due to releasing before and during his performances, David literally has no fear, and many times he has lived through all of the circumstances he once feared. A school principal might turn a loud assembly over to him, or perhaps there will be a smart aleck in the room. He simply lets the tension in his stomach release and is peaceful as he looks out and says, "I look forward to doing what I'm here to do for you, and, in a moment, I'll continue as though I haven't stopped and spoken. But I won't be able to do that as long as you're also doing a show while I work." The kids are then entirely on his side. His commitment to freedom has enabled him to have a much greater impact with his vital message to the at-risk students he serves. David says, "When I contribute from a state of courage and acceptance, I bring harmony to the world. That only happens by letting go inside me. Then my actions are automatically more loving and compassionate."

Words and phrases that describe courageousness:

- Adventurous
- Alert
- Alive
- Assured
- Aware
- Centered
- Certain
- Cheerful
- Clarity
- Compassion
- Competent
- Confident
- Creative
- Daring
- Decisive
- Dynamic
- Eager
- Enthusiastic
- Exhilaration
- Explorative
- Flexible
- Focused
- Giving
- Happy
- Honorable
- Humor
- I can
- Independent
- Initiative
- Integrity
- Invincible
- Loving
- Lucid
- Motivated
- Non-resistant
- Open
- Optimistic
- Perspective
- Positive
- Purposeful
- Receptive
- Resilient
- Resourceful
- Responsive
- Secure
- Self-sufficient
- Sharp
- Spontaneous

- Strong
- Supportive
- Tireless
- Vigorous

- Visionary
- Willing
- Zest

Allow yourself to take a few moments and remember the last time that you or someone you know experienced courageousness. Then give yourself a few moments just to be with whatever feeling this memory brings up in this moment.

Could you allow yourself to welcome this feeling as best you can?

Could you allow yourself to let it go?

Would you let it go?

When?

If you are having a hard time letting go of a good feeling, please remember that, as you let it go, you are allowing it to get better. We all have an infinite supply of the positive emotions that are being covered over by our limiting ones. That is why positive emotions are often strengthened when we release, while negative emotions get weaker. You are also weakening your lifelong tendency to suppress and hold on.

Repeat the releasing process a few more times until you feel as though you are able to let go of some or all of what you are feeling. Then move on to the next emotion.

Acceptance

When we experience acceptance, we have and enjoy everything as it is. We have no need to change anything. It just is, and it's okay. It's beautiful just as it is. Our bodies have a lot more energy than in courageousness. That energy is mostly at rest, yet available if we need it. Our energy is light, warm, and open. Our minds are much less cluttered than in courageousness, and mostly quiet and content. Our pictures and thoughts are in love with the exquisiteness of what is. Life is joyous.

Ralph and his wife were attending a Seven-day Retreat with me in Sedona. Before the course began each morning, they usually took a hike. On one particular day, they went up to a spot known as Bell Rock, where Ralph spent some time releasing on his goals. When the familiar feeling of "It'll never happen" came over him, he had an instant recognition that the message was *only a feeling*. He didn't even have to grab onto it. What made the experience so special was how visual it was. As he stood there, he could see a whirlwind of feelings arising within him, and he observed himself merely accepting the feelings without reaching out to hold onto them. The image of the whirlwind arose several times with less and less force until it ultimately vanished.

Although the whole vision lasted only a minute or so, it was very powerful. Ralph says, "Like having a stray dog come to the door, I knew that if I fed the feeling, it would come back. But if I didn't, it would eventually go away." Back in class, he shared how truly wonderful and free he felt.

Words and phrases that describe acceptance:

- Abundance
- Appreciative
- Balance
- Beautiful
- Belonging
- Childlike
- Compassion
- Considerate
- Delight
- Elated

- Embracing
- Empathy
- Enriched
- Everything's okay
- Friendly
- Fullness
- Gentle
- Glowing
- Gracious
- Harmonious
- Harmony
- Intuitive
- I have
- In tune
- Joyful
- Loving
- Magnanimous
- Mellow
- Naturalness
- Nothing to change
- Open
- Playful
- Radiant
- Receptive
- Secure
- Soft
- Tender
- Understanding
- Warm
- Well-being
- Wonder

Allow yourself to take a few moments and remember the last time that you or someone you know experienced acceptance. Then give yourself a few moments just to be with whatever feeling this memory brings up in this moment.

Could you allow yourself to welcome this feeling as best you can?

Could you allow yourself to let it go?

Would you let it go?

When?

Remember to do your best to let go of the positive emotions.

As with the previous emotions, do this a few more times until you feel as though you are able to release some or all of what you are feeling. Then continue with the final emotion: peace.

Peace

When we experience peace, we feel, "I am. I am whole, complete, and total unto myself. Everyone and everything is part of myself. It is all perfect." The body has a lot more energy than in acceptance but is totally at rest—still. The energy is quiet and calm. The mind is clear and empty, yet totally aware. There is no need for pictures or thoughts. Life is as it is, and all is well.

My editor Stephanie told me about a moment of peace and oneness she recently experienced when she was holding her friend's six-week old baby. As he innocently snuggled against her chest, she relaxed into the experience of his trust. She entirely released her expectations and concerns. She was neither planning for the future, nor worrying about the past, only resting in the NOW with the tiny infant. There were no obstacles to loving and being loved. All she needed was a heart. For peace, she only had to *be*.

Words and phrases that describe peace:

- Ageless
- Awareness
- Being
- Boundless
- Calm
- Centered
- Complete
- Eternal
- Free
- Fulfilled
- Glowing
- I am
- Light
- Oneness
- Perfection
- Pure
- Quiet
- Serenity
- Space
- Still
- Timeless
- Tranquility
- Unlimited
- Whole

Allow yourself to take a few moments and remember the last time that you or someone you know experienced peace. Then give yourself a few moments just to be with whatever feeling this memory brings up in this moment.

Could you allow yourself to welcome this feeling as best you can?

Could you allow yourself to let it go?

Would you let it go?

When?

Exploration: You Are Not Your Feelings

Notice how you feel after your journey through the nine emotional states. If you allowed yourself to feel the import of what you were reading (as best you could), you probably already feel a little more relaxed, in touch,

"An interesting thing happened to me while I was listening to the audio program in my truck. Hearing disturbing sounds, I pulled into the nearest gas station and parked. No sooner had I dialed their payphone to call a tow truck than a man ran up, saying, 'Your truck is on fire!' Then he got a fire extinguisher, popped the hood, and put the fire out before I had a chance to react. I'm generally a person who stays calm in emergencies, but in this case, it was like I was an observer to an event that was happening to someone else."

—Victoria Menear,
Pleasant Hill, CA

and open to your emotions. If you are not sure, or feel no change at all, don't worry about it. Remember that you're learning a new skill, and it may take a while to become proficient. You have a lot more practice at suppressing and expressing your emotions than you do so far at letting go. Soon, you'll be more in touch with your emotions and have an easier time identifying them and letting them go.

Let's take a few moments and explore the following statement to conclude our journey through the nine energy states: "Emotions are just emotions. They are not you, they are not facts, and you can let them go." This simple statement epitomizes much of what the Sedona Method is about. But what does this actually mean?

The first part, "Emotions are just emotions," may seem obvious, yet this is not how most of us live. We live in a culture that mainly deals with emotions on either end of a broad spectrum. On one end of the spectrum, we deny our emotions and the effect they have on our rational thinking processes, on our health, or on our experience of life. On the other end, we deify our emotions, investing way too much importance on the supposed messages that they are here to deliver and what they mean about who we are.

There are grains of truth in the perspectives of both acting rationally and of not denying our emotions. However, most of us lose ourselves, and our ability to choose, in each perspective. Depending on how our rational mind is interpreting our sensory input in the moment, we can often swing wildly between the two.

Most of us tend to identify with our emotions as though they are who we are. As I commented in both the Introduction and Chapter 1, this identification is even found in our language, such as when we talk about "being angry" as opposed to "feeling angry." It is our identification with feelings that often makes it more difficult than it needs to be to let them go. We often cling to our identification with a feeling because we think, "It is who I am." We believe, "I feel, therefore I am."

From the releasing perspective, this is not true. The next part of the statement, "They are not you," is a reminder that this is a false identification. I recommend that you examine this idea for yourself. See whether it is more accurate to notice that emotions come and go, while who you truly are always remains.

If you are not sure who you are beyond your emotions, allow that to be for now. As you explore the Sedona Method and you start to practice releasing throughout the day, you'll uncover your true nature beyond the self-imposed limitations created by your emotions.

When you find yourself lost in identification with an emotion, you can ask yourself, "*Am I* this feeling, or am I just *having a feeling*?" This simple question can help you separate yourself from a false identification. You may also use the question in the first step of the Method, "What am I feeling?" to help recognize that you are not the feeling. You are merely having one. This allows for the opportunity to let it go.

As we explore the statement further, we come to: "They are not facts." Have you ever been sure of what you thought was a fact—such as that someone you knew liked you—only to find the opposite was true? Or have you ever been sure that something was about to go wrong only to have it go very right? These are just two examples of how we relate to the input that we get from our feelings. We live in a world of assumptions, thinking we are relating to facts. In some ways, our feelings are just stories that we have made up about a particular set of sensations. These stories often, if not always, come after the feeling has already arisen in our consciousness. We then use them to explain why we feel the way we feel.

Treating emotions like facts can be a problem, because we often don't realize that we have made an assumption until it is too late. By then we have made what we thought was a rational decision, only to find out later that it was just based on an automatic emotional reaction.

The final part of the statement focuses on what this whole book is about: "You can let them go." The more you accept and employ your natural ability to release, the more every part of your experience of life will be transformed.

Make a Commitment to Your Growth

Before you move on to the next chapter, I recommend you practice releasing on the nine emotional states a few more times. Every time you reread this chapter, you'll get more out of it and deepen your use of the Method. Take the opportunity to examine your life from the new perspective of high and low energy, and allow yourself to notice how the different emotional states are affecting your life. Also, do your best to incorporate the releasing process more fully into your life. Using the Method throughout your day is where the rubber meets the road, so to speak. It is also where you'll start to see the profound results that are mentioned throughout this book.

Chart of the Nine Emotional States

Your Roadmap to Emotional Freedom

freedom
imperturbability

Apathy	Grief	Fear	Lust	Anger
Bored	Abandoned	Anxious	Abandon	Abrasive
Can't win	Abused	Apprehensive	Anticipation	Aggressive
Careless	Accused	Cautious	Callous	Annoyed
Cold	Anguished	Clammy	Can't wait	Argumentative
Cut-off	Ashamed	Cowardice	Compulsive	Belligerent
Dead	Betrayed	Defensive	Craving	Boiling
Defeated	Blue	Distrust	Demanding	Brooding
Depressed	Cheated	Doubt	Devious	Caustic
Demoralized	Despair	Dread	Driven	Defiant
Desolate	Disappointed	Embarrassed	Envy	Demanding
Despair	Distraught	Evasive	Exploitive	Destructive
Discouraged	Embarrassed	Foreboding	Fixated	Disgust
Disillusioned	Forgotten	Frantic	Frenzy	Explosive
Doomed	Guilty	Hesitant	Frustrated	Fierce
Drained	Heartbroken	Horrified	Gluttonous	Frustrated
Failure	Heartache	Hysterical	Greedy	Fuming
Forgetful	Heartsick	Inhibited	Hoarding	Furious
Futile	Helpless	Insecure	Hunger	Harsh
Giving up	Hurt	Irrational	I want	Hatred
Hardened	If only	Nausea	Impatient	Hostility
Hopeless	Ignored	Nervous	Lascivious	Impatience
Humorless	Inadequate	Panic	Lecherous	Indignant
I can't	Inconsolable	Paralyzed	Manipulative	Irate
I don't care	It's not fair	Paranoid	Miserly	Jealous
I don't count	Left out	Scared	Must have it	Livid
Inattentive	Longing	Secretive	Never enough	Mad
Indecisive	Loss	Shaky	Never satisfied	Mean
Indifferent	Melancholy	Shy	Oblivious	Merciless
Invisible	Misunderstood	Skeptical	Obsessed	Murderous
It's too late	Mourning	Stage fright	Overindulgent	Outraged
Lazy	Neglected	Superstitious	Possessive	Petulant
Let it wait	Nobody cares	Suspicious	Predatory	Pushy
Listless	Nobody loves me	Tense	Pushy	Rebellious
Loser	Nostalgia	Terrified	Reckless	Resentment
Lost	Passed over	Threatened	Ruthless	Resistant
Negative	Pity	Timid	Scheming	Revolted
Numb	Poor me	Trapped	Selfish	Rude
Overwhelmed	Regret	Uncertain	Voracious	Savage
Powerless	Rejected	Uneasy	Wanton	Simmering
Resigned	Remorse	Vulnerable	Wicked	Sizzling
Shock	Sadness	Want to escape		Smoldering
Spaced out	Sorrow	Wary		Spiteful
Stoned	Tearful	Worry		Steely
Stuck	Tormented			Stern
Too tired	Torn			Stewing
Unfeeling	Tortured			Stubborn
Unfocused	Unhappy			Sullen
Useless	Unloved			Vengeful
Vague	Unwanted			Vicious
Wasted	Vulnerable			Violent
What's the use?	Why me			Volcanic
Why try?	Wounded			Wicked
Worthless				Willful

Pride	Courageousness	Acceptance	Peace
Above reproach	Adventurous	Abundance	Ageless
Aloof	Alert	Appreciative	Awareness
Arrogant	Alive	Balance	Being
Bigoted	Assured	Beautiful	Boundless
Boastful	Aware	Belonging	Calm
Bored	Centered	Childlike	Centered
Clever	Certain	Compassion	Complete
Closed	Cheerful	Considerate	Eternal
Complacent	Clarity	Delight	Free
Conceited	Compassion	Elated	Fulfilled
Contemptuous	Competent	Embracing	Glowing
Cool	Confident	Empathy	I am
Critical	Creative	Enriched	Light
Disdain	Daring	Everything's okay	Oneness
Dogmatic	Decisive	Friendly	Perfection
False dignity	Dynamic	Fullness	Pure
False humility	Eager	Gentle	Quiet
False virtue	Enthusiastic	Glowing	Serenity
Gloating	Exhilaration	Gracious	Space
Haughty	Explorative	Harmonious	Still
Holier than thou	Flexible	Harmony	Timeless
Hypocritical	Focused	Intuitive	Tranquility
Icy	Giving	In tune	Unlimited
Isolated	Happy	Joyful	Whole
Judgmental	Honorable	Loving	
Know-it-all	Humor	Magnanimous	
Narrow-minded	I can	Mellow	
Never wrong	Independent	Naturalness	
Opinionated	Initiative	Nothing to change	
Overbearing	Integrity	Open	
Patronizing	Invincible	Playful	
Pious	Loving	Radiant	
Prejudiced	Lucid	Receptive	
Presumptuous	Motivated	Secure	
Righteous	Non-resistant	Soft	
Rigid	Open	Tender	
Self-absorbed	Optimistic	Understanding	
Self-satisfied	Perspective	Warm	
Selfish	Positive	Well-being	
Smug	Purposeful	Wonder	
Snobbish	Receptive		
Special	Resilient		
Spoiled	Resourceful		
Stoic	Responsive		
Stubborn	Secure		
Stuck-up	Self-sufficient		
Superior	Sharp		
Uncompromising	Spontaneous		
Unfeeling	Strong		
Unforgiving	Supportive		
Unyielding	Tireless		
Vain	Vigorous		
	Visionary		
	Willing		
	Zest		

Chapter 4

Dissolving Your Resistance

Rather than allowing the flow of life to carry us where we want to go, most of us spend a lot of time swimming upstream. We assume that we have to struggle to get what we want and push against the current. But what if that's not true? What if we could actually use the natural flow of life to support us in having what we want? No doubt you've already experienced what being in a state of flow is like. Think of a day when everything worked perfectly! You just seemed to be in the right place at the right time doing exactly the right thing. Now think of a TYPICAL day. Which would you prefer? The greatest obstacle to being in the flow all day long, every day, is resistance to what is.

Good news: You can let go of resistance just like any other feeling.

Resistance prevents us from moving ahead in all areas of our life, especially in the area of personal growth and happiness. If you've read this far, you've already had experience in releasing many different types of feelings. You've probably noticed how willing you are at certain times to release, where-as, at other times, you find it easier to put the book down and do something—*anything*—else. It is exactly this kind of resistance that prevents us from following through on our good intentions, even when they pertain to an activity as obviously beneficial as the work we're doing in this book.

It is important to note that letting go of resistance does not mean you must allow others to control you. You can still stand up for what's correct without resistance. If you have ever studied a martial art, such as aikido, karate, or tae kwon do, you know that if you hit someone with a tight fist, you'll get hurt. But if your fist is slightly relaxed—without resistance—you have a lot more power and a lot more strength. Martial artists also understand that when opponents attack you, by *not* resisting, you can turn that energy against them. The same things are true every time you let go of the feeling of resistance. You have more strength with less effort and greater emotional resilience and stamina.

What Is Resistance?

Have you ever started a project really gung ho and lost enthusiasm somewhere in the middle? That's resistance. Resistance is quite insidious. It's one of the main things that stop us from having, doing, and being what we want in life. In fact, we often resist the things we really like and care about. And if someone *tells* us to do something, that's a sure-fired trigger for resistance. It may come up even if we would like to do what we're being told to do. Resistance can be self-sabotaging and counterproductive, and it's operating constantly, because we live in a sea of "shoulds" and "have to's" and "must do's" and other imperatives. Any time there is an imperative, it stirs up resistance.

When you are told you *should* do something, or you *have to* do something, what do you feel inside? "No way! Don't tell me what to do!" The exact same thing happens when you tell yourself what to do. If you say to yourself, "You *have to* work on your bills," what happens? You probably respond, "Oh, yeah?" Or, if you say to yourself, "You'd better not do this anymore," perhaps referring to a habit you want to break, you may find yourself doing whatever it is even more. That's just the nature of our minds. We simply do not like being told what to do. Yet, we are continually "shoulding" on ourselves and then wondering why we are not having fun and why things are not getting done.

The first time I remember resistance operating in my life, I was a young child. A pattern of resistance got initiated one day when I was feeling introspective and just did not want to go out to play. Although I loved going out and playing with my friends on the block where I lived, on this day I wanted to be by myself and play with my own toys. But my being alone disturbed my mother, so she insisted that I go out to play with my friends. Because this happened a few times in a row, it quickly turned into a point of contention between us. Soon, I hated going out to play with my friends and started avoiding it at all costs. Unintentionally, my mother had thrown me into resistance about playing with my friends. Although I was only feeling resistant to her *should*, I spent many years believing that I didn't like to play with others, which was just not true.

Resistance manifests in many different ways, some of them subtle. Maybe you forget things that are important to you. Or perhaps you find yourself gradually moving away from things that are really helpful. Let's say, for instance, that you're doing great with releasing. You're really enjoying it, and you think it's the best thing since sliced bread. Then a few days, weeks, or months later, it's hard for you to persuade yourself to do it, even though you've had firsthand experience of how much it can help you. What happened? You hit resistance. Most likely, you turned releasing into a "should." In situations like this one, the "should" creates an opposing force equal to, or greater than, the force that you're exerting when you're trying to get something to happen.

Here are some definitions of resistance that may help you recognize it:

- Resistance feels like trying to move forward with the brakes on.
- Any time you feel like you have to, must, or should do anything, you're in resistance.
- Resistance is opposition to force, real or imagined.
- Resistance is pushing against the world so that it will push back.
- The feeling or thought "I can't" is resistance. It takes a conscious effort to overcome the unconscious effort (habit) of holding down the feelings. That unconscious habit is resistance.
- Resistance is just another program that we have manufactured to protect the other programs. (I will explain what programs are and how they affect us in Chapter 12.)
- Resistance is when you haven't yet decided whether or not to do something, but you do it anyway, and it's difficult. To make it easy to do, all you need to do is decide to do it and do it—or decide not to do it and don't do it.

112

Releasing Resistance

You can use the basic three-step releasing process that you learned in Chapter 1 to let go of resistance any time you notice that you're feeling it. Either read the questions to yourself, or have a releasing partner work through them with you.

Step 1: Allow yourself to welcome the resistance in this moment.

Step 2: Ask yourself one of the following three questions:

Could I let go of this resistance?

Could I allow myself to feel resistance in this moment?

Could I welcome the feeling of resistance?

Then ask:

Would I?

When?

Step 3: Repeat the preceding two steps as often as needed until you feel free.

"For 30 years, it has always been an effort to clean my apartment. I hated it every time I had to tackle the problem. Now I am in 100 percent motivation mode to clean and throw out old stuff. For the first time in my life, I can actually take more than a couple of steps in my room without tripping. I always made the excuse that I never had the time to clean up. Now get this: I work 4 jobs totaling about 80 hours a week, but I can still find the energy and time to do it. And I am no spring chicken with boundless energy. What I do have, and what the Sedona Method has given me, is the freedom to do it."

—Terence O'Brien,
Tokyo, Japan

Once you truly understand that you can let resistance go, you'll find yourself doing so without a lot of excess thought.

As always, remember that "yes" or "no" are both acceptable answers. You will often let go even if you say "no." So, answer the questions that you choose with a minimum of thought. Stay away from second-guessing yourself, or getting into an internal debate about the merits of releasing your resistance, or the consequences of letting it go. Whatever your response, move on to the next step.

At first, the results may be quite subtle. Very quickly, however—particularly when you are persistent—the results will become more pronounced. You may find that you have several layers of resistance about a particular topic, so it may take a while to release entirely. However, every layer you let go of is gone for good.

Jane has been teaching time management courses in corporations for years. Still, her own ability to procrastinate is, as she says, "alive and well." But, rather than beating herself up about the procrastination, she finds it easiest to let go of her resistance, which is part of the procrastination. She asks herself: *Could I welcome how much I dislike this dreadful task?* Then she can pick small pieces of the task to get started on, and she finds she develops momentum. No, she doesn't always leap forward with choirs of angels singing in the background, but she does move forward more easily. She does get unstuck.

"Like anything else, letting go of resistance is not going to work unless you actually do it," says Jane. "But when you do, it's a masterful technique. Afterwards, there's a sense of movement and a change of perspective."

Three More Ways to Dissolve Resistance

Since each of us carries around a backlog of resistance, we can actively look for things in the environment to which we feel resistant and let go on them. Try the following:

1. Look around the room you're in right now and pick any item.
2. Focus your resistance on it by asking: Could I allow myself to feel my resistance to that item as best I can?
3. Then use the three basic releasing steps to let it go: Could I let it go? Would I? When?
4. Repeat this exercise several times in a row, and then go about your day. You will notice that everything in your life gets easier the more you let go of resistance.

This is a great excise to do when you have down time at work, while you're commuting, or any time you simply want to feel more in the flow and have more "get up and go."

Another terrific way to release resistance is to admit that when you're resisting having, being, or doing something, you are probably also resisting *not* having, being, or doing it. When this happens, apply the following process:

1. Think of something that you resist doing.

   Now ask yourself:

   Could I allow myself to let go of resisting doing ____?
   Would I?
   When?

2. Then ask yourself the opposite:

   Could I let go of resisting not doing _____?
   Would I?
   When?

3. Keep going back and forth between both sets of questions until you feel the resistance dissolve. Then notice how much easier it is to do this particular thing.

The same process is useful for releasing on items you resist having and being. Simply substitute the words *having* or *being* for the word *doing*.

Are you wondering about how to put this technique into practice in your life? Here are two possibilities. Let's say you are resisting not having money—a common feeling, for sure. Consider that you are also probably resisting having it. If you were not resisting having money, you'd probably already have more than enough. Or let's say you resist being alone—not having a relationship. I guarantee that you're also resisting having a relationship. Release on both sides of these issues and watch what happens in your life. I think you're in for a pleasant surprise.

Often, when we're trying to release and it's not happening, we know we're hitting a wall of resistance. If this happens to you, giving yourself permission to hold on to your stubborn resistance is another effective way to approach it. Once you have permission to do what you are already doing, enough space will be created inside for you to let go. Simply ask yourself: *Could I give myself permission to hold on for a moment?* Often, you'll spontaneously release at this point. If the resistance does not let go completely, however, go back to the basic releasing questions: *Could I let go of holding on? Would I? When?* You can go back and forth several times between giving yourself permission to hold on and gently allowing yourself to let go in the usual manner.

Bob describes himself as a person who has a fair amount of trouble with resistance. "Normally, I am decisive and directed, but, a couple of days ago, I had a day where I couldn't decide on anything. It was as though my pencil was stuck in a fan. Finally, I decided to let the pencil be stuck, and the situation righted itself immediately." He generally finds that his resistance dissolves by diving into it or asking: *Could I just allow myself be as resistant as I am?*

Exploration: Getting in Touch with Resistance

During Sedona Method courses, we frequently do a very simple, yet powerful, exercise that's designed to help us get in touch with how resistance feels on a physical level. The more we can connect to the feeling of resistance, the easier it is to let it go. I therefore recommend approaching this exercise from your heart rather than your mind. In other words, don't try to figure out the *correct* outcome. There isn't one.

This exercise may be done in two ways. The first version is done alone. The second version is for partners. Most people find it a great aid in letting go both of resistance and of the feelings that are hidden beneath it.

Exploring Physical Resistance on Your Own

To begin, place your hands together in front of you in an isometric or prayer position, with the palms touching. Arbitrarily decide which hand will push and which will resist. With the hand that you decide is the pushing hand, allow yourself to push gently against the other hand, which is resisting, and have that hand hold its position.

While you are doing this, allow yourself, as best you can, to get in touch with what it feels like to resist.

Next, let go of resisting the push without trying to control or do anything in particular with your hands. Just let your hands do what they do.

Repeat this activity several times, switching which hand is pushing and which is resisting, and allow yourself to notice your emotions as you let go.

Spend some time after you're done reflecting on the exercise and using the basic releasing process to let go of whatever thoughts and feelings come up.

Exploring Physical Resistance with a Partner

When you do this version of the exercise, remember that it's only an exploration. It is not about who is the strongest or who can knock the other one over. It is very important never to do anything that's physically or emotionally hurtful to your partner.

To begin, both partners stand facing each other and make eye contact. Select which partner will push and which will resist. For the purpose of this description, let's say that your partner is the first "pusher." Then, reaching both arms out to the sides, you and your partner will touch your palms together.

Now, your partner will push gently against your hands. As he or she pushes, simply resist the push, holding both your hands steady. The pressure being exerted should be strong enough so you both can feel the resistance, but not enough so that the partner who's the "resister" has any concern about falling over.

As your partner pushes against your hands, allow yourself to get in touch with what it feels like to resist. Then, let go of the resistance as best you can, without trying to control or do anything in particular with your hands. Just let your hands do what they do.

Next, switch roles and run through the same exercise. Whoever was the pusher now becomes the resister and vice versa. Reverse the roles several times until both partners have a clear feeling sense of what it's like to resist and to let go of resistance.

In the process of doing this exercise, you may discover some patterns in yourself and in others that relate to resistance. Feel free to share your discoveries with your partner *after* you've completed the exercise, but avoid getting into an intellectual discussion. Take turns supporting each other in releasing whatever gets stirred up.

> "With the Sedona Method at my disposal, I no longer feel helpless when negative feelings arise. I have a tool to prevent them from causing me to enter a downward spiral, and even to reverse my outlook."
> —Dr. Saul Weiner,
> Buffalo Grove, IL

Written Releasing: The "Things I Have to Do" Worksheet

The following process is designed to assist you in releasing your resistance. It's simple to use. To prepare, make two columns across the top of a clean sheet of paper in your releasing journal. The first column is labeled "Things I feel I have to do." The second column is labeled "What is my NOW feeling about that?"

Begin by make a list of everything that you feel you "have to" do in the first column.

Now, take each item, one at a time, and write down your NOW feelings about it. There may be several emotions involved. Check especially for resistance as you do this exploration, along with any other emotions that arise.

Then, release each feeling—and any resistance—to completion. Once you are fully released, either put a check mark next to it or cross it out.

THINGS I HAVE TO DO

Things I feel I have to do ...	What is my NOW feeling about that?
Pay the bills	~~Anger~~ R ✓
Clean the house	✓ Depressed ~~R~~
Go to work	~~Tired~~ ~~R~~
Be nice	~~Fear~~ R ✓

Repeat the above steps and continue releasing your NOW feelings until you are fully released on that item from the first column. Remember also to release your so-called positive feelings, so you can keep moving to higher energy states.

Process for Letting Go of Resistance

You can use this process to start or continue letting go of your resistance. It can be done on a specific topic you pick from the "Things I Have to Do" worksheet above, or it can be used simply to free you from the inner holdback that we all experience as resistance. Either read the questions to yourself or have a releasing partner read them to you. By the way, when you release on your own, you have the option to substitute the first person pronoun "I" for the second person pronoun "you," if that would feel more natural.

Begin by thinking of something that you believe you should do, must do, have to do, or it's important that you do—any one of those. Notice how you tighten up inside when you think about it, how you push back.

Could you welcome that feeling of resistance?
Could you just allow it to be here?
Then, could you let it go?
Would you?
When?

Now, think of that same thing or something else that it seems extremely important to get yourself to do, or that someone else told you that you must do—like losing weight, stopping smoking, making more money, paying your bills, or being out of debt. Notice how that immediately engenders resistance inside of you.

Could you welcome that feeling of resistance?
Then, could you let it go?
Would you?
When?

Next, think of something else in your life to which you have resistance. We also tend to resist things that we have to do repeatedly, even simple things like brushing our teeth, taking out the garbage, or mowing the lawn. Maintenance tasks that we do frequently, such as washing the dishes, are big issues for a lot of people. Truly feel what it's like to resist. Welcome it. Allow it to be here.

Then, could you let it go?
Would you?
When?

Find something else in your life that you resist. There are

certain sensations that we resist, like loud noises or bright lights, or certain inflections in people's voice, even certain smells. Find one of those kinds of items that you resist.

Could you welcome that resistance into your awareness?

Could you just embrace it?

Then, could you let it go?

Would you?

When?

We also resist certain people. So, think of a person in your life right now to whom you have resistance. Remember, resistance doesn't mean you don't care about them. Sometimes we even resist the people whom we love. Do you have someone in mind? This could be an in-law—that's a popular one—or anyone else in your experience that you resist.

Could you allow that resistance into your awareness?

Could you welcome it?

Then, could you let it go?

Would you?

When?

Another big thing we resist is our feelings. We very often don't want to feel what we're feeling, especially if we've labeled the emotion as "unpleasant." Most people resist certain emotions more than others, like fear or anger. Right now, can you sense how you resist certain feelings?

Could you welcome that resistance into your awareness?

Could you just allow yourself to resist for a moment?

Then, could you let it go?

Would you?

When?

Next, think of something you resist doing even though you

enjoy it. Ironically, many of us resist things that are good for us, things that we like to do. There's still hesitation. That's why it can seem as though we never find time for pleasurable activities.

Could you just allow yourself to feel the resistance? Welcome it into your awareness.

Then, could you let it go?

Would you?

When?

We also resist things about our body—certain sensations, or the way it looks. Even when we are at an ideal weight (as if that were possible in our weight-obsessed culture), most of us just obsess about our weight and the way we look, and we resist however we look, even if we're having a good-hair day. So, find something about your physicality that you resist, something about your body, either the way it feels or the way it looks, or something like that.

Simply welcome the resistance into your awareness.

Could you let it go?

Would you?

When?

Any one of the topics above would be ideal for further exploration. Use this process any time you feel resistant or would simply like to get more into the flow of life.

Staying in the Flow

If there were no resistance, we would all go free very quickly. Therefore, it's important for us to keep releasing constantly on resistance in order to allow our feelings to come up and move out. As you continue reading this book and working on

123

the processes it contains, remember to release on resistance any time you feel stuck.

Here are three important tips for handling resistance and staying in the flow:

- *Ask, don't tell.* We've already discussed what happens when someone tells you that you have to, or should do, something. It immediately brings up resistance. Conversely, your imperatives also trigger resistance in others. So be clever. Avoid bringing up unnecessary resistance in others by asking them to do what you want them to do rather than telling them. If you get into this habit, you'll find that you get a lot more cooperation. By the way, I would also recommend that you communicate in this fashion with yourself, in order to get more cooperation and less resistance from within, as well.

- *Do what you do—and don't do what you don't do.* Very often we feel that we should be doing something differently than we're doing it, or that we should be doing something that we're not doing. The way around this dilemma is to allow yourself to do what you're doing when you are doing it, and to not do what you're not doing when you are not doing it— without the extra dimension of "shoulding" on yourself. Any time you find yourself shoulding, take a moment to release your resistance.

  Please understand that this doesn't mean staying stuck in a rut. Actually, the results will be the exact opposite. As you let go of shoulds and the corresponding

Dissolving Your Resistance

resistance that shoulding engenders, you'll find yourself easily doing whatever you're doing and not obsessing over that which you are not doing. This includes anything that you've been trying to get yourself to do or to stop doing. You will be breaking out of the ruts that resistance has already created in your life.

- *Ease off the pressure.* Does what you're doing feel hard? This is a clear indication that you've hit a wall of your own resistance. You are probably pressuring yourself or feeling pressure from someone else. If you are pressuring yourself, make a conscious decision to take the pressure off. As a result, you'll probably find that you're getting done whatever you are trying to do a lot more easily, more quickly, and even more efficiently and enjoyably. Here's an interesting fact: You can't feel others pushing you. You can only feel yourself pushing back. Thus, if you feel that others are pressuring you, let go of your feelings of wanting to push back or resisting their pushes. As a result, you'll find that whatever you're doing will be done with much more ease and grace.

Before you go on to the next chapter, explore how resistance is blocking the intentions you wrote down at the end of Chapter 1 (see page 46). As you let go of your resistance in these areas, begin noticing the ease and flow that's always there as well as the increased ease and flow that shows up as you let go of resistance. The more you practice letting go of resistance, the better you'll feel, and the easier life will become.

Resistance can be a major obstacle to having what you want and feeling the way you want to feel. However, you can easily let it go and enjoy the benefits of a life without resistance filled with all that you choose.

Chapter 5

Your Key to Serenity

"God grant me the serenity to accept the things I cannot change, courage to change the things I can, and wisdom to know the difference."

—*The Serenity Prayer*, Reinhold Niebuhr

You have probably heard the Serenity Prayer. And if you're like most of us, at times you still find yourself waiting for an answer. Well, here it is! As you do the work in this chapter, you'll discover a way to accept the things that you cannot change. You will find that you're easily and bravely changing the things in your life that need to be changed. In addition, the wisdom to distinguish between the two will suddenly be at your fingertips.

What is the answer? It is so simple that it may confound you. Let go of the feeling of wanting to change it—"it" being anything in your life, or within the scope of your personal experience, that you do not like and want to be different than the way it is, including events in the past. If you remain open to the elegance and simplicity of this solution, it has the power to set you free.

How does letting go of wanting to change things help us? Besides the obvious outcome of feeling better as we let go, there are several ways. Let's start by looking at acceptance. Accepting what we can't change is not always easy. The mind rebels at the whole notion. However, when we let go of wanting to change the way things are, we naturally move into greater acceptance without having to try to force it to happen.

In regards to changing the things that need to be changed, examine your personal experience. Quickly review your life and make a mental list of anything you want to change. It is probably quite lengthy, and many of the items on this list are longstanding. So far, many things you've wanted to change have not changed, right? Although the mind informs us that the desire to change something can actually change it, or that wanting to change what needs to be changed will cause us to take an action, in most cases the exact opposite is true. When we are focused on wanting to change a problem, our awareness of the problem causes it to persist. We hold the issue in mind in order to change or resist it.

Here's how this works. Perhaps we have an experience that we don't like (the boss yells at us), or something happens to a person we care about (a friend gets sick or has a car accident), or maybe we don't like the news we hear that day (the stock market takes a nose dive). Therefore, we want to change it. Either we think, "I hope this doesn't happen to me," or, "I hope this never happens again," which is where we get stuck. Since the mind sees and creates in pictures, it doesn't accurately translate negations—words like *not*, *never*, or *don't*. As a result, it interprets our hopes in reverse and sustains them.

If you don't believe me, try right now to *not* picture a shoe. What happened? If you're like most people, you immediately saw a shoe in your mind's eye. The harder we try to *not* create what we do not want, the stronger we're holding on to the idea; thus, the more likely we are to create it in our reality.

So, what is the solution? Easy. Let go of the sense of wanting to change something, and the unwanted pictures about it that you were holding in mind will dissolve; then, you'll courageously move into action to make the changes that are necessary.

Lastly, how can we distinguish between what we can and cannot change? There's a simple process. Any time you're not sure whether something in your life needs to be changed or allowed to be as it is, make a decision to let go of the feeling of wanting to change it. If you let go of that feeling, and it's something that cannot be changed, you'll find yourself effortlessly accepting it as it is. On the other hand, if it's something that does

"This is the best self-help method I have ever found! I originally used the Method to help me control my angry outbursts. As a child, I was very mentally abused. I became a counselor to help others who suffered the same as I, or worse. But, despite my training and education, everything I tried always fell short. Since I've learned the Sedona Method, I have had many realizations about the reasons and feelings behind my destructive behaviors. It has given me the freedom I have always been searching for. I thank you. My family thanks you. I've finally found myself."
—Donna B. Gisclair, Morgan City, LA

need to be changed, letting go helps you shift easily into action to get things done.

Experiment with this principle in your life and see what happens. As with everything else in this book, please do not take my word for it alone.

Stuck on a Feeling?

Letting go of wanting to change what you are feeling in the NOW is the key to achieving serenity when you've been finding it difficult to let go of specific feelings or beliefs, or when you have any indecision about releasing. When we feel hesitant to let go, it's often because we want to maintain control. This step can help us release our need for control. In Chapter 4, we explored different processes for letting go of resistance. This is another approach to that same sort of dilemma. Since you can use it as a step at any point in your releasing process, letting go of wanting to change what is acts as the safety valve of the Method.

If you are stuck, let go of wanting to change the stuckness. Simply ask yourself: *Would I like to change that?* The answer will invariably be "yes." Then release on it. Here's a brief process with which you can play around. Read these questions to yourself in the second person (*Could you . . . ?*) or the first person (*Could I . . . ?*) whenever you're having difficulty letting go or feeling a particular way that you don't like. This is also a process that a releasing partner can help you to do.

First, see if you feel a little stuck about something in your life or have become stuck somewhere in the process of letting go. *Could you allow yourself to welcome that feeling of stuckness as best you can?*

Then, check whether you have a sense of wanting to change the stuckness. *If you do, could you allow yourself to have that feeling as well?*

Now, could you let go of wanting to change the stuckness?

Would you?

When?

Check to see how you feel now. *Do you feel as stuck? Less stuck? Either way, is there any more feeling of wanting to change it?*

Could you let go of wanting to change it?

Would you if you could?

When?

Again, notice how you feel inside. If you have been open to this experience, you probably feel a little, or a lot, lighter already.

Now, take another look within. Check to see if there is still more of that sense of wanting to change how you feel. *If there is, could you let go of wanting to change that?*

Would you?

When?

Yes, releasing stuckness can be this simple. So, I recommend cultivating the habit of noticing when you want to change what you are feeling. Even though this process may seem painfully obvious to you, when I was learning the Method, I frequently forgot that this approach to letting go existed. But whenever I remembered to ask myself if there was something I wanted to change—and then was able to let go of wanting to change it—the feeling that had seemed insurmountable a moment before would just dissolve.

The instructors in the early Sedona Method classes that I attended knew this was an easy way to get me to release. It even became a joke among them. First, I'd spend several minutes whining about how significant and important a particular problem was, or how much work I had done on it, yet it *refused* to move. So then they'd simply ask me, "Would you like to change it?" This was usually enough to cause me to release spontaneously, often with waves of uncontrollable laughter.

Lester Levenson found this technique an early key to freeing himself of inner limitations. Once he discovered it, he reviewed his life and noticed how he wanted to change just about everything, including small things like the endings of movies and insignificant events from many years earlier. As he let go of wanting to change what was, he was able to dissolve huge chunks of his inner limitations with ease and became much happier than he had ever dreamed possible. Of course, he did not stop there . . .

Frank: Serenity amidst Chaos

Frank is an attorney who prosecutes misdemeanors in a major city courthouse. The cases he tries, he says, are like "slime in the icebox"—traffic violations and petty theft, for the most part. The docket is always full, so there's a lot of chaos. In the past, he found it easy to become frazzled when the scene got hectic. But ever since studying the Sedona Method a couple of years ago, handling his workload and the different personalities in the courtroom has become much easier and nearly effortless. What some prosecutors take many hours to accomplish, Frank can now calmly get done in a few hours.

He reports: "One judge told me, 'When most prosecutors get interrupted, they need time to reorganize themselves. If it happens six times, they get testy. If it happens 10 times, they're ready to chop somebody's feet off. But I saw you get interrupted about 40 times. You quietly helped each person, and then immediately focused and got right back in groove.' She was impressed by the imperturbability I'm developing. Granted, I'm still a work-in-progress. But when people annoy me, I release on them. So, I'm having fun and acting much more loving to others, even in the courtroom. I feel much freer and lighter."

Frank often asks himself: *Could I allow myself to have an easy and effortless day? Could I allow myself to treat everyone with respect? Could I let go of all self-sabotaging behavior past, present, and future?* A while ago, he realized he could let go on anything and everything. If he stopped wanting to change what was going on around him in the courtroom, the mood altered naturally. Frequently, releasing wanting to change a particular person helps him win cases.

"Strange things can happen in a courtroom," he says. "Many times, I'll help defendants with court processes. Most defendants are grateful when they realize I'm going to treat them with dignity. I can honestly tell them, 'You're not a bad person at the core; you just did a specific thing wrong at a specific time.' With other defendants, it's as though they're energetically slapping me in the face across the room. They believe I'm out to get them and so reject my help and make their situations harder. I keep on loving them and releasing them in my mind when they do this, and I don't worry about the result anymore. That's up to the judge and jury, not me. Should these

133

defendants subsequently lose, which often happens, I feel sorry for them—but I release on that, too."

Frank has found serenity because he's chosen to accept everything that occurs in the NOW. Nothing is more important to him than his peace of mind. Using the Sedona Method, he's discovered: "Life is to be lived and enjoyed in each moment."

Releasing Wanting to Change

Let's do a little more work together now on the issue of wanting to change the way things are. A few pages ago, I asked you to do a quick mental review of things in your life you don't like and want to change. For the purpose of this exercise, let's explore that list and also revisit one or more of the issues that you wrote down at the end of Chapter 1 (see page 46) as your intentions for this self-study course.

Begin by taking a moment to focus inside and relax. Feel free to close your eyes. Please understand, however, that you may keep your eyes open without missing any of the benefits, since the Method is a tool to be used in action throughout the day. Either way, allow your focus to shift to a more inward direction. Notice how you can do that and become more aware of your feelings and your inner state even with your eyes open. Just making this shift has probably started to calm you down already.

Please note, if you're reading this material on your own, always remember to go at your own pace, and allow yourself to feel like I'm asking you the questions, or that you are asking them to yourself in the second person.

Now, think of a specific person, place, or thing in your life that you wish were different, that you want to change. *Could*

you welcome whatever feeling is engendered by it as it is?
Allow it fully.

Could you let go of wanting to change it?

Would you?

When?

*Now how do you feel? Is there any more of the feeling of
wanting to change the way this particular situation is?*

If so, could you let go of wanting to change it?

Would you?

When?

Check again to see if you still want to change it. If you've
been open to the process, you may be seeing the situation now
from the perspective of finding solutions rather than being
stuck with the problem. You may also have discovered that
that there is nothing that needs to be changed, and the situation is perfect the way it is. Continue asking the questions until
you no longer want to change it and can fully accept it as it is.

Remember to allow for the possibility of letting go on any
of the steps along the way. For instance, when you're having
difficulty letting go of wanting to change something, ask yourself if you want to change the degree of difficulty and then let
go. You will be right back on track again.

If you still can't let go, use another question: *What if I
wanted it to be this way?* If you can get the hang of this excellent question, it will free you to let go.

You might even expand your questions to extremely
ridiculous parameters. You could ask: *What if I have spent
my whole life trying to develop this degree of stuckness or
to create this degree of difficulty?* You may find yourself
spontaneously letting go.

Also, please remember that it's always a good idea to give yourself permission to hold on for a moment if you're having trouble letting go. This invariably creates more space for releasing.

Focus inside again, and allow yourself to become aware of something else that you want to change. It could be a person, a place, a thing, or a situation. Whatever it is, simply focus on it and feel what it's like to want to change it.

Then, could you let it go?

Would you?

When?

Now, focus on that same thing, or something else in your life that you'd like to change.

And, could you let go of wanting to change it?

Remember, there's nothing wrong with changing things in life that you'd like to change. We very often get stuck in "wanting" rather than in taking action. So it's a good idea to experiment with letting go of wanting to change it.

Again, focus on that same situation or on something else in your life that you'd like to change.

Could you, just for now, as an experiment,
let go of wanting to change it?

Would you?

When?

Notice how you feel inside right now. Perhaps you have a sense of space opening up, deep inside you, as you let go of wanting to change things. *Does letting go of wanting to change things make you feel a bit uncomfortable? Does it make you feel a little out of control? Could you welcome the feeling?*

Then, could you let go of wanting to change it?

Would you?

When?

See if there's anything about the way you feel right now that you'd like to change.

If so, could you let go of wanting to change it?

Would you?

When?

When we want to change things, we're saying they're not okay the way they are. We're telling ourselves that they need to be changed, fixed, or improved somehow. But this is often not true. Or, if it is true that something needs to be changed, wanting to change it keeps us stuck. Holding on to the yearning for change doesn't really help us to move on and take the action that's necessary.

Now, could you allow yourself to feel exactly the way you feel in this moment? Could you welcome it? Whenever you welcome the way you feel, whenever you allow it, you're embracing a natural way of letting go of wanting to change it.

If you've been willing to let go of wanting to change both how you feel and the circumstances in your life, you should now

"The most noticeable gain from the Method is the feeling of patience. At first, the process seemed redundant. As time went on, I started to see the sense of it all and got into sticking to the process of redundant release. The more I did, the more I realized that the things that bothered me were of my own making. I created more problems by reiterating each troubling scene in my mind, rehearsing my point and how important it was for me to make my point, that I never realized that nothing is really that important—at least not more important than being happy."

—M.M., Bronx, NY

feel calmer, more relaxed and centered—and more able to go out and actually change things. This truly is the key to serenity.

Allow Yourself to Dig Deeper as You Move Forward

Before you read the next chapter, spend some time exploring how you want to change various events, memories, and feelings, as well as letting go of wanting to change them. In the process, see if you are able to keep taking on deeper and deeper issues. Also, allow yourself to notice the areas in your life where you already feel grateful and fulfilled, and that you already accept as they are. Even if you do this only a little bit every day, I promise that it will have a profound effect on your life. The results are likely to surprise and delight you.

Chapter 6

Taking Your Releasing to a Deeper Level

If you've read this far and worked experientially on the releasing processes suggested in the previous chapters, I'm sure you've already begun to discover that feelings greatly color your performance and mental clarity; also, that you have the ability to let go of unwanted feelings. As you let them go, not only do you feel better, you also function better. In this chapter, we're going to explore the Sedona Method at an even deeper and more powerful level: underlying motivations or *wants*. As you engage in releasing at this new level, you'll notice that your results are much more rapid, effective, and easier to achieve.

Are You Motivated by What You Want?

Yes and no. Consider what you want for a few minutes. Do you want more money or less debt? Do you want to enjoy better relationships with family and friends, or to begin a special love relationship of your own? Do you want better health, or at least to diminish your suffering and pain? Do you want to be successful, or at least to stop feeling like a failure? Do you want more free time and less pressure? Do you want a new car, a new dress, a new stereo, a new hairdo, a new life? Your list could go on and on.

Do you *truly* want these things? Or are you seeking the happiness that these things represent? What if you could have that happiness without needing the stuff that you associate with it?

Wanting equates to lack. It does not equal having. Our lives are limited by our tendency to focus on the struggle that leads up to having, rather than having itself. When we let go of wanting, we therefore feel more like we can have. We also notice a corresponding increase in what we actually do have. Anyone who's ever been in sales knows that when you want to make the sale, it's often much more difficult. Conversely, when you feel like you don't need the sale, you often make it. That's because the most powerful place to create what we choose is from the position that it's "okay" whether we get it or not. This model applies to all areas of our lives.

Everyone is motivated by four basic desires that exist beneath our thoughts: emotions, beliefs, attitudes, and behavior patterns. These underlying motivators—the desire for approval, control, safety, and separation—form the core of all our limitation. When we release these *wants*, we can have what we desire and stay motivated. In the process, we simply let go of our sense of deprivation and lacking.

We enter life with tendencies dictated by heredity and the environment—and, if you believe in reincarnation, by the past. These tendencies can be anything from genetic or environmental predispositions to simple preferences. But, in general, these mostly subconscious tendencies don't take over and run our lives until we get older. Throughout childhood, they merely add dimension to what is being experienced. By the time we reach adulthood, however, we have learned to sublimate our underlying needs or wants with more adult desires—items that are a few steps removed from the true motivation. We might equate a car, for instance, with control, or money with security. (Each of us assigns different meanings to different objects.) This is one reason that the happiness we derive from getting the things that we want is often short-lived. We only *believe* we want them.

> "I have experienced a great overall quality of confidence because of releasing, especially the fear of strong emotions. The strong emotion may arise, but it is gently dissolved or reduced to a level that enables me to continue to think, listen, and respond rationally, often while I'm continuing to release."
> —Deborah Dineen,
> Port St. John, FL

From my experience, the other reason that we're not completely satisfied by "getting what we want" is that we cannot obtain what we truly want from anything external. Nonetheless, many people deny themselves the things they believe they want, because they feel they can never have them, or they've been told that it's wrong even to want them. The Sedona Method has literally helped tens of thousands of people let go of imposing such limitations on themselves—and you can, too.

How It All Began

The following story is merely a story. Its resemblance or lack of resemblance to your life is purely coincidental.

141

Although it is designed to give you a taste of how your underlying motivations may have evolved, it is neither meant to be a new theory of early childhood development, nor to confirm or dispute any other theory. It is also not meant to take the place of, or challenge any particular spiritual belief. Your life experience may be similar or different. Either way, do your best to identify with the evolution of the character in this story, without being too concerned yet about how it applies to you.

We begin with the premise that we are now, and have always been, unlimited Beingness. Thus, you—the main character—start out as undifferentiated consciousness, aware of nothing in particular, whole and complete unto yourself. This is the canvas on which the story is painted, and which allows for even the possibility of it to unfold. Furthermore, the canvas is uninvolved with, and unchanged by, the unfolding of the story.

At some point, sounds, sensations, and pictures start to arise in this effortless, choiceless awareness that you are. Some sounds are repetitive, like the gentle thumping of your mother's heart and breathing, which resemble the ebb and flow of an ocean's tides. Off in the distance, there are also muffled sounds, including your mother's voice and the voices of other people and events in her environment. There are sensations of warmth, floating, and gentle rocking, as her body moves through life, and your world moves in unison. There is also an undulating semidarkness that envelopes and fills awareness. All these sensations, sounds, and pictures drift in and out of consciousness at rest.

This Beingness continues until stronger sensations arise in consciousness when your world starts to contract. For however long it takes, there is a transition from a world filled only with relatively muted sensations, sounds, and pictures to a world filled with much more distinct, stronger ones. The birth experience is occasionally violent. Yet, no matter how apparently traumatic the transition is, once you've come through it, these sensations also drift in and out of consciousness. For a while, you spend most of your time asleep.

Soon, pictures have more definition as your eyes begin to function in this new world. Your ears and the rest of your body also become accustomed to living in a world filled with air instead of amniotic fluid. Over time, patterns appear in consciousness as different groups of sensations, sounds, and pictures arise at varying intervals. Soon, some of these will be recognized as "your" body. There is still an underlying sense of unity between you, as the background, and any perceptions that are arising.

There is a background feeling of love, even towards experiences that could be labeled as traumatic. Perceptions, including those of the body, do not yet have names or meanings. They merely arise and then subside into that which you are. Body parts become objects of play once you discover that certain inner shifts cause them to react. They are enjoyed but not owned by anyone in particular.

If you're having what most people would consider a normal infancy, benevolent presences come in out of consciousness that will later be called Mommy and Daddy. These presences come with particular patterns of perception. Over time, and through the hopefully patient repetition of different sounds and movements of these benevolent presences, you begin to be introduced to the world of concepts and symbols.

Mommy and Daddy point to themselves over and over again and say, "Mommy," or, "Daddy," and then point to your body and repeat your name. They also point to various patterns of light, sound, and sensation and give those names as well. This game is fun, and you get rewarded for almost every attempt to play it. Eventually, you discover that certain inner shifts of perception cause your body to be able to make sounds like theirs. Now, as you start to enter the world of concepts and symbols, it begins to be harder—except during sleep—to remain at rest as the background unity that you are. You have an increasing sense of separation from your basic nature.

Of course, not everything in life is fun and games. Some people's stories up to this point are quite traumatic. But this unfolding play that you'll later call your life has not taken you in completely. Consciousness continues to move in and out of identifying with the central character, in the same way you probably identify now with the characters in a good book or movie. As you start to use language, you may even go through a period where you refer in the third person to the person who, you later believe is you. "It's Hale's toy" or "It's Mary's toy," not "mine." Yes, you cry if you get hurt, or scream if you don't get what you want, but without the personal stickiness that arises later.

Then, around the age of two, two-and-a-half, there is another transition. You have now been so persuaded that you are a separate identity (e.g., Hale or Mary) that suddenly everything becomes about *my* toy, *my* needs, and *me*. Now, the sensations, pictures, and sounds that arise in consciousness are given meaning and a history based on this growing belief in a "me." And that's when you begin wanting to change the way things are. You resist what is. You want things to go your way. The name for this phase is the "terrible twos." It is often a very difficult period for both parent and child. The world is no longer as secure as it may have once appeared to be. You may be in competition with siblings for attention. Since everything is separate from you, everything is a potential threat. To get Mommy and Daddy's approval becomes hugely important, and failing to get it is potentially life-threatening. You want to control what used to appear to be a perfect world.

You long for the ease and simplicity of your parents and your world controlling you; simultaneously, you want to assert your will over your world. You want to get approval or even disapproval from outside of you, yet you also want to go back to being in love with all that is. You want to be safe and secure, and survive, but you also want the sense of being a separate entity to die and disappear. You long to be in unity again—one with all that is—yet you are driven to assert your separate, unique identity.

Now, for some of us, developing separation is a gradual

> "I have gained more desirable results (changes in attitude and behavior) in six months with the Method than all my wanting has achieved in a decade! I always understood the concept of 'oneness' with the universe, but recently, while I was releasing, it became fully animated in my life. The realization is hard to explain. Just knowing and feeling that everything is part of me, and I am a part of everything, is an unbelievable experience."
> —Michael McGrath,
> Belfast, Northern Ireland

process, starting way before we are two; for others, it is quite sudden. But there appears to be no turning back for anybody, unless, as they get older, they do a process such as the one you are learning in this book. No matter how much we long for the security and unity we felt when we were very young, the developmental process runs its course.

Does any of this sound or feel familiar? We could expand on it endlessly, taking in all the subtle and not-so-subtle nuances of each birth and how each baby's life unfolds. This is enough, however, for you to get the picture—specifically, that as we lock into identifying with a particular body/mind as our own, we begin to be more highly motivated by some basic needs (the underlying wants) that reinforce our sense of separation and cause us endless suffering.

Five Basic Steps to Release Underlying Wants

Every time you let go of your limiting feelings and thoughts at the underlying level of the wants, you will accelerate your progress. As stated in Chapter 1, you may notice that some areas of your life clear up, even though you never release on them directly. Since all issues relate directly to the wants, many areas shift at once as you let go of the wants.

Would you rather *want* approval or *have* approval? Would you rather *want* control or *have* control? Would you rather *want* security or *have* security? The answer is obvious.

Here is an easy five-step procedure for letting go of the wants. As you incorporate it into your daily activities, you'll find that it gets easier. Merely bringing a want into conscious awareness will often cause you to let it go spontaneously, even before you ask the questions. These questions replace, or may be added at the end of, the series of Basic Releasing questions that you have been working with until now. From this point forward, we no longer ask the two follow-up questions "Would you?" or "When?" because, as we let go at this deeper level, the decision to let go happens more quickly and with greater spontaneity. However, please feel free to use them any time you need to, in order to support yourself in the releasing process.

You may do this process on your own by reading the following questions silently to yourself, or do it with the assistance of a partner.

Step 1: Focus on your issue and allow yourself to welcome whatever you are feeling in the NOW moment.

Step 2: Dig a little deeper to discover whether the NOW feeling comes from a sense of wanting. Ask one of the following two questions:

- *Does the feeling come from wanting approval, control, security, or separation?*
- *What is the sense of wanting underneath this feeling?*

If you're not sure which want is underneath the feeling, or if you feel like it may be several wants at the same time—as it often is—pick the one that you feel is dominant, is most likely, or is the one that you'd like to let go of first. Then proceed to Step 3.

Step 3: Ask yourself one of the following three questions:

- *Could I allow myself to want (approval, control, security, or separation)?*
- *Could I welcome wanting (approval, control, security, or separation)?*
- *Could I let go of wanting (approval, control, security, or separation)?*

When you are releasing on the wants, simplify your questions. After you realize you can let the wants go, you'll find yourself doing so without a lot of excess thought. Remember "yes" or "no" are both acceptable answers, and you'll often let go even if you say "no." Also, if you'd like to, give yourself permission to hold on for a moment before you let go, as this often creates the space for an even deeper release. Partners should keep asking the questions even when they hear a "no" answer. As best you can, answer the chosen question with a minimum of thought. Stay away from second-guessing yourself or getting into a debate about the merits of an action or its consequences. Whatever the response is, move on to the next step.

Please be mindful that you're not being asked to let go of control, approval, security, or separation, merely to let go of your feeling of lacking them, of wanting.

Step 4: You may use this step at any point during the releasing process to address any feeling, want, or sense of indecision and stuckness. As you learned in Chapter 5, Your Key to Serenity, it is the safety valve of the Method.

Simply ask: *Would I like to change that?*

The answer will invariably be "yes." But if you're not entirely sure, check to see whether you like it the way it is. Any time that something is not okay with you the way it is, this indicates that you want to change it.

Then ask: *Could I let go of wanting to change it?*

In most cases, even if you are stuck, you'll be able to answer "yes" to this question. Letting go of wanting to change it will dissolve the stuckness and put you right back on track. As you'll recall, wanting to change is a subset of wanting to control.

Step 5: Repeat the preceding four steps as often as needed until you feel free of the specific want on which you're working.

Lester believed it was more important to focus on wanting approval, control, and security than on wanting to be separate when we release. He felt that if we were to let go enough of the first three wants, the sense of wanting to be separate would drop away by itself. This was certainly part of his process. Except in this chapter and the next, our releasing questions throughout most of the book will focus almost exclusively on approval, control, and security. Of course, if you find yourself aware of wanting to be separate, please feel free to let go of this want as well.

> "My daughter and I had a dysfunctional relationship and had lost touch. After learning how to release, I began looking for her again, and we have now reconnected. We not only have resolved our differences, but my daughter is now releasing, too! We communicate better now than we have in years."
>
> —Carole Dunham,
> Miami, FL

Exploration: Seeing Through to Perfection by Letting Go of the Wants

Lester Levenson used to say, "Release and allow yourself to see the perfection where the seeming imperfection seems to be." During this process, welcome your thoughts, your sensations, your feelings, and the stories that you tell yourself. Just allow them all to be here, and know that everything is okay as it is. Part of what happens when we release this is that we start to recognize the perfection underlying our thoughts and feelings.

Begin by making yourself comfortable and focusing your attention inwardly.

Now, bring to mind one of the main issues that you've been working on in this book so far, or a new or different issue that's currently up in your awareness. As you think about that situation, problem, intention, or goal, allow yourself to get in touch with your feelings about it right in this very moment.

Could you welcome that feeling?

Now, dig a little deeper and see if you can determine whether the NOW feeling comes from wanting approval, control, security, or separation. As you let go of the wants, remember that there is nothing wrong with *having* approval, control, security, or oneness; you are merely letting go of the sense, or feeling, of lacking them.

Whichever want it is, ask: *Could you just allow yourself to feel it?* Embrace it fully.

Then, could you let it go?

Look at the same issue again and see what your NOW feeling is about it.

Does the feeling come from wanting approval, control, survival, or separation?

Could you let that sense of wanting go? Could you allow it to release?

Now, focus on your issue again and see if there's anything about it that's stirring up resistance. You could be resisting it changing, you could be resisting it the way it is, or there might be a specific aspect of it towards which you feel resistant.

Could you allow yourself to feel the resistance?

Then, could you allow yourself to let it go?

See if there's something else about this issue that you're resisting.

Could you let go of resisting it?

Remember, resistance is pushing against the world so that it will push back. It is saying that things aren't okay the way they are and digging our heels in against them.

Repeat the last few steps on resistance two or three more times, then move on.

Now, see if there is anything about this issue that you'd like to change.

Could you let go of wanting to change it?

Find something else about the issue, or the way you feel about it, that you'd like to change.

Could you let go of wanting to change it?

Is there anything about the issue that seems stuck in any way?

Do you want to change that sense of stuckness?

Could you let go of wanting to change that sense of stuckness?

Check again: *Is there anything about the way you feel about the issue or your attitude about the issue that seems stuck?*

When we feel stuck, we want to make things different, but that makes us even more stuck. To let go of stuckness, all we need to do is let go of wanting to change what is.

So, could you let go of wanting to change whatever sense of stuckness you might be feeling right now?

Now, notice how you feel about the issue right now. Observe how your feelings have already shifted. This bit of the process has probably made a huge difference already.

Underneath your issue, is there anything that you'd like to control, such as the way you feel about it or the way that it seems to be?

Could you welcome that sense of wanting to control?

Then, could you let it go?

Repeat the above series of questions several more times, each time noticing how your energy about the issue is shifting and clearing up any remaining sense of wanting to control that's associated with it.

Now, is there anything about this issue—how you feel about it, how you're interacting with other people in relationship to it, or how you're relating to yourself about it—that stirs up a sense of wanting your own or anyone else's approval?

Could you welcome how much you want approval?

Could you let the wanting go?

Repeat the above series of questions several more times, clearing up any remaining sense of wanting approval there is.

Now, let's dig even deeper. *Is there anything about this situation, problem, or issue that stirs up a sense of wanting safety, security, or survival?*

Could you just allow yourself to feel the sense of wanting security?

Then, could you let it go?

Focus on the situation again and see if you can find anything about it that makes you feel a little insecure or a little threatened, and notice how that comes from wanting security or survival.

Could you let go of wanting security or survival?

Repeat the above series of questions several more times,

clearing up any remaining sense of wanting safety or security there is.

Now, simply tune in and become aware of how you're feeling inside. Notice that you're probably feeling a lot more space and lightness. If there's any sense of wanting to hold on to that good feeling, notice how it comes from wanting to control. Also, realize that there are plenty more good feelings where that came from. Our feelings of limitation are finite, whereas good feelings are infinite.

So, could you let go of wanting to control the good feeling and just let it be?

Now, relax into whatever you're feeling in the moment. Welcome it fully. Every time we welcome a feeling fully, we're letting go of wanting to change or control it. We are accepting it as it is, at least for the present moment. If there's still a remaining sense of contraction or negativity about your issue, switch your focus to the increased lightness that you're aware of—just for now—and give yourself over to that.

Let it have you as best you can.

Relax into it.

Allow yourself to be at rest.

The natural goodness that you're feeling inside is always present, no matter how extreme your feelings may become. The goodness resides underneath your emotions and thoughts, and it's available to you any time you shift your focus in its direction. All the power of your unlimited potential is available to you, and it can naturally dissolve your remaining sense of limitation if you allow it.

Could you allow yourself to let go even more into this present moment and trust the power that knows the way?

Allow yourself, even for this moment, to see the perfection where the seeming imperfection seems to be.

For a moment, could you entertain the idea that maybe all is well and everything is unfolding as it should?

Now, in a moment, gradually start shifting your awareness outwardly again and know that everything you've gained from this process is with you forever. Every process is a beginning, an opening to the life that you've always wanted, and a discovery of what's really true for you.

So, allow this to flow easily into your life.

Use this process—and the perspective it offers—as often as you'd like to gain more freedom on a specific issue, or simply to feel happier and more alive.

Chapter 7

Letting Go of the Four Basic Wants

As he explored his own process, Lester Levenson spent a good deal of time reviewing his past and letting go of his inner motivations. He discovered that, as people clean up the past relating to the four basic wants, the heavy burdens they've been carrying from their personal histories can easily be put down, never to be picked up again.

In this chapter, we're going to explore the four basic wants in greater detail and do some written releasing targeted to each category. Interestingly, each want includes an opposite or opposing force. So, not only does wanting create a sense of lack for us, we also experience varying degrees of conflict between wanting to control and to be controlled, wanting approval and disapproval, wanting security and insecurity, and wanting separation and oneness. Depending on our individual personalities, we each have these desires in different percentages. Furthermore, every situation we find ourselves in triggers these opposing forces to a greater or lesser extent in our conscious awareness.

Is it any wonder that most of us get stuck somewhere in the middle? We're a little like the push-me-pull-you in *The Story of Doctor Dolittle*, which is an animal resembling a llama, but with two heads that face away from each other. Due to conflicted wants, most of us take three steps towards our goals in life and two steps back before we can move forward again.

If you find releasing in this section a little confusing at first, allow yourself to ease into it. I highly recommend working more extensively on the primary wants and getting comfortable with them before you begin focusing on their opposites. Of course, if you become aware of the opposites during the process, let them go. Just allow the opposites to reveal themselves to you as they do. You can relax, though, because the process is holistic. When we're letting go of a given want, we're always letting go of some of its opposite at the same time. Like flipping a coin, you can't throw it up in the air unless you toss both the head and the tail together.

Wanting to Control

When we want to control, we feel like we don't have control. It may help you to recognize the sense of wanting to control if you understand that it is not a feeling, although it has a feel to it. It feels hard and pushy, like: "It has to be my way." When we want to control, we feel out of control and like we need to take action to get it back. Synonyms for wanting to control include resistance and wanting to change, as well as wanting to understand, to manipulate, to push, to fix, to force, to have it be our way, to be right, and to be on top, among others. As we let go of wanting to control, we feel more in control.

Do you recall the Serenity Prayer at the beginning of Chapter 5? As you start to let go of wanting to change or control things in your life, you'll find yourself accepting things that you cannot change, changing things that are appropriate to change, and feeling a lot less tension about things that are truly out of your control. There is nothing wrong with taking appropriate action to change things that need changing in business or your personal life. However, too many people get stuck in wanting to change or control things that are fine the way they are, or can't be changed—like the past or the weather. Because we want to control or change them, we can't see that they're okay as they are.

As I mentioned in Chapter 4, Dissolving Your Resistance, resistance is the reason you may lose motivation in the middle of a project that you started with great enthusiasm. Resistance is also synonymous with wanting to control. It can sabotage your personal growth and stop you from moving forward in every area of your life. It can even prevent you from doing things you like to do or that bring you the most benefit, such as the Sedona Method. Resistance feels like trying to move forward with the brakes on. As I've mentioned, it will come up any time you feel as though you *have to*, *must*, or *should* do anything. As you let go of resistance, your life will begin to flow in the direction of what's best for you.

Wanting to Be Controlled

A subset of wanting to control is the built-in opposing force of *wanting to be controlled*. When this is motivating us, we long to have someone else to blame or take responsibility for our lives and feelings. We want to be told what to do. We would rather follow than lead. You can recognize wanting to be controlled, because it feels soft and wishy-washy, like: "I want to give my power away." When we want to be controlled, we feel like we want to be out of control and that we should not do anything unless we get permission first.

Synonyms for wanting to be controlled include resistance and wanting to change (these appear on both sides of the control equation), as well as wanting to be confused, to be manipulated, to give in, to be fixed, to be forced, to follow, to be the underdog, to blame, and to be the victim, to name a few. As we let go of wanting to be controlled, we feel more in control and more willing to have control of our lives.

During releasing, when you work on the sense of wanting to control, check for its opposite inside of you, at least occasionally. Even the most self-motivated and controlling of us have some of this opposing desire inside of us.

Written Releasing: Wanting to Control

This two-part written process is designed to assist you in releasing *wanting to control*. It's very simple. To prepare for

Releasing *Wanting to Control*

Remember a specific instance in which I wanted control	What is my NOW want about that?
The last time I went to the dentist	I was scared— ~~w/c~~
It rained all weekend	Bored —✓w/c, ~~w/a~~
My checkbook didn't balance	Frustrated—w/s ✓

part one, create two columns across the top of a clean page of paper in your releasing journal. You may also type this format into a computer file. The first column is labeled "Remember a specific instance when I wanted control." The second column is labeled "What is my NOW want about that?"

Begin by writing down in the first column as many instances as you can remember when you wanted to control. Then, in the second column, write down your NOW want (e.g., wanting approval, wanting control, or wanting security).

Releasing *Wanting to Control*

Ways I try to control	Ways I try to be controlled
Asking questions ~~w/a, w/c~~	Not taking responsibility ~~w/c~~
Making demands w/c✓	Not speaking up for myself ~~w/a,~~ w/c ✓
Being right w/a,✓ ~~w/c, w/s~~	Letting my feelings run me ~~w/c, w/s~~

It is perfectly appropriate to jot down "w/a" for wanting approval, "w/c" for wanting control, and "w/s" for wanting security. When you have fully released that want, either put a check mark next to the abbreviation for the want or cross it out. Repeat the above steps and continue releasing your NOW want until you feel that you are fully released on that incident. Remember also to release your so-called positive feelings so you can keep moving to higher energy states.

When you feel ready to move on, create a second worksheet for part two of the process. Across the top of another blank page in your journal, create two columns. The first is labeled "Ways I try to control." The second column is labeled "Ways I try to be controlled."

Now, make a list of all the ways you try to gain control in your current life (business, relationships, etc.). Take each item, get in touch with your NOW want, write down whether it relates to wanting approval, control, or security, and then release it completely. When you have fully released that want, either put a check mark next to the abbreviation for the want or cross it out.

Next, make a list of all the ways you try to be controlled in your current life (business, relationships, etc.). Take each item, get in touch with your NOW want, write down whether it relates to wanting approval, control, or security, and then release it completely. When you have fully released that want, either put a check mark next to the abbreviation for the want or cross it out.

Be mindful that there's not necessarily anything wrong with your actions, even if wanting control motivates them. This process simply helps you continue to be aware of which actions come from your desire to control, which will give you a better chance to release it on the spot. Then you can take the action or not—by choice.

Process for Letting Go of Wanting Control

Begin by making yourself comfortable and shifting your perspective to an inward focus. If you're aware of holding on anywhere in your consciousness, see if that comes from wanting control.

Could you welcome the sense of wanting control?

Could you allow it to release?

Do you have a physical sensation right now that you want to control or change?

Could you let go of wanting to change it?

Repeat the last two questions for as many physical sensations as you'd like.

Now, find something in your life that you'd like to control.

Could you let go of wanting to change that?

Find something else in your life that you want to control.

Could you let go of wanting to control that?

Repeat the last series of questions for as many issues as you'd like, and then move on.

Next, think of a situation in the past that you remember wanting to control. Welcome the feeling of wanting to control it again.

Could you let go now?

As you focus on that issue, and any other issues of control from the past, allow yourself to see how wanting to control has affected your life, how it made you feel, how it made you act. Is there a recurring theme in your life that relates to control?

Could you welcome that tendency or any action that comes from wanting to control?

Check to see if you have a desire to control your sense of wanting control.

Could you let go of wanting to control or change that?

Now, allow wanting control to come into your awareness—if need be, stir it up by recalling an event—and then relax into the very core of it.

Could you dive into its very center?

And even deeper?

And deeper still?

Allow yourself to notice from where the sense of wanting to control arises.

If you haven't already, could you let it go?

Now, focus on your NOW feeling. Notice the shift in awareness that has come from releasing at least a little bit of your sense of wanting to control. Imagine what your life would be like if you always felt in control, at ease, at home, and there was nothing that you felt you needed to change. Everything was already perfect the way it was.

If you're aware of any remaining desire to control, could you let it dissolve now?

Allow yourself to rest in the moment, and be at home.

Wanting Approval/Love

When we want approval, we feel like we don't have approval. Therefore, we act in ways designed to help us get it, while all the time sabotaging actually getting it. We are focused on ourselves, and we feel self-conscious. We become overly concerned with what people think of us. We may say "yes" when we mean "no." We may allow others to give us the runaround or control us in order to get them to like us. We may take on too much responsibility or not delegate tasks, because we think it will make us more popular.

You can recognize wanting approval, because it feels soft and exposed and also like: "Gimme," or, "Do-it-for-me." When we want approval, we feel like we don't have love and that we need to do something to get it back. Synonyms for wanting approval include wanting love, acceptance, admiration, caring, to be noticed, to be understood, to be stroked, to be nurtured, and to be liked, among others. As we let go of wanting approval, we will feel more loving and caring, more loved and accepted.

Wanting approval actually has two opposing forces, each with a very different feel to it. They are the sense of wanting

163

disapproval and the sense of wanting to love. Each is described separately below.

Wanting Disapproval

When we want disapproval, we feel like we don't want approval. Therefore, we act in ways that are designed to help keep it away. As with wanting approval, we are focused on ourselves, and we feel self-conscious. We are overly concerned with what others think of us, yet we pretend that we don't care. We will often say "no" when we could just as easily have said "yes." We give others the runaround in order to make sure they don't like us. We may avoid responsibility or leave tasks undone. We go out of our way to make ourselves unpopular.

This want is recognizable because it feels raw, exposed, and has a slippery or "leave me alone" feeling to it. When we want disapproval, we feel we don't want love, and that we need to do something to make sure we don't get it. Synonyms for wanting disapproval include wanting to be disliked, to be rejected, to be looked down on, to hide, and to be misunderstood, to name a few. As we let go of wanting disapproval, we feel more able to be loved and accepted, and more able to love and care for others.

Wanting to Love

When we want to love, we feel like we can't give enough. Therefore, we act in ways designed to help us feel loving, while all the time sabotaging actually feeling love. We are focused on others, and we feel self-abdicating. We become overly concerned with other people's feelings. As with wanting approval, we may say "yes" when we mean "no." We may allow others to give us the runaround, or control us in order to get them to feel better. We may take on too much responsibility or not delegate tasks, because we think this will be better for others.

You can recognize the sense of wanting to love because it feels soft and vulnerable and has an overly giving, or "let me do it for you" feeling to it. When we want to love, we feel we can't give enough love or approval, and that we need to do something to get others to understand how much we care. Synonyms for wanting to love include wanting to approve, to accept, to admire, to care, to mother, to be understanding, to stroke, to sacrifice, to nurture, and to like, as well as others. As we let go of wanting to love, we feel more whole and complete within, while at the same time being able to love and care for others without having it come at our expense.

Written Releasing: Wanting Approval/Love

This two-part written process is designed to assist you in releasing *wanting approval*. As you did when you were releasing on wanting to control (see page 158), to prepare for part one, create two columns across the top of a clean page of paper in your releasing journal. The first column is labeled "Remember a specific instance when I wanted approval." The second column is labeled "What is my NOW want about that?" And, of course, you may abbreviate the labels.

Begin by writing down in the first column as many instances as you can remember when you wanted approval. Then, in the second column, write down your NOW want (e.g., wanting approval, wanting control, or wanting security) or abbreviate it. When you have fully released that want, make a check mark next to it or cross it off. Repeat the above steps and continue releasing your NOW want until you feel that you

Releasing Wanting Approval/Love

Remember a specific instance when I wanted approval	What is my NOW want about that?
My first date	*Awkward—* *embarrassed w/a*
Making the presentation	*Nervous—w/c,*✓ *w/a*✓
The cocktail party	*Self-conscious—* *w/c, w/s*✓

are fully released on that incident. As always, also remember to release your so-called positive feelings, so you can keep moving to higher energy states.

When you feel ready to move on, create a second worksheet for part two of the process. Across the top of another blank page in your journal, create two columns. The first column is labeled "Ways I seek approval." The second column is labeled "Ways I seek disapproval."

Now make a list of all the ways you try to gain approval in your current life (business, relationships, etc.). Then, take each item, get in touch with your NOW want, write down whether it relates to wanting approval, control, or security,

Releasing Wanting Approval/Love

Ways I seek approval	Ways I seek disapproval
Looking good ~~w/a, w/c~~	*Rebelling—w/c,* ✓ ~~w/a,~~ *w/s* ✓
Giving gift ~~w/a~~	*Failing* ~~w/a, w/c~~
Being a martyr w/a ✓	*Arriving late—* ✓ *w/c, w/a* ✓

and release it completely. Check off or cross out the NOW want afterwards and focus on the next action.

Next, make a list of all the ways you seek disapproval in your current life. Then, take each item, get in touch with your NOW want about it, write down whether it relates to wanting approval, wanting control, or wanting security, and then release it completely. When you have fully released that want, either put a check mark next to the abbreviation for the want or cross it out.

Process for Letting Go of Wanting Approval

Begin by making yourself comfortable and shifting your focus inwardly. Bring to mind any time that you can remember when you wanted approval.

Could you welcome the sense of wanting approval?

Could you let it go?

Focus on a situation in your life in which you felt that someone disapproved of you, didn't like you, or didn't give you the acknowledgment you felt you deserved. Notice what it feels like to want approval.

Could you welcome that sense of wanting approval?

Could you let it go?

Now, think of a specific person, either from your business or personal life, whose approval you often and repeatedly want.

Could you let yourself want their approval now, just for a moment?

Could you let go?

Repeat this last series of questions for as many other people as you would like.

Now, think of a time when you wanted your own approval. Maybe you disapproved of something you did or did not say or do. Perhaps you didn't accomplish something you thought you should have done, and you really took it to heart.

Could you welcome your desire for approval into your awareness right now?

Then, could you let it go?

Repeat with as many instances of wanting your own approval as you'd like.

Now, let's explore wanting approval further. It's usually a pattern in someone's life. So, what are some of your recurring thoughts, feelings, and behaviors that come from wanting approval? Perhaps: "It's not my fault," or, "They don't care." You may feel ashamed, exposed, vulnerable, or hurt. Your behaviors might include doing things to get attention, acting nice, paying false compliments, or saying "yes" when you really mean "no." Let all of those types of wanting approval come into your awareness.

Could you allow that sense of wanting approval to be here?

Then, could you let it go?

Repeat the steps above a few more times, releasing on the images that arise.

Next, welcome wanting approval into your full awareness.

Could you allow yourself to dive into the very core of it?

And even deeper?

And deeper still?

Go to the very core of it, to the point where it arises, and let it dissolve.

Now, imagine what life will be like as you let go of wanting approval. You'll be self-confident and assured and know that people care about you. Whether or not they approve of you, you're okay.

By the way, this is a real possibility. As you let go of wanting approval, people will mysteriously approve of you more than they do already.

Wanting Security/Survival

When we want security, we feel like we don't have security. We approach life as though it's a battle for survival. We see everyone, at least on a subtle level, as an enemy. We may often feel and react to even the smallest changes or decisions as if our lives are threatened. We may avoid taking risks, even if that means giving up success. We may avoid confrontation, even if it's necessary. We may walk around expecting the next disaster.

You can recognize wanting security, because it may include

a sense of being threatened, uneasy, in danger, on guard, or impending doom. In the extreme, it's a paralyzing fear—we feel like we're about to die. We also feel like we'll do anything to get it back. Synonyms for wanting security include wanting safety, to survive, to get revenge, to protect ourselves and others, to attack, to defend, to kill, and to be safe, to name a few. As we let go of wanting security, we feel safer, more secure, and at home wherever we are without feeling like we have to achieve safety at others' expenses.

Wanting to Die

The built-in opposing force to wanting security, or survival, is the sense of wanting to die. When we want to die, we feel as though life is too much. We are afraid of living, so we want to get it over with. We approach life like a minefield. We are our own worst enemies. As with wanting survival, we often feel and react to even the smallest changes or decisions as if our lives are threatened. However, unlike wanting survival, we may seek risks and confrontation, secretly hoping for the worst to happen. We may walk around expecting the next disaster, secretly hoping for it.

Wanting to die is sometimes hard to distinguish from wanting security. It also may include a sense of being threatened, uneasy, in danger, on guard, or impending doom. You can recognize it, however, because it may also feel hopeless and defeated, like the end is near. In the extreme, it's either paralyzing fear or paralyzing apathy—we feel like we're about to die, and we don't care. When we want to die, we feel that we don't want security and may even do things to make sure we aren't safe.

Synonyms for wanting to die include wanting danger, to end

it all, to expose ourselves and others, to be attacked, to be defenseless, to be killed, to be annihilated, and to be threatened, among others. As we let go of wanting to die, we feel safer, more secure, and at home in life. We are willing to live and enjoy life to the fullest without worrying about the consequences.

Written Releasing: Wanting Security

This two-part written process is designed to assist you in releasing *wanting security*. Again, as with releasing wanting to control and releasing wanting approval, to prepare for part one, create two columns across the top of a clean page of paper in your releasing journal. The first column is labeled "Remember a specific instance when I wanted security." The second column is labeled "What is my NOW want about that?"

Begin by writing down in the first column as many instances as you can remember when you wanted security. Then, in the second column, write down your NOW want (e.g., wanting approval, wanting control, or wanting security) or abbreviate it. When you have fully released that want, make a check mark next to it or cross it off. Repeat the above steps and continue releasing your NOW want until you feel that you are fully released on that incident. As always, remember also to release your so-called positive feelings so you can keep moving to higher energy states.

When you feel ready to move on, create a second worksheet for part two of the process. Across the top of another blank page in your journal, create two columns. The first column is labeled "Ways I seek security." The second column is labeled "Ways I challenge my security."

Now, make a list of all the ways you seek security in your

Releasing *Wanting Security*

Remember a specific instance when I wanted security	What is my NOW want about that?
Going to the doctor	*Fear -* w/c, w/s ✓✓
The car accident	*I almost died –* ~~w/c, w/a, w/s~~
Got fired from job	*No money –* w/c, ✓ ~~w/s, w/a~~

current life (business, relationships, etc.). Take each item, get in touch with your NOW want, write down whether it relates to wanting approval, control, or security, and release it completely. Check off or cross out the NOW want afterwards and focus on the next action.

Next, make a list of all the ways you challenge your security in your current life. Take each item, get in touch with the NOW want, write down whether it relates to wanting approval, control, or security, and then release it completely. When you have fully released on that want, either put a check mark next to the abbreviation for the want or cross it out.

Releasing *Wanting Security*

Ways I seek security	Ways I challenge my security
Insurance ~~w/s~~	Taking risks ✓ w/c, w/s ✓
Saving money ✓ w/a, w/s ✓	Getting sick ✓ w/a, w/s ✓
Maintaining status quo ~~w/a,~~ w/s ✓	Change — w/s ✓

Process for Letting Go of Wanting Security

Begin by shifting your focus inwardly. Give your body permission to relax. Tune in to your overall feeling sense in this moment.

Could you welcome the NOW feeling and know that it's okay?

Now, bring to mind a situation in your life when you felt threatened or challenged, a time when your sense of wanting security or survival was stirred up.

Could you welcome the sense of wanting security into awareness?

Could you release it?

Now, focus on that same situation or another in which you felt strongly threatened. *Could you welcome that sense of wanting security?*

Then, could you let it go?

Repeat the steps above as many times as you'd like, and then move on.

Now, allow yourself to experience the fullest extent of wanting security or survival that you can right now without forcing it. Gently stir it up if you need to, while realizing that all wants are merely energy. They're not "good" or "bad." They just are.

Could you allow the sense of wanting security to release?

Again, invite your sense of wanting survival to enter your awareness.

Could you let it go?

Repeat several more times, noticing how the things that formerly threatened you now seem less and less threatening.

Remember, the wants are belief systems—programs that we use to operate our lives. Therefore, we experience recurring thoughts, feelings, and behaviors. When you want security, you may think, "Oh, this is not good. Something bad is about to happen," or, "This doesn't feel right. This is going to be a big mistake." You may feel scared, threatened, or out of control. You could have a panic attack. It's possible that you'll freeze up right in the middle of an important meeting or situation. Behavior may include over-planning, hyper-vigilance, fighting even when there's nothing to fight about, running away, and doing whatever you can to preserve the status quo.

Think of what you do when you're feeling as though you

want security: a recurring thought, an action you take, or a feeling. *Could you truly welcome that into your conscious awareness?*

Then, could you let go of the sense of wanting security from which this tendency is arising?

Repeat the step above four or five times, releasing the images that come to mind.

Now, could you let the sense of wanting security to arise again?

Could you dive into the core of wanting security or survival?

Could you allow yourself to go deeper still?

And even deeper?

And just a little deeper?

If you're still aware of any remaining wanting security or survival in this moment, could you just set it free?

Notice how much more secure you feel right now after releasing. Imagine what your life will be like as you're increasingly secure and let go of more of the sense of lacking security, as you feel more at home and at ease.

Rest for a moment in the inner security you've discovered.

Wanting to Be Separate

When we want to be separate, we feel that we don't want to belong or that we need to maintain a separate identity. Therefore, we act in ways designed to help maintain a distinct identity. We are constantly engaged in differentiating from everyone and everything else. We want to prove how we are different, better, and special. We often give the message to the world, "Leave me alone." For most of us, the desire to be separate is so prevalent, yet subtle, that, although it colors everything we say, do, or think, it is often as difficult to discern as the air we breathe.

Wanting separation can have a strong feel to it, or it can be very subtle. At full strength, it feels rejecting and pushing away from. Many of us think separation is the essence of who we are. When we want to be separate, we are pulled in two directions: We want to get away from everyone else, or we want to stand out from the crowd. We don't want to be ordinary and fit in.

Synonyms for wanting separation include wanting to be alone, to reject, to look down on, to stand out, to be special, to detach, to disassociate, and to disconnect, to name a few. As we let go of wanting to be separate, we feel more able to be in union, connected with others, without losing our uniqueness.

Wanting to Be One

When we want to be one, we feel that we want to belong, or as though we need to dissolve our separate identity and merge with others—or with everything. People who've been seekers on a spiritual path are often highly motivated by this desire. We are constantly engaged in seeking unity, while ignoring the underlying unity that is already effortlessly present. As with wanting separation, the desire to be one is so prevalent, yet subtle, for most of us that it colors everything that we say, do, or think. But as long as we have any sense of wanting to be one, we always feel a little—or a lot—alone and isolated, and we have a desire to end that loneliness and isolation. We often fill our lives with external signs of connection in order to hide or avoid our feelings of isolation.

Wanting oneness may have a strong feel to it, or it may be

very subtle. It feels like a sense of yearning, of longing for connection. Synonyms include wanting to unite, to accept, to be equal with, to be ordinary, to attach, to associate, to join, and to connect. As we let go of wanting to be one, we are more able to feel the oneness that is already here and now, without having to look for it outside of ourselves.

Written Releasing: Wanting Separation

This two-part written process is designed to assist you in releasing *wanting separation*. Again, as with the earlier written releasing processes, in order to prepare for part one, create two columns across the top of a clean page of paper in your releasing journal. The first column is labeled "Remember a specific instance when I wanted separation." The second column is labeled "What is my NOW want about that?"

Begin by writing down in the first column as many instances as you can remember when you wanted separation or you wanted to be one. Then, in the second column, write down your NOW want (e.g., wanting approval, wanting control, wanting security, or wanting separation or oneness) or abbreviate it. When you have fully released that want, make a check mark next to it or cross it off. Repeat the above steps and continue releasing your NOW want until you feel that you are fully released on that incident. Again, also remember to release your so-called positive feelings, so you can keep moving to higher energy states.

When you feel ready to move on, create a second worksheet for part two of the process. Across the top of another blank page in your journal, create two columns. The first column is labeled "Ways I seek separation." The second column

Releasing *Wanting Separation*

Remember a specific instance when I wanted separation	What is my NOW want about that?
My divorce	Anger ~~w/c,~~ w/sep. ✓
Got a promotion	Proud – w/a, ✓ ~~w/sep.~~
Visit from my aunt	Overwhelmed – ~~w/c,~~ w/a ✓

is labeled "Ways I seek oneness."

Now, make a list of all the ways you seek separation in your current life (business, relationships, etc.). Then, take each item, get in touch with your NOW feeling, write down whether it relates to wanting approval, control, security, separation, or oneness, and release it completely. Check off or cross out the NOW want afterwards and focus on the next action.

Next, make a list of all the ways you seek oneness in your current life. Take each time, get in touch with the NOW feeling, write down whether it relates to wanting approval, control, security, separation, or oneness, and then release it completely.

Releasing *Wanting Separation*

Ways I seek separation	Ways I seek oneness
Accomplishment	*Meditation*
~~*w/a, w/c, w/sep.*~~	~~*w/o, w/c*~~
Go in the other room —w/c, ✓ ✓*w/sep.*	*Talking on the phone—w/a,* ✓ *w/o* ✓
Judging people	*Sex —w/a,* ✓ ~~*w/s,*~~
~~*w/a, w/c, w/sep.*~~	*w/o* ✓

When you have fully released the want, either put a check mark next to the abbreviation for the want or cross it out.

Process for Letting Go of Wanting Separation

Begin by making yourself comfortable and shifting your focus inwardly. Then allow yourself just to be.

Could you welcome the NOW feeling and know that it's okay?

Now, bring to mind a situation in your life when you either felt alone or wanted to push others away, a time when your sense of wanting separation or oneness was stirred up.

*Could you welcome that sense of wanting separation
or wanting to be one into awareness?*

Could you release it?

Now, focus on that same situation or another in which you felt "leave me alone" or were longing for separation or oneness. *Could you welcome that sense of wanting separation or oneness?*

Then, could you let it go?

Repeat the steps above as many times as you'd like, and then move on.

Now, allow yourself to experience the fullest extent of wanting separation or wanting to be one that you can right now without forcing. Gently stir it up, if you need to, while realizing that all wants are merely energy. They're not "good" or "bad": they just are.

*Could you allow the sense of wanting to be separate
or wanting to be one to release?*

Again, invite your sense of wanting separation or oneness to enter your awareness.

Could you let it go?

Repeat several more times, noticing how things that formerly separated you now seem less and less important, and you feel more with the flow.

Remember, the wants are belief systems—programs that we use to operate our lives. Therefore, we experience recurring thoughts, feelings, and behaviors. When you want separation, you may think, "I am truly special," or, if you want oneness, "I am all alone, cut off from all that truly matters to me." You may feel isolated, alone, or rejected. It's possible that you merely feel cut off, blank, and dissatisfied with what is.

Think of what you do when you feel as though you want

to be separate or you want to be one: a recurring thought, an action you take, or a feeling. *Could you truly welcome that into your conscious awareness?*

Then, could you let go of the sense of wanting separation, or wanting to be one, from which this tendency is arising?

Repeat the step above four or five times, releasing the images that come to mind.

Now, could you allow that sense of wanting separation, or wanting to be one, to arise again?

Could you dive into the core of this wanting?

Could you allow yourself to go deeper still?

And even deeper?

And just a little deeper?

If you're still aware of any remaining wanting separation or wanting to be one in this moment, could you set it free?

Notice how much more at one and at home you feel right now after releasing. Imagine what your life will be like as you're increasingly connected to the flow of what is and at home with life as you know more of the time that all is well, and everything is unfolding as it should be.

Rest for a moment in the inner oneness you've discovered.

The Anatomy of an Imaginary Tree of Limitation

Imagine that you are lost amid a dense forest of imaginary limitation. What's the anatomy of these trees? At the subtlest level, they are made up of atoms, which, in our world, we call "thoughts." Moving toward a little more density and structure, the leaves on this imaginary tree represent your individual feelings. The branches represent the nine emotional states. The trunk and the roots spreading out laterally from the bottom of the trunk represent wanting approval and wanting to control, as well as their opposites. The taproot, growing straight downward into the soil, represents wanting security and its opposite. Lastly, the soil represents wanting to be separate and its opposite, wanting to be one. (See illustration page 183)

If we wanted to fell these imaginary trees of limitation and clear a path through this imaginary forest by releasing, there are several ways we might go about it. We could let go of one atom at a time by working to change our thinking. But that would take a long time. We could be even more active and proceed by plucking off individual leaves (feelings). But leaves tend to grow back. Or we could start pruning the branches (the nine emotional states). If you've ever pruned a tree, however, you know that branches often come back healthier than before. We would only start making significant progress once we began chopping at the trunk and lateral roots (the wanting approval and wanting to control). Of course, many trees have grown back from stumps even after some of their roots were removed.

There is not much certainty of eliminating this imaginary tree until we set about severing its taproot: wanting security and its opposite, wanting death. Now remember, in the forest of limitation where you're lost, every tree is imaginary.

All limitation is imaginary. At any point in this process, you can get a glimpse of what lies beyond the trees, the background of perfection and infinity that supports yet is unaffected by the forest. So, allow for the possibility as you use the Sedona Method that big chunks of the forest itself can fall away. Often, when you least expect it, you'll let go of big chunks of your imaginary limitation quite spontaneously. This will happen more and more frequently as you release at the level of the four basic wants.

The Imaginary Tree of Limitation

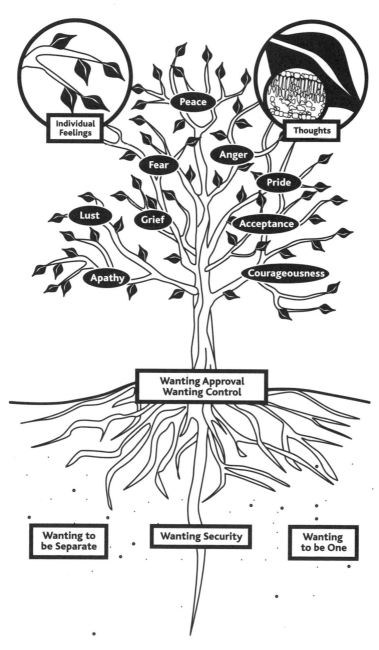

Chapter 8

Setting and Attaining Your Goals

In this chapter, we're going to explore a very powerful application of the Sedona Method: setting and attaining goals. While I cannot guarantee that the process described here will help you achieve every goal that you set, I am able to promise that it will dramatically improve the odds in your favor. Not only can this process help you discern which goals are ones that you truly can and should pursue, it will also help you to let go of goals that are inappropriate. In addition, you'll begin to feel better about goal setting in general.

When you hear the word "goal," does it conjure up strong positive or negative feelings? We live in an extremely goal oriented culture, yet most of us have mixed feelings about setting and attaining goals. We have internalized so many *shoulds* and *shouldn'ts* that dictate what we're supposed to want and strive for in life that the goals we pursued in the past, or that we're pursuing now, often do not feel like our own.

Do you work in a business environment that imposes goals upon you? Does your family have an undue influence on your life choices? Do you feel as though only certain goals are acceptable to your friends and peers? If you answered "yes" to any of the preceding questions, you are not alone. At times, most of us have felt pushed or cornered into pursuing goals that we probably would not have chosen if we were given the choice.

We have also had diverse experiences when we were striving to achieve our goals: some good, some so-so, others frustrating. Although we've pursued certain goals with our full hearts and minds, we've ultimately given up on them, because they took too long to realize. Other goals we've achieved without even trying. These kinds of experiences color our impressions of goal setting and generate a broad spectrum of emotional responses. In short, there's a lot of confusion around the whole topic.

As Lester Levenson stewarded the creation of the Goal Process you're about to learn, he was aware of the confusion so many people feel. By designing a simple system, he hoped he could alleviate much of the suffering associated with goals. He purposefully crafted the process in such a way that, besides creating what we wanted in our lives, we would gain another major benefit from releasing on our goals: imperturbability.

Becoming "Hootless"

We all spend much of our time either moving away from, or moving towards, the actual or potential contents of our lives as a result of our attachments and aversions. These are the real or imagined objects that we hold in awareness and grant the power to bestow or take away our natural state of happiness. Attachments are those things that we desire to hold close. Aversions are those things that we desire to hold away. In both cases, the operative word is "hold." Since they are the leading cause of our unnecessary suffering, a primary definition of freedom would be having no attachments and no aversions.

When you set a goal and use releasing to achieve it, you bring up into your awareness the attachments and aversions that you have about that particular issue. Then, as you release your attachments and aversions to the goal, you'll either achieve it or you won't. But, either way, you'll have lightened your load of suffering. You'll become free.

The way results are achieved is by reaching an internal feeling state that Lester called "hootlessness." Hootlessness is when you do not give a hoot whether you achieve a particular goal or not. Contrary to popular belief, you do not attain your goals when you desire them strongly enough. In fact, if you honestly examine your past experiences, you'll discover that most of the goals you've achieved are the ones that you let go of wanting—even if not by choice. Most people focus on the struggle that leads up to the letting go and then attribute their results to the struggle rather than the release. They miss the point.

As you journey through this process, you'll discover that the struggle is unnecessary. This does not mean, of course, that you won't take action steps to achieve your goals. It simply means that the actions you do choose to take will come with less effort and drama. When you allow yourself to release to the point where you are hootless about getting your goal, two things may happen. Either you'll find that you abandon the goal altogether and feel lighter because of it, or you'll be much more likely to achieve the goal than you were when you wanted it. As Lester used to say, "Even the impossible becomes completely possible when you are fully released on it. And you know when you are fully released on it when you don't give a hoot."

Now, you may be concerned that if you become hootless you won't enjoy the fruits of your labors. Let me put this fear to rest. In my experience, it couldn't be further from the truth. The more hootless you feel, the freer you are to enjoy whatever you have in this moment without the usual fear of loss or disappointment.

In Chapter 6, Taking Your Releasing to a Deeper Level, we looked at our motivations and how we have a tendency to confuse objects with feelings. We want approval, control, security, and separation—as well as their opposites—and we erroneously believe that objects give them to us. So, another reason why we may have mixed feelings about goals is that, even when we do get something we believe we want, it never truly satisfies us.

After all, how long do we enjoy a new car, stereo, or pair of shoes? Usually, not long enough. Almost as soon as we get one item on our list, we move on to the next, because the happiness we seek is not truly contained in any object. Rather, it is our natural state of being. When we get past seeking objects and outcomes, we become hootless.

Does this mean that you should stop pursuing goals? Absolutely not! I highly recommend that you pursue your goals using the process in this chapter until you achieve them or you let go of wanting them. Denying that you want something will not cause the desire to go away. Until you acknowledge a desire, and either achieve it or let it go, it will eat away your insides. Rest assured, you'll find it fun to pursue your goals using this process, because you'll feel freer and happier every step of the way.

Robert: Manifesting Without Fretting about It

At age 63, Robert had been thinking of retiring. He was managing a multimillion-dollar project for the federal government that was turning sour and he felt desperate for it to work out. Then, he found himself in the midst of an acrimonious divorce, and his ex-wife took a large settlement. Suddenly, he was in bad financial shape, and he was furious. That's when he purchased a set of Sedona Method audiotapes and began listening to them.

Robert had made a personal discovery about hootlessness years earlier. He found that if he really needed or wanted some material object to be his, the first thing to do was to articulate clearly in his mind exactly what it was that he wanted. The second and most important step was to expel any feelings of need or want, just let it go. Then, sooner or later, whatever he wanted would materialize! Whenever he could do this, he enjoyed amazing results. Conversely, if he fretted or lusted after it, it would never happen. It was a revelation to him when he heard this phenomenon explained by the Sedona Method. He finally understood how it relates to the basic needs of acceptance, control, and security. He honestly believes that it was no coincidence that, halfway through the tape program, he enjoyed a "miracle" that made him a millionaire overnight—literally! An investment of his tripled in value through an unpredictable sequence of events.

That isn't the end of the story, however, for Robert had several goals. His top priority was to rid himself of any negative feelings about the people in his life. This was accomplished almost immediately by daily releasing. He also wanted more money than he got in his stock windfall, and to have a job where he could work at home and set his own hours. He was ready to quit his job and travel, but his boss wouldn't let him go. So, he became a consultant. And even though basically nobody in the federal government works from home, Robert now did. He doubled his income after his "retirement." In addition, he wanted to live in a house by a lake. By using the Goal Process, he manifested his dream home within a year. He simply would visualize watching a sunset over the lake from a position seated behind his desk. Then, he would use the three basic releasing questions and let it go entirely. He didn't angst about it.

One day, Robert happened to be driving by a lake and saw a sign listing several properties for sale. He stopped and looked at a few nice houses that for different reasons just didn't appeal to him. Then, he noticed a path leading to another house nearer the water. When he walked into that house, he could see the lake out a front bay window. In fact, every single room, except the two bathrooms, faced the lake. It was the right size for him: not too big, not too small. The previous owners had taken out some walls, and he'd only have to make minor modifications. As the price was good, he bought it on the spot.

In Robert's own words, "Hootlessness is important and dear to me. Everything I have that I really like, and that I've wanted to have, has appeared through that state. I can't tell you how often it happens. The mind is precious real estate. Before I learned the Method, I already understood the need to set goals and relax the mind. It gave me a way."

Releasing Your Feelings about Setting Goals

Before we actually work on the Goal Process, let's do some general releasing on goals. As I explained at the beginning of the chapter, most of us have a lot of different feelings about pursuing goals. We live in a goal oriented society that's often unforgiving. If we've achieved them in our past attempts, we may be enthusiastic about goals. But even when we have succeeded in the past, we may feel some trepidation about adopting a new way of working on goals and about moving forward. And what if we haven't succeeded? If we've tried to achieve goals before and failed, we're likely to transfer our feelings about these past failures into any future efforts.

So, see how you feel about your past history with goals. Notice what you feel about goals in general.

Allow yourself to feel however you feel in the NOW about goals. Welcome the feeling as best you can. Allow it to be here.

Then, could you allow yourself to notice from which want it's coming (approval, control, or safety)?

Could you let that want go?

Now, think of a specific time when you didn't achieve a goal. You set the goal up. You took steps to achieve it, and yet it didn't happen. *How do you feel about that now?*

Embrace how you feel in this moment about not having achieved that goal.

Could you allow the feeling just to be here?

Check to see if it's coming from an underlying sense of wanting approval, control, or security.

Then, whichever want it is: *Could you let it go?*

Repeat this process focusing on the same memory if you still have feelings about it. Or move on to another time that you set a goal you did not attain, and let go on that. Welcome your feelings into awareness, determine which wants are stirred up in the moment, and release them as best you can.

Next, recall whether anyone has ever pressured you into going for a goal. Maybe you work in sales, or in a corporate environment that dictates a particular goal for you. Very often, we're pressured into going for goals that we may not feel able to reach. Perhaps your parents or your spouse imposed a goal upon you. Once you have a situation in mind, notice what your NOW feeling is about it.

Simply allow yourself to feel however you feel in this moment about that time you were pressured to go for a goal.

Then check to see from which want it is coming.

Could you let that want go?

Focus again on that specific time in which you were pressured to go for a goal, either by yourself or someone else, and see how you feel about that now.

Is there any sense of wanting in association with that memory?

Could you let go of that want?

Now, think of a current goal that you feel like you *should* do, you *must* do, or you *have to* do. Maybe you don't really want to do it, but you feel like you have to do it. *How does that make you feel inside?*

Could you allow that feeling to be here, just to let it be?

Does that stir up some resistance or another want?

Could you let that go?

Focus on the pressure to achieve goals, either exerted by yourself or someone else, and welcome that sense of pressure to have, to do or to be into your awareness.

Could you allow the pressure to be here and embrace it fully?

Check to see which want that pressure stirs up inside of you.

Then, could you let it go?

Going after our goals should always feel like a choice. The more often we can start freshly in every moment, without any preconceived notions, and without carrying around excess baggage from the past, the better our chances are to be truly successful at achieving the goals we've set for ourselves. Once you feel that you've let go of enough of your limiting beliefs and feelings, you're ready to continue below with the Goal Process.

Crafting Your Goal Statements
Wording a Goal Statement

Writing down your goals is one of the keys to achieving them. In fact, studies of groups of successful people have shown that those who write down their goals are more likely to achieve them than people who only think about them. Furthermore, wording a goal correctly can make the difference between whether or not it is finally achieved. Before you move on to wording your goals, here are a few important points to keep in mind:

- *Phrase your goal in the NOW, as though it is already achieved.* Most of us fall into the trap of thinking that we're going to create what we want in the future. But the future never seems to come. How many times have you said to yourself, "I'll do that tomorrow," and you didn't do it? Whenever you're holding in mind, "I'm going to do this later," or " . . . next week," or " . . . next year," you're projecting your goal forward. Phrasing it as a future event tends to keep it always out of reach.

  This reminds me of a clever sign that one of my

193

British students saw in a pub, which read: Free Beer Tomorrow. Nobody was ever able to collect on that offer!

- *Phrase your goal in the positive.* Put in what you want, not what you don't want. Focus on the solution. Your goal statement should reflect the end result that you'd like to achieve. Avoid including anything you want to get rid of in your statement, because keeping in mind what you don't want creates it. What if you would like to stop smoking, for instance? It would be inappropriate to phrase your goal: "I allow myself to stop smoking."

  Do you recall the earlier discussion about how the mind doesn't translate words of negation, such as not, don't, or stop, because it thinks in pictures? Right now, try not to think of a white elephant, and what do you think of? A white elephant.

  Always put something in the goal that the mind can visualize. For example, "I allow myself to be a non-smoker." You can picture being a nonsmoker, as that's something you can see—other people who aren't smoking. You can also imagine a kinesthetic sensation of breathing deeply and freely or climbing a long flight of stairs without gasping for air. It makes a huge difference to word your goals in this manner.

- *Your goal should feel realistic and right for you.* It should seem possible—with a sense of "I can have it!" Suppose you are making $1,000 a week, but what you'd really like to earn is $10,000 a week. Upping your income from $1,000 to $10,000 might be too big a jump for you to accept in a single goal statement. Instead, you might start by wording the goal, "I allow myself to effortlessly make $2,500 a week." That's a stretch from where you currently are, but it seems more realistic.

The more attainable you make a goal—phrased so the mind can at least accept it as a possibility—the more easily you'll be able to release the obstacles that you hold within you toward that goal's achievement.

- *Include yourself in the goal statement.* In other words, if you want to clean your house, you might phrase your goal as, "I allow myself to clean my house," rather than, "The house is clean." When you say, "The house is clean," you may not believe it. If you were to phrase it that way, on some level you might also start waiting for a miracle to happen so that the house gets clean by itself. Whereas, if you've had tremendous resistance in the past to cleaning your house, and then you release on the goal, "I allow myself easily to clean the house," you could find yourself easily cleaning your house. That's much simpler.

- *Be precise and concise.* Focus on one goal per statement. Don't diffuse your energy by creating multiple goals. Also, use as few words as possible, while being sure to make it a complete statement of what you want. Choose the exact words that convey a specific meaning that makes you feel enthusiastic. Enthusiasm is important.

Years ago, a man in a workshop set up a goal: "I allow myself to have an abundant income, so that I can have a new sports car, a house in the country, the maids to take care of the second house, and the perfect woman to have a relationship with to share all this." As you can see, there were several goals within that one goal, and they were pulling him in different directions. The instructor helped the man simplify his goal by breaking it down into specific individual goals. They then created an umbrella goal that was appropriate for the whole situation: "I allow myself to have all the good things in life and enjoy them." See how that includes everything?

- *Be specific, but not limiting.* Leave things as open as possible to allow for your results being upgraded from what you initially project.

- *Eliminate the word "want."* As we've already discussed at length in Chapter 6, wanting bars you from having. Would you rather want to have a lot of money, or would you rather have a lot of money? Would you rather want the perfect relationship, or would you rather have the perfect relationship? Would you rather want good health, or would you rather have good health? "Want" is always equated with a feeling of lack or deprivation, so avoid putting the feeling of lack in your goal statement.

- *Word your goal to facilitate letting go.* Make sure to word the goal statement in a way that does not build in wanting approval, control, security, or separation.

One area where you could get yourself into trouble is in the area of relationship. For example, if you set a goal: "I allow Mary (or Joe) to love me," you might get locked into wanting approval. First of all, you'll be running around doing all sorts of things to try to get the person to love you. Secondly, what if the person is not even the right match for you? The goal would be more open and inclusive if you phrased it, "I allow myself to have a loving relationship." That's easier to release on, and the result could be a relationship with the person with whom you're currently interested, or it could not.

Another goal that could get you into trouble is, "I allow _____ (another person's name) to have/be/do _____ (something that you want them to have/be/do)." If you set up a goal statement in this way, it indicates that you want to control that other person's experience. If someone in your experience appears to need assistance, it's much more freeing to word your goal as follows: "I allow _____ (the person's name) to have whatever it is he or she wants for him or herself." This approach is especially helpful for people who are suffering in any way. It grants them their own inner strength and knowingness—their Beingness.

- *State the end result, not the means of achieving it.*
  Let's go back to the earlier example of netting an income of $2,500 a week. When you phrase your goal statement, don't explain how you're going to get the

money. I've seen people word statements like: "I allow myself to make $2,500 a week by working eighteen hours a day, six days a week," and a whole list of other actions that they thought they needed to take in order to achieve their goals. In fact, these are limitations. The actions we think we need to take very often have absolutely nothing to do with the goal itself. They're just artificial obstacles that we're putting in the way.

As we work on your goals later in this chapter, you'll learn to release specifically on each action step you can take. Always allow for the unexpected. What if someone gives you a large amount of money? What if you win the lottery? There are so many things that could happen to allow a goal to come into your awareness.

- *Word your goal so it relates to courage, acceptance, or peace.* "I allow myself to . . . ," "I can . . . ," or, "I open myself to . . ." are good ways to begin a goal in courageousness. "I have . . ." is a good way to begin a goal in acceptance. "I am . . ." is a good way to begin a goal in peace. These ways of starting a goal statement enable the mind to use its creativity to generate possibilities of how the goal can happen.

By the way, if you're not feeling courageous yet about a particular goal, getting there will be a great step forward. Later on, you can always reword the goal to raise the energy even higher to acceptance or peace.

Sample Goal Statements

These can be used as a basis for creating your own individual goal statements. Simply adjust the final wording to reflect your particular situation.

Job/Career/Financial

- I allow myself to have a net income of _____ or more a month/year.
- I allow myself to have a positive net worth.
- I allow myself to be paid well for doing what I love.
- I allow myself to run my _____ (business/department) efficiently and successfully.
- I allow myself to release with ease throughout my workday.
- I allow myself to easily have and enjoy the best job for me at this time in my _____ (life/career).
- I allow myself easily to find and develop a career that will greatly utilize my creative abilities (and/or skills), and which will provide abundant financial rewards.
- I allow myself to have, be, and do whatever I choose with ease.
- I allow myself to have enough in all areas of my life.
- I allow myself to have all the good things in life and enjoy them.
- I allow myself to feel like I have all the time in the world.

Relationships/Communication

- I allow myself to have the perfect relationship for me.

- I allow myself to have a loving relationship that supports me in my freedom and aliveness.
- I allow my relationship with _____ to be _____ (choose from the following list: easy, relaxed, comfortable, friendly, harmonious, loving, constructive, supportive, open, honest, kindly or mutually beneficial).
- I allow myself to communicate easily and effectively with my _____ (choose from the appropriate category: spouse, co-workers, boss, subordinates, children, friends or a person's name).
- I allow my situation with _____ to be resolved with fairness and mutual benefit for all concerned.
- I allow myself to love and accept (or forgive) myself or _____ (insert person's name), no matter what.
- I allow myself lovingly to support _____ (insert name) in his/her growth and freedom.
- I allow _____ (insert name) to have what he/she wants for himself/herself.
- I allow myself to accept that I am enough exactly as I am.

Diet/General Health

- I allow myself easily to achieve and maintain my ideal body weight.
- I allow myself to enjoy eating foods that keep my body slender, healthy, and fit.
- I allow myself to be attracted to and eat the foods that are best for me.
- I allow myself to enjoy a regular exercise routine.

General Health and Well-being

- I allow myself to release naturally and with ease.
- I allow myself to have a radiantly healthy, relaxed, and energized body and mind.
- I allow myself to approach each moment from a feeling of wholeness and well-being.
- I allow myself to sleep well and to awake refreshed and well rested at _____ a.m.
- I allow myself to easily and cheerfully establish and maintain a lifestyle that promotes good health and fitness.
- I allow myself to enjoy being a non-smoker.
- I allow myself to love myself as I am.
- I allow myself to enjoy life moment to moment.
- I allow myself to be at peace, relaxed in the knowing that all is well and everything is unfolding as it supposed to be.
- I allow myself to rejoice in the present moment.
- I allow this moment to be enough.
- I allow myself to rest as the presence of awareness that is always here and now.

Activity: Writing Down Your Goals

Now that you understand the subtleties of wording a goal statement, refer back to the list of intentions for this course that you made in your releasing journal, as I suggested in Chapter 1, and pick one or two items on which to work. Although you may select more than one goal to reword using the above guidelines and samples, I recommend that you limit the number of goals

"I started this course during a period of intense turmoil in my business life. In the past 22 months, we've experienced four major setbacks, and my company's sales were off at an unprecedented level—80 percent of normal. I needed to make a lot of hard choices and still have the energy to develop and implement a recovery plan. Through the tools of the Method, there was a methodology for me to make the choices, to act, and to sleep at night. Moreover, each action became easier, clearer, and more focused. Business has turned around rather dramatically. We are not out of the woods completely, but we can see the rays of the sun."

—M.P., New York, NY

that you actively work on at any given moment for a couple of reasons. First, you are more likely to take your goals to completion (either achievement or full release) if you can avoid scattering your energy by focusing on too many of them at once. Secondly, since the Method helps us to let go at such a deep level, you will find that many of the items on your list are achieved without you ever having to work consciously on them.

On a blank sheet of paper in your releasing notebook, rewrite the goals you've selected using the preceding guidelines. You'll benefit from having optimally worded goal statements when you work on the Goal Process and Action Steps Process below.

The Goal Process

The Goal Process is incredibly simple. One at a time, you will focus on the positive goal statements that you've written and use each one like a magnet to pull whatever negativity you have about that goal up from your subconscious mind—and

Goal Process

GOAL: *I allow myself to easily achieve and maintain my ideal body weight.*

What is my NOW feeling about my goal?

Lust - I like to eat—w/a, w/c ✓ ✓

Anger - I hate to diet—w/c ✓

Frustration—I don't have time to exercise—w/a, w/c ✓ ✓

Courageousness—I can do this—w/a ✓

then you'll let it go. If you feel nervous or skeptical about this process, keep one idea in mind: If you always do what you've always done, you'll always get what you've always gotten.

The Goal Process is an opportunity to learn to do what you do *in a new way.*

Step 1: Write your goal at the top of a blank piece of paper, using correct wording (see page 193).

Step 2: Read the goal silently or aloud and, below the goal, write down the first thought or feeling that comes to mind in relationship to it.

Step 3: Ask yourself which want underlies the thought or feeling, using this question: Does that come from a sense of wanting approval, control, or security? Make a note of which want it is by writing an abbreviation next to the question. For wanting approval, write w/a. For wanting to control, write w/c. For wanting security, write w/s. If more than one want is stirred up, simply write down all the appropriate abbreviations.

Step 4: Release any wants that are stirred up in the NOW moment about the feeling or thought that you wrote down. Simply ask: *Could I let go of wanting the approval, control, or security?* As you let go of a given want, cross it out or check it off.

Step 5: Repeat Steps 2 through 4 until you feel courageousness, acceptance, or peace about your goal. Once you're feeling one of these higher emotional states, you can be confident that you've taken off a layer of limitation about that particular goal. You then have three options of what to do in Step 6.

Step 6: Your first option is to continue repeating the process above in order to eliminate several more layers of limitation about that particular goal.

Your second option is to put the Goal Process down for now and go about your life. Do your best to let go whenever you think about your goal during the day.

A minor caution about stopping too soon: Before you discontinue the process, it's best to reach at least a state of courageousness, acceptance, or peace. Otherwise, you'll be holding in mind an outcome that's less than ideal. Furthermore, you probably won't be eager to return for more releasing on any of the energy levels below courage.

Your third option at Step 6 is to continue the Goal Process by working on the Action Steps Process below.

The Action Steps Process

The Action Steps Process is designed to complement the Goal Process by helping you release more of the inner limitations—emotional, mental, and behavioral barriers—that prevent you from taking action and effectively pursuing your goals. In addition, this process will help you to discern between action steps that are truly necessary to attain a particular goal and those that are not. This can save you a lot of time and effort.

Many of us avoid pursuing a particular goal, because we imagine that the actions we must take to achieve it are actions that we're unwilling to take. As you release on your action steps, you may discover that it's possible to release your resistance to taking those specific actions or that the actions are in fact unnecessary and were mental fabrications.

Okay, get out a clean sheet of paper or your releasing journal and begin.

Step 1: Write your goal statement at the top of the page, using the full wording. For this purpose, it's better not to abbreviate.

Step 2: After you read the goal silently, ask yourself: *What actions do I believe I need to take to achieve this goal?* Then, on separate lines, write down any actions that come to mind. A few will usually pop into your awareness right away.

You also have the choice to write down a single action at a time and go through Steps 3 to 5 before proceeding to the next action.

Step 3: On the line next to a particular action, write down any thoughts and feelings you have about taking it.

Step 4: Ask yourself which want underlies the thought or feeling, using this question: *Does that come from a sense of*

Action Steps Process

GOAL: *I allow myself to easily achieve and maintain my ideal body weight.*

What actions do I believe I need to take to achieve this goal?	What is my NOW feeling about doing it?
Join the gym	*Embarrassed (I don't like exercising in public)* — ~~w/sep.,~~ ~~w/a, w/s,~~ w/c ✓
Start diet	*Resistance (I don't want to)* — w/c ✓, w/a ✓
Stop eating snacks	*Grief (But I like to)* — ~~w/c,~~ w/s ✓

wanting approval, control, or security? Make a note of the want, as you did during the Goal Process, by writing an abbreviation next to the question: w/a (approval), w/c (control), and w/s (security). If more than one want is stirred up, simply write down all the appropriate abbreviations.

Step 5: Let go of any wants that are stirred up in the NOW moment about the feeling or thought that you wrote down. Use the question: *Could I let go of wanting approval, control, or security?* As you let go of a given want, cross it out or check it off. Continue to release on each action step until you feel courage, acceptance, or peace.

Step 6: Repeat Steps 2 through 5 until you've completed the Action Steps Process for all the action steps you've listed. If you're pressed for time, you can spend a few minutes completing the process on a few and return later to complete the remainder of them. But spend at least as much time as it takes to feel courageous about every step you do work on.

Step 7: Where appropriate, get into action. In addition, make sure to continue to release before, during, and after you take your action steps.

If you already use time management software on your computer, or a book that contains a daily action planner, you can abbreviate the process above by doing all of the same seven steps—without writing down your thoughts and feelings—as you plan your day. Simply jot down the abbreviations for the wants and cross them off or delete them as you release.

As you get into the habit of releasing on your action steps before you take them, you'll begin to accomplish them more quickly and easily. You will also approach your goals and action steps with a sense of fresh enthusiasm and greater self-motivation. In addition, you'll often think of much more creative action steps to take than you would have if you were not releasing.

Releasing on Your Goals and Action Steps

For best results, go through this process as often as you can on your own and/or with a releasing partner. The more you work on it, the more layers of obstacles you'll let go. It is not necessary to write anything down. Simply allow yourself to work on the goal and action steps internally. You can always make some notes afterwards about your insights.

Begin by thinking of a goal that you've set, and which you've already written down. Then say the goal quietly to yourself, noticing any thoughts that come to mind. Simply allow yourself to feel your overall feeling about the goal.

Check to see whether the feeling comes from a sense of wanting approval, control, or security?

Could you let that want go?

Read the goal quietly again and notice what comes to mind. Again, allow yourself to get a sense of your overall feeling about the goal in this moment.

Which want does that stir up inside?

Could you let that want go?

Repeat the above steps three or four more times. As you read the goal quietly to yourself each time, be sure to notice how your feeling about it is starting to shift. You may already feel very positive about the goal, or you may only be getting closer to feeling positively about it. No matter how you feel, allow yourself to feel that way and continue releasing on any underlying sense of wanting.

Once you're feeling courageousness, acceptance, or peace about the goal, you have a choice about how to proceed. You may set the goal aside and come back to work on it later, or you may move on to releasing on your action steps, as follows:

Read your goal again, and then think of an action you can take to get your goal.

What is your NOW feeling about the action step?

Could you simply allow that feeling to be present?

Is that feeling coming from a sense of wanting control, approval, or security?

Could you let that want go?

Now, focus on that same action step or another action step that you can take in order to achieve your goal. Just see how you feel about taking that action.

Could you welcome the feeling more fully into your awareness?

Would you allow yourself to identify which want it is coming from?

Then, could you let that want go?

Repeat this last series of releasing questions on several more action steps.

Now, notice how much more positively you feel about the goal, having released on it directly, and also having released on the action steps that are involved in getting the goal.

Exploration: Experience It, Let It Go, and Make It So

You may already be using visualization to achieve your goals. If you are, I bet you'll enjoy the results of the following process, for visualization combined with releasing is a lot more powerful than visualization on its own. A great number of

Sedona Method graduates have reported very profound gains from the marriage of the two. I highly recommend spending a few minutes a day exploring this process.

Make yourself comfortable. Sit back, relax, and focus inwardly. You may do this process with eyes open or closed, however the majority of people I've worked with seem to find it easier to visualize with their eyes closed. So, if you're doing it on your own, simply read each instruction, and then close your eyes to carry it out. Once you feel that you're completely finished doing as requested, open your eyes and read the next question or instruction. Then, close your eyes again while you carry it out. Remember also to take your time and go at your own pace. There is no reason to rush.

After you've worked through the process a few times, no doubt you'll be able to do it on your own from memory without even needing to read the instructions. Another choice is to have a releasing partner read it to you, step by step.

Begin by thinking of a specific goal, perhaps the goal that you just worded.

Now, using your imagination, paint a picture of what it will be like when you have attained this goal. If you're a visually oriented person, you're likely to see an actual image. However, if you're a feeling oriented person (kinesthetic), you may get a physical sensation instead. And if you're an auditory person, you may hear a narration in your mind about it. Use whatever sense or combination of senses is comfortable to you. Some people struggle with visualizing, because they believe it must be visual. Please let that go.

So, allow yourself to create as vivid an image as you can right now of what it's going to be like to have fulfilled your goal.

Really get into it as best you can. Indulge your senses, if you can. How does it look? What does it feel like? What are you hearing? Notice your perceptions on every level of your being.

Now, check whether there's any feeling inside of you that says, "No, I can't have this," or, "This isn't real," or, "This is just a fantasy." Identify any feeling that comes up to the contrary of allowing your ideal image to come into reality.

Could you welcome that contrary feeling?

Ask: *Does it come from wanting approval, control, or security?*

Whichever want it is: *Could you let it go?*

Now, using the sense or senses with which you are most comfortable, picture attaining your goal again. What is it going to be like when you have achieved it?

Then, check to see if there's anything else inside of you that's saying, "No, I can't have it," "I shouldn't have it," "I don't have it," and bring that belief, thought, or feeling into the foreground of your awareness.

Does it come from wanting approval, control, or security?

Could you let it go?

Repeat this process five or six times, releasing on everything that comes up in opposition to your goal. Observe how your goal feels more attainable and easier to accomplish each time you go back to your visualization and release. You have more of a sense of, "I can do this," or, "I can have this."

Now, allow yourself to picture having or doing whatever it is that's in your goal. Experience it as if it's happening right now. Let it be as vivid and full-blown as possible.

Check whether you have any resistance, even on a subtle level, to having your goal be here right now. *Are you holding back from experiencing that outcome?*

If there is, could you let go of the fight and welcome that resistance in your consciousness for a moment? Just let it be.

Could you let go of resisting the goal from coming into your experience?

Next, go back to the visualization one more time, allowing yourself to see, feel, and hear yourself having or achieving exactly what you want.

Could you fully welcome that image into your awareness, embrace it, own it, and truly allow it to be?

Just rest now. Know that it's okay to have what you want. It's okay to allow the fulfillment of that goal into your awareness. You deserve it.

When you're ready, gradually shift your awareness to an external focus.

Going Two Steps Further

In the next two chapters, you'll learn two additional techniques to help you achieve a state of hootlessness: the Likes/Dislikes Process and the Advantages/Disadvantages Process. Both techniques enable us to become neutral about our various attachments and aversions, which makes them liberating adjuncts to the Goal Process. Before moving on, however, allow yourself to do some additional work on your goals. I am confident that the material in the chapter you've just read can and will make a profound difference in your life and in your ability to achieve everything you choose.

Chapter 9

Beyond Attachments and Aversions

If you've read the preceding chapters and diligently applied the techniques they describe, I'm sure you've already made substantial progress on your path to emotional freedom. By the time most workshop participants arrive at this section of the Sedona Method Basic Course, they are smiling and laughing and report feeling lighter, calmer, and clearer than ever before. It's hard for them to believe how quickly and painlessly they've been moving through the terrain of unwanted emotions and beliefs in which they've been stuck, often for years. They feel excited that the Method's approach to goal setting, in particular, puts the freedom and power to choose their destiny in their own hands. Furthermore, once they've had positive experiences with releasing, they are more open to the genuine promise of what it can deliver. They begin using it more frequently, as well as looking for additional areas to apply it in their lives.

As soon as you get interested in real life applications of the Sedona Method, such as those described in Part Two of this book, the Likes/Dislikes Process that you're about to learn will become enormously valuable to you. It is an excellent way to dig deeper into a single issue in a short span of time, and can be especially helpful in letting go of your attachments and aversions to people, places, and things. However, you may use the Likes/Dislikes Process to do some additional releasing on any topic you choose.

As we discussed in Chapter 8, we all tend to hold on to things that we like, developing attachments to them. We also tend to hold away things that we don't like, developing aversions to them. Every time we release both our likes and dislikes about a given topic, we free ourselves from our attachments and aversions to it. If we use this technique often enough, our whole lives become freer, which ultimately increases both our happiness and our peace of mind.

> "The biggest and most important gain is that I have always had an abnormal fear of crowds, groups of people, and gatherings—social or otherwise—and the Method has now eliminated that fear!"
> —G.H. Malinoski,
> Normandy Park, WA

What Purpose Does this Process Serve?

Throughout this book, you've had the opportunity to work on paper. Many people find written releasing comparable to working with a releasing partner, but it is only one of your options. You can also use the Method effectively, in fact *very* effectively, without ever picking up a pen or a pencil. When you're doing the Likes/Dislikes Process, it may be helpful to objectify your experience of your releases by writing them down. However, doing a rapid series of internal Likes/Dislikes releases as you go about your day can help keep the events in your life flowing smoothly.

One of the key areas that can be positively impacted by the Likes/Dislikes Process is the area of relationships. For even in our most intimate relationships, most of us have both likes and dislikes about particular people. In fact, most of us maintain unconscious or semiconscious lists of things that we like and don't like about our life partners, family, friends, and business associates. We then compare everything they do to these internal lists, which tends to reinforce our expectations about them and our habitual ways of relating to them. Unfortunately, the patterns we're reinforcing are not the healthy ones, even in healthy relationships. Rather, they're patterns motivated by the four basic wants. As you'll soon discover, the result of releasing both your likes and dislikes for a given person is that you can truly open up more to that individual.

In personal relationships that we're enjoying, we become obsessed with the things that we like and sweep the things we don't like under the rug. But, of course, the dislikes sit festering just below our conscious awareness, until they eventually explode to the surface. In relationships that are not "working," the opposite is true. We forget all the things we like about these relationships and the people to whom we're relating. We start suppressing the good and intensively focus on all the things we don't like about them. Because it restores the balance between both sides of the relationship equation, the Likes/Dislikes Process is extremely helpful. It enables us to be more deeply connected.

Of course, this process is not reserved for personal relationships. It is also very effective for working on professional relationships. Most of us have someone in our business lives— at least one person—with whom we believe we must interact even though we don't really like him or her. This could be a key supplier, a key customer, or anyone else with whom we must maintain an ongoing relationship, feeling as though we don't have much choice about it. We wish the relationship could improve or would end. You might try applying this process to a difficult person such as this. If you release both the likes and the dislikes, I am sure you'll find that you feel better about him or her.

In addition, you can use the Likes/Dislikes Process to release personal tendencies and beliefs that keep you stuck in a rut. You might, for instance, believe that you talk too much or think too much, or that you act too shy, too proud, or too judgmental. You get the point. The value in doing Likes/Dislikes about a tendency such as being overweight is that you might be hard put to imagine that there are any likes about it, especially if it's a problem for you. But when you explore the topic, you would find that there are even some hidden reasons why you think it's good to be overweight. Discovering those likes and letting them go could be the key to changing that pattern.

Similar to our lists of likes and dislikes about others with whom we're in relationships, most of us keep lists about ourselves—and they're usually much less complimentary than the ones that we keep on our partners. Thus, I highly recommend that you also do the Likes/Dislikes Process on yourself at some point. This can be an eye-opening and extremely liberating experience.

The Likes/Dislikes Process

Ordinarily, people do the Likes/Dislikes Process on a sheet of paper. For now, however, I suggest that you don't write anything down. Just read this process to yourself or have your partner read it to you, and do your own releasing as best you can. After some initial imaginative releasing, I'll give you instructions for preparing a worksheet.

Begin by allowing yourself to bring a topic to mind. Because you can use this process for so many different kinds of subjects, if you have difficulty coming up with a topic right now, refer back to the intentions you set in your releasing journal, as suggested in Chapter 1, or to a goal you set in Chapter 8 and select one of those.

What's something that you like about this person, place, or thing?

Feel whatever feeling is engendered inside of you. Welcome it fully.

Does it come from wanting approval, control, or security?

Could you let that want go?

Now, think of your topic again.

What's something that you dislike about this person, place, or thing?

Again, allow yourself to feel whatever feeling that engenders in this moment.

Could you allow that feeling to be here?

Does it come from wanting approval, control, or security?

Could you let it go?

Repeat the steps above, shifting between aspects of the topic that you like and aspects that you dislike, and then releasing your NOW feelings and underlying wants. You may find that the same aspect comes up as both a like and a dislike, or that an item on your list will come up more than once. That's okay. Release on it each time. Also remember that it's important to let go of your "good" feelings; this practice will help you gain clarity and deepen whatever goodness there already is in any given situation.

Once you've done about nine rounds of releasing in total, stop and notice how differently you're starting to feel about what you've been releasing on. Together, each pair of likes and dislikes makes up a layer of limitation, or a holdback, on a particular topic. Often, there are many layers on a particular topic. The first few times you use the Likes/Dislikes Process, you may be amazed at how effective it is.

Suzanne: Increasing Comfort with Sales Calls

Using the Likes/Dislikes Process helped Suzanne, a Sedona Method instructor, to overcome her resistance to cold calling corporations to promote her classes. As a self-employed individual, she felt for a long time that she was playing it small and safe. "I am a person with amazing experiences who has done all sorts of things. I have lived abroad, and I speak several languages. But I could never step into my public work—my greatness, or true self—and bring that into my life in a big way," she says. "I think a lot of people have an inside that doesn't match their outside like that, so maybe my story will be useful." She set a project goal to sell corporate trainings and began releasing on it until her beliefs changed and her phone calls became a source of good feelings.

"Making phone calls can be challenging. When I set my goal, I'd sometimes hear negative self-talk like, 'Oh gosh, I can't sell this because they're not going to want it. The market is down, and corporations have no money right now for trainings. They're not going to pay what we want them to pay. They're too busy, and I'm never going to get the person I need on the line.' Little ideas like that. So, I began working on likes and dislikes: I really like laughing and talking with people on the phone. I dislike getting voicemail. I love making new friends. I dislike the time it takes. I like telling people about the Method because it inspires me. As a result, I got through my calls. As I released on the things I resist and the things I embrace, the calls took care of themselves and are producing phenomenal results."

Written Releasing on Your Likes/Dislikes

On paper, the Likes/Dislikes Process is exactly the same as what we were doing above, except you write down your responses to the questions as a way to monitor yourself. So, get out your releasing journal, and let's begin. Before you begin, draw a line down the center of the paper, leaving room at the top for your topic. There are eight steps in total.

Step 1: Write your topic at the top of the page. Remember, this could be the name of a person, place, or thing, or a few words that describe a situation from any area in your life where you'd like to experience greater freedom. For example, you might write down the name of a city that you're considering moving to, such as New York. At the top of the left-hand column, create a label: Likes. At the top of the right-hand column, create a label: Dislikes. Now you're ready to move on to Step 2.

Step 2: Ask yourself: *What do I like about ____ (your topic)?* Then write down the first thought or feeling that comes to mind in the left-hand column. Using the same example of New York, you might write down "Excitement," or "Broadway theater."

Step 3: Check to see which basic want your like comes from by asking: *Is there a sense of wanting approval, control, or security?* Once you've identified it, write down the want from which the thought or feeling comes using the usual abbreviations: w/a for wanting approval, w/c for wanting to control, and w/s for wanting security.

Step 4: Allow yourself to let go of the underlying want by using either one of the following questions:

- *Could I welcome this want fully?*
- *Could I let go of wanting _____ (whichever want it is)?*

Cross out the want as you let it go, then move on to a dislike. Do only one like at a time.

Step 5: Ask yourself: *What do I dislike about _____ (your topic)?* Then write down the first thought or feeling that comes to mind in the right-hand column. Using the example of New York again, you might write down "Overcrowded," or "Noisy."

Step 6: Check to see which basic want your dislike comes from by asking: *Is there a sense of wanting approval, control, or security?*

Step 7: Allow yourself to let go of the underlying want by using either one of the following questions:

- *Could I welcome this want fully?*
- *Could I let go of wanting _____ (whichever want it is)?*

Cross out the want as you let it go, then move on to

Likes/Dislikes Process

Topic: *What do I (like/dislike) about moving to New York City*

Likes	Dislikes
Excitement—~~w/a~~	Overcrowded— ~~w/s, w/c~~
Broadway theater— ~~w/a, w/c~~	Noisy—w/c, ✓ ~~w/sep.~~
New job—~~w/s, w/c~~	Far from family— ~~w/s, w/o~~
Many conveniences— w/c ✓	High rent—~~w/c~~

another like. Do only one dislike at a time.

Step 8: Repeat Steps 2 through 7 many times, alternating between a like and a dislike, then another like and dislike, and so on until you feel a positive shift in attitude towards your topic. You can work on it for as long or as short a time span as you decide. The more you put into the Likes/Dislikes Process, the more you'll get out of it.

Opening Doors

As you work with the Likes/Dislikes Process, you'll find that it opens many inner doors that you may not even have realized you once slammed shut. In opening these doors, you will be letting go of the limitations that they've trapped inside of you. This will free you to truly enjoy your relationships and your life. I highly encourage you to experiment with this process before you move on to explore the next chapter.

Chapter 10

Power Decision-making

At the end of Chapter 8, I promised to teach you two additional techniques that would help you achieve a state of hootlessness. The Advantages/Disadvantages Process is the second of these. It is an excellent tool whose function is to help you uncover areas where you've become stuck and subsequently let them go. With just the right amount of focused releasing, you can easily shift these recurring thought patterns, behaviors, and situations. As of today, 26 years after being introduced to the notion, I still use Advantages/Disadvantages worksheets on a regular basis. I even worked on one this morning before I sat down to write. In fact, it's probably my favorite worksheet.

Use the Advantages/Disadvantages Process to further your work on a host of different things, including:

- *Goals.* In addition to working on a goal directly, ask: *What advantage is there to me to have this goal?* And: *What disadvantage is there to me to have this goal?*

- *Decisions.* When an opportunity arises, such as being offered a new job, and you're not quite sure whether or not to take it, doing advantages and disadvantages will help you get a lot clearer. The process cuts through confusion about career changes, purchases, taking trips, and starting new projects.

- *Problems.* You can use this to let go of overspending or not saving appropriately. Other problems it would be useful to address include difficulty with particular types of people, leaving things incomplete, or procrastination, to name a few.

- *Habits and Tendencies.* Not sure why you can't quit smoking or feel the need to shop all day long? Advantages/Disadvantages may reveal hidden attachments and aversions.

- *Positives.* I find it freeing to do advantages/disadvantages on positive feelings, such as having abundance, more joy, feeling more alive, or recognizing your true nature. These may not necessarily be goals that you're pursuing right now, although most people would like to experience many of these qualities. When you release on a positive feeling, it always deepens your releasing and cleans out that area—even if you're already feeling good about it.

I think you can tell I'm pretty enthusiastic about this process, so why don't we do some work on it together?

Think of an area in your life that would apply to this process: a decision you need to make, a problem you'd like to resolve, or a goal you'd like to fulfill, or any other topic that you'd like to do some in-depth releasing on. If you need inspiration, revisit the work you did in your releasing journal as you were reading the sections "What Do You Want in Your Life?" from Chapter 1 (see page 46) or "Writing Down Your Goals" from Chapter 8 (see page 200).

The Advantages/Disadvantages Process

This process is similar to the Likes/Dislikes Process we explored in Chapter 9 (see page 217), however it captures the imagination in a slightly different way. After using both, you'll discover which process works best for which kinds of issues in your life.

Begin by making yourself comfortable and shift your focus within. Bring to mind the topic that you're going to be releasing on—a goal, a problem, or whatever it is.

What is the advantage to you in it being that way? Remember to accept the first thought or feeling that comes to mind.

Does the advantage come from wanting approval, control, or security?

Whichever want it is: *Could you let it go?*

What's the disadvantage to you in your topic being the way it is?

Go a little deeper and see if the disadvantage comes from wanting approval, control, or security.

Could you simply let it go?

Repeat the steps above, shifting between aspects of the topic that are advantageous and aspects that are disadvantageous,

"The best part of releasing old issues using the Sedona Method is that it is a one-time event. No other tool or technique I have encountered is so instantly and permanently effective in removing conscious and unconscious barriers to living in comfort, ease, and joy. Since learning and utilizing the Method, I live with less fear, more peace, and from a much deeper, more spiritually connected part of myself. Even amidst the apparent harried and 'emergency' situations that I encounter, I am able to remain calm and to approach challenges from a balanced perspective."

—Jeff Goodman,
San Jose, CA

and then releasing your NOW feelings and underlying wants. Remember, if you're having a hard time coming up with new advantages or disadvantages, allow yourself to release on *that*—and keep going. Be diligent. The deeper you go into this process, the more you'll get out of it.

Once you've done about nine rounds of releasing in total, stop and notice how differently you're starting to feel about the topic you've been releasing on. Each advantage and disadvantage together forms a layer of unconsciousness or limitation on a particular topic, so the process is like drilling for oil. The deeper a stratum you penetrate, the more insights, the more understanding, and the more freedom comes on that particular topic.

Although you may never arrive at a specific big "ah-ha" moment, there is likely to be a series of small ones along the way. If you persistently release on advantages and disadvantages, I'm certain profound changes will occur. I have yet to see it produce a less than positive effect either for myself or for those I've assisted in focusing on it.

Laura: Uncovering a Forgotten Decision

Here is a story that shows how significant the Advantages/Disadvantages Process can be. Many years ago, I met a woman named Laura who had a genuine issue about being overweight. The instructor working individually with her in class was leading Laura through the Advantages/Disadvantages questions, but every time she was asked, "What advantage is there to you in being overweight?" none came to mind. Laura kept responding, "There aren't any." She was having absolutely no problem thinking of disadvantages, however. Nonetheless, the instructor was persistent. She had Laura release on her NOW feeling about the fact that she couldn't think of an advantage.

Finally, around the ninth time she was asked, Laura started getting frustrated and blurted out, "Why are you asking me what advantage there is to being overweight? How could there possibly be an advantage to being as overweight as I am?" She was ready to pick a fight. The instructor calmly asked again, "What advantage is it to you to be overweight?" Suddenly, Laura flashed on a suppressed memory and she started to cry. Twenty years earlier, she'd been an exquisitely beautiful woman, and her body was an ideal weight. While she was hospitalized for a couple of days, her husband took it upon himself to make an investment that he knew his wife wouldn't approve. He figured he would get away with it by being able to report wonderful rewards afterwards. But it was an irresponsible investment, and it didn't do well.

Towards the end of Laura's stay in the hospital, her husband showed up one day and sheepishly said, "Honey, I'm sorry, but I've lost our investment money. It's all gone." She was so furious in that instant that she had a fleeting thought,

227

"Oh, I know how to get back at him!" Soon after she left the hospital, she went from being the type of woman who turned everyone's head when she walked into the room to being overweight. In fact, she kept growing more obese and had absolutely no understanding of why it was happening. She had totally forgotten that she'd made a specific decision.

Well, 20 years later, she was still very overweight, even though it had been a long time since she and her husband had divorced. She had tried dieting in the past, but nothing had helped. When she rediscovered her decision to punish her ex-husband, and released her feelings, she let go of a very large hook in her subconscious and the main reason she'd been holding on to being overweight. The very next day after class, she phoned a specialized diet doctor to whom a friend had referred her a year and a half earlier. Now, she immediately began taking actions to lose weight—and those actions finally started to work. About a year later, Laura was a normal weight. Years later, she still maintains it.

Written Releasing on Your Advantages/Disadvantages

On paper, the Advantages/Disadvantages Process is exactly the same as what we were doing above, except you write down your responses to the questions as a way to monitor yourself. So, get out your releasing journal, and let's begin. There are eight steps in total.

Step 1: Write your topic at the top of the page. Then, draw a line down the middle of the page. At the top of the left-hand column, create a label: Advantages. At the top of the right-hand column, create a label: Disadvantages.

Step 2: Ask yourself: *What is the advantage to me of*

_____ *(your topic)?* Write down the first thought or feeling that comes to mind in the left-hand column, without any censoring.

Step 3: Check to see which basic want your advantage comes from by asking: *Is there a sense of wanting approval, control, or security?* Once you've identified it, write down the want from which the thought or feeling comes using the usual abbreviations: w/a for wanting approval, w/c for wanting to control, and w/s for wanting security.

Step 4: Allow yourself to let go of the underlying want by using either one of the following questions:
- *Could I allow this want to be here?*
- *Could I let go of wanting* _____ *(approval, control, or security)?*

Cross out the want as you let it go, then move on to a disadvantage. Do only one advantage at a time. Please refrain from the impulse to make a list. However, if more than one advantage or disadvantage spontaneously occur to you at the same time, write them all down, and then release the wants associated with each, one at a time.

Step 5: Ask yourself: *What is the disadvantage to me of* _____ *(your topic)?* Write down the first thought or feeling that comes to mind in the right-hand column, without censoring.

Step 6: Check to see which basic want your disadvantage comes from by asking: *Is there a sense of wanting approval, control, or security?* Write down an abbreviation next to the disadvantage.

Step 7: Allow yourself to let go of the underlying want by

Advantages/Disadvantages Process

Topic: *What is the (advantage/disadvantage) in accepting a job promotion?*

Advantages	Disadvantages
Higher salary— ~~w/a,~~ w/s ✓	Greater responsibility— ~~w/c,~~ w/s ✓
More interesting assignments— ~~w/a~~	Possibility of failure— ✓ w/c, ~~w/s~~
Get to travel— ~~w/c,~~ w/s ✓	Less leisure time— ✓ w/c, ~~w/sep.~~

using either one of the following questions:

* *Could I allow this want to be here?*
* *Could I let go of wanting* _____ *(approval, control, or security)?*

Cross out the want as you let it go. Do only one disadvantage at a time.

Step 8: Repeat Steps 2 through 7 many times, alternating between an advantage and a disadvantage, then another advantage and another disadvantage and so on until you feel complete, or at least ready to take a break for a while.

Carol Sue: Creating an Amicable Divorce

According to Carol Sue, when she told her ex-husband that she wanted a divorce, he got very angry and began screaming at her. She spent the next day releasing her feelings about their relationship, using the Cleanup Procedure—which will be covered in Chapter 11—and other techniques. But the Advantages/Disadvantages Process really helped her navigate her divorce smoothly and rapidly without barely making a dent in her finances. After doing advantages and disadvantages on the topic of lawyers, she went for a consultation. Her husband came with her. The lawyer wanted to charge them $7,000. The disadvantages of lawyers included time consumption and expense. Because Carol Sue had released, she and her husband were able to speak calmly together, and they decided to hire a paralegal who had the divorce papers finished in only a day and charged only a few hundred dollars.

Even though Carol Sue calls herself materialistic, she didn't try to hang on to anything in the divorce. In her words: "It worked out perfectly. Originally, I was divorcing my husband, but after doing the Advantages/Disadvantages Process, I allowed him to legally divorce me. If I had divorced him I would have had to stay in the house for 30 more days. But I wanted to leave right away. That was an advantage. Now, this may sound like a disadvantage, but to me it was an advantage—I allowed him to keep everything: the car, the house, and the furniture. I took what I wanted when I left. It's a huge advantage to me to be free. I don't even need an apartment,

231

since I am traveling and staying with friends and relatives now. My stuff is stored at my daughter's house. Letting go of things was a major advantage."

Persistence Pays Off

Whatever comes up first is going to be the obvious. But if you're willing to be persistent, you'll strike oil by making a profound shift in your awareness. Sometimes I've worked for days on the same Advantages/Disadvantages worksheet, returning to it until I knew it was complete, and gaining tremendous insights and benefits. Before you proceed to the next chapter, I highly recommend that you explore at least one Advantages/Disadvantages worksheet on your own. I promise, you'll be glad you did.

See the list below for just a few topic ideas.

What Are the Advantages/Disadvantages of . . . ?

- Abundance
- Poverty/Debt
- This Decision
- Calmness
- Stress
- Joy
- Sorrow
- Fear
- Exercise
- Smoking
- Drinking
- Overeating
- Freedom
- Illness
- Health
- Marriage/Partnership
- Being Single
- Work
- Play/Leisure
- Being Unemployed
- Giving
- Receiving

Chapter 11

The Cleanup Procedure

Lester Levenson originally created the Cleanup Procedure for the exclusive use of the Sedona Method instructors, because he understood how critically important it was for them to let go of wanting approval, control, or security, as well as any reactions they might have to participants in their classes. Our instructors are trained to be 100 percent supportive. Even though I didn't become an actual instructor until several years later, I've been using this process since 1977; it's another of my favorite applications of the Method. You can use it to complete an interaction—positive or negative—with anyone, including yourself.

Now, why would you release on positive interactions? You might want to feel even better than you already do about the person you're using as the object of this process, so you can relate to that individual with more openness, honesty, and love. We all have people in our lives with whom we repeatedly interact—our husbands, wives, or lovers, our children or business associates—all sorts of people. I am sure you don't want to carry excess baggage you've picked up from a previous encounter with any of these people into your next and future encounters with them.

The Cleanup Procedure is designed to accelerate your gains from the Sedona Method. It is made up of a series of questions that can be asked before, during, or after meetings, gatherings, and random interactions—especially those with difficult people.

"Since we learned the Sedona Method, there is even greater harmony and better communication between my husband and myself. Our future looks rosier. I am also dealing with several extremely difficult situations with work and family with greater ease. I no longer become severely depressed, and my downs are less frequent and much less severe. My husband is happier, and he is doing better financially."
—Carolyn Graham,
Brick, NJ

As you work with the cleanup questions on a regular basis, you'll begin to understand how much they can help you improve your relationships, communicate more effectively, resolve conflicts, and incorporate letting go into your life more easily. The process will also increase your effectiveness and contribute to the integrity of all of your interactions.

The Cleanup Procedure has a special place in my heart, because it helped me break through to truly experiencing my emotions. When I first started using the Sedona Method, I was a "from-the-neck-up releaser," meaning that I was letting go of more thoughts than feelings. Although the Method was making a huge impact on my life and on me personally, I knew I could go deeper. It was while doing the Cleanup Procedure on my relationship with my mother that I finally became able to feel all the way down to my toes.

While I was growing up—partially due to my relationship with my mother—I went from being a sensitive, tuned-in young child to a teenager very out of touch with my emotions. My mother was in psychoanalysis for over ten years, and she always used to bring home her latest insights, which she would use to try to fix me. In order to opt out of this way of relating, I trained myself over time not to be in touch with my feelings.

Using the Cleanup Procedure, as I released on my mother, I felt as though a wall had melted in my heart, allowing a warm, loving energy to flow throughout my whole body. Ever since then, I've been able to feel and know my feelings fully. My relationship with my mother now, as I write this book, is excellent. We both use the Method, and it has helped us to become friends as opposed to estranged mother and son.

When you begin to use the Cleanup Procedure, you will find that it has an almost magical ability to help you shed whatever unresolved feelings you're carrying from an interaction you just had with another person. Perhaps you just spoke to a friend on the phone or went out to a movie on a date. Or perhaps you were speaking with your husband, wife, son, or daughter, and you still feel bothered or incomplete about your discussion. Maybe you finished a confrontational business meeting or had a conflict with a bank teller or supermarket cashier. This incredibly simple releasing process will help you let go of whatever just happened, so you can move forward with your life without dragging around so much extra mental and emotional weight.

The Cleanup Procedure can bring you peace of mind even about people who are no longer alive. You can clean up on past relatives or past relationships, on people you may be separated from but for whom you still carry around a lot of feelings.

As I mentioned in the Introduction, for part of my history I sold real estate. I would always use this process before and after meeting with clients. If I'd previously met with a client, whether or not that meeting ended favorably, I'd often use the Cleanup Procedure before seeing them again in order to insure even greater success. My clients often commented that I wasn't like other real estate salespeople with whom they'd dealt. That it was much easier to work with a broker who was relaxed and friendly, yet still got the job done.

You can do the Cleanup Procedure in the car. You can do it walking down the street. You can do it between phone calls at the office. You can do it sitting quietly by yourself. You can do it while you work out at the gym. You can use it in any situation where there is human interaction that you'd like to feel better about.

Here's how.

The Cleanup Procedure

The Cleanup Procedure is composed of three groups of questions, each focusing on a separate want: first control, then approval, and finally security/survival. Follow these basic steps and guidelines as you work:

1. Begin by visualizing the face of the person you have chosen to release about. (Remember, this may also be an auditory or kinesthetic experience for you.)

2. Then, ask yourself one cleanup question at a time and allow your underlying wants to surface. Often, the first question in each set will be enough to cause you spontaneously to let go of the want you are focusing on at

that moment. Welcome the want fully or let it go.

3. Start with the set of cleanup questions about control, and stay with that set of questions until you feel that you can "grant that person the right to be" the way he or she is. Most times, completely letting go is just a decision. If you are open to it, it's possible to reach this point very quickly, but feel free to take all the time you need.

4. Repeatedly ask the first two cleanup questions in each subsequent set, and keep releasing whatever is stirred up until you can honestly answer "yes" to the third question. Being honest produces better results. The third question in each set is designed to help you see if you are fully released on that particular want about that individual.

5. Do the same thing with each set of cleanup questions in order. You will know that you're fully released on a person when you can see his or her face and have only acceptance/love for him or her.

The Cleanup Questions

The questions in **bold** type are the standard cleanup questions. The questions in italics are suggestions to facilitate letting go of each want. Feel free to release the wants without the use of any additional questions, or to come up with questions of your own.

Step 1: Control

1. *Did this person try to control you? (Or did it feel that way?)*

   Pause to allow for spontaneous releases, or ask one of the following questions.

- *If so, could you let go now of wanting to control them back?*
- *If so, could you let go of resisting them?*
- *If so, would you like to change that?*

2. **Did you try to control this person? (Or did it feel that way?)**

   Pause to allow for spontaneous releases, or ask the following questions.
   - *If so, could you let go now of wanting to control them?*
   - *If so, would you like to change that?*

3. **Do you now grant this person the right to be as this person is?**

   Remember that the third question is simply a decision.

Repeat the three control questions above until you grant this person the right to be as this person is.

Step 2: Approval

1. **Did you dislike or disapprove of anything in this person? (Or did it feel that way?)**

   Pause to allow for spontaneous releases, or ask the following questions.
   - *Could you let go, just for now, of your dislike or disapproval for this person?*
   - *If so, would you like to change that?*

2. *Did this person dislike or disapprove of anything in you? (Or did it feel that way?)*

    Pause to allow for spontaneous releases, or ask the following questions.

    * *Could you let go of wanting their approval?*
    * *If so, would you like to change that?*

3. *Do you have only love/acceptance feelings for this person?*

    Remember, the third question is just a decision.

Repeat the three approval questions above until you feel only love/acceptance.

Step 3: Security/Survival

1. *Did this person challenge, oppose, or threaten you? (Or did it feel that way?)*

    Pause to allow for spontaneous releases, or ask one of the following questions.

    * *Could you let go of wanting to challenge, oppose, or threaten him/her back?*
    * *Could you let go of wanting security with this person?*
    * *If so, would you like to change that?*

2. *Did you challenge, oppose, or threaten this person? (Or did it feel that way?)*

    Pause to allow for spontaneous releases, or ask one of the following questions.

    * *Could you let go of wanting to challenge, oppose,*

or threaten this person?

- *Could you let go of wanting to protect yourself in this way?*
- *If so, would you like to change that?*

3. *Do you have only a feeling of well-being, safety, and trust with this person?*

   Remember, the third question is just a decision.

Repeat the three security questions above until you have only a feeling of well-being, safety, and trust with the person you're releasing about.

When you've finished Steps 1 to 3, visualize the face of the person you are working on again (or hear them, or feel them) and allow yourself to bask in your feeling of acceptance/love for him or her. If there are any other feelings than love/acceptance, go back to the cleanup questions.

Why Does Completion Benefit You?

Many people struggle inside themselves to reach a genuine "yes" on the third question in each set, even though they know it will produce a profound shift in their consciousness. They may see how granting people the right to be the way they are is important, even after they've had some difficulty with them. They may even be able to love and accept people after a conflict. But they may still find it hard to imagine having only a feeling of well-being, safety, and trust with certain people.

What if the person you were releasing about was someone who just tried to cheat you in business? Why would you want

240

to feel trusting towards him or her? Very simple: when you feel distrust, you're holding in mind that someone is going to cheat you. Remember, whatever you focus your attention on gets created in your reality. When you feel threatened, you're giving your power away to another person, and he or she can sense it and acts accordingly. If you're feeling insecure, other people feel more powerful, because they know intuitively that they can control, manipulate, and threaten you.

If you allow yourself to experience a feeling of well-being, safety, and trust at the end of the Cleanup Procedure, it puts you in charge. Then you don't have to worry about doing business with anyone. You can discriminate better, because the Method helps you see the way you and others interact more clearly. While you still may choose never to do business again with someone who cheated you, as long as you're holding on to a feeling of mistrust, you may attract new people into your experience who aren't trustworthy.

You're rarely releasing on behalf of another person. In a close, healthy relationship, you might do your releasing to improve the relationship, which benefits your partner. When my wife Amy and I first met, for instance, she loved it when I did the Cleanup Procedure in class. As I released and got lighter, I was more fun to be around. But if you're

"I have got my sense of humor back—a great ally in times of need—and now I have the freedom to go on creating and recreating myself every day. After all, isn't that what life is truly about?"
—Amanda Kanini,
London, England

in a difficult relationship, you're probably not doing releasing for your partner; you're doing it for your own freedom and happiness.

It is to your advantage to get to that point of completion on all three questions. You can get big releases very easily doing this process, and you'll see from practical experience as you work with the process that it truly helps you in all your relationships.

Tom: Resolving a Professional Misunderstanding

For several years, Tom had a mentor who was also his good friend. At some point, they had a communication problem that became adversarial. His mentor accused Tom of using his materials without permission, and, even when the truth came out that Tom hadn't, there didn't seem to be a way to resolve the tension in their relationship. Tom had a lot of strong feelings about the situation. He felt angry and betrayed, disappointed, and even guilty. So, for a few days in a row, he did the Cleanup Procedure on his mentor while he walked his dog around the loop in his neighborhood.

Did he try to control me? *You bet.* Could I let go of trying to control him back? *Sure.* Did he disapprove of me in any way? *Absolutely.* Could I let go of it? *Yeah.* Did I feel threatened? *Uh-huh.* This was the way Tom's process went, asking the questions and releasing deeply. He finally decided that it had been time for their relationship to change.

While the friendship never returned to where it had been before, the emotional charge around it was neutralized, because there was actually no real substance to it. Tom sums it up well: "I've noticed that the content of a disagreement is usually minor compared to the emotional stuff we attach to it. When we do the Cleanup Procedure, we're usually able to move on in relationship, whether or not we ultimately reconcile."

A Short Cleanup Process

Make yourself comfortable and focus inside. Think of a person you'd like to try this out on. Pick someone for your first exploration that you don't feel highly charged about, so you won't feel overwhelmed. But make sure to choose a person for whom you have a tiny bit of resistance, or a tiny bit of wanting approval, control, or security. That way you will feel a real sense of completion by the end of this process.

So, allow yourself to focus on the person you've chosen.

Did that person try to control you?

If so, could you let go of wanting to control him/her back?

Did you try to control this person?

If you did, could you let go of wanting to control him/her?

Did this person try to control you?

And did that stir up some resistance inside of you?

If it did, could you let it go?

Did you try to control this person?

If so, just for now, could you let go of wanting to control him/her?

Cycle through those questions a few more times on your own. Allow yourself to let go of wanting to control, as best you can, by welcoming it into your experience.

When you are ready, move on to the third question in this series: *Could you grant this person the right to be the way this person is? Just could you?*

Would you grant this person the right to be the way this

person is? Remember, this is just a decision.

Do you now grant this person the right to be the way this person is?

Now, did you dislike or disapprove of anything in this person?

If so, could you let go of withholding your love or approval from him/her?

Did this person dislike or disapprove of anything in you?

If it seems that way, could you let go of wanting their approval?

Did you dislike or disapprove of anything in this person?

If so, could you let go of withholding your love from this person—withholding your approval? Could you let go of disapproving of them, just for now?

Did this person dislike or disapprove of anything in you?

If so, could you let go of wanting this person's approval—wanting him/her to like you or care about you?

When you are ready, move on to the third question: *Could you have only love or acceptance feelings for this person? Just could you?*

Would you allow yourself to accept or love him/her? Again, remember that it's just a choice.

Do you now have only love feelings for this person?

If the answer is "yes," continue with the next set of questions. If not, go back and do a little more work cycling through those questions.

Did this person challenge, oppose, or threaten you?

If so, could you let go of wanting to protect yourself from this person?

Did you challenge, oppose, or threaten this person?

Could you let go of wanting to challenge, oppose, or threaten him/her?

Did this person challenge, oppose, or threaten you?

If so, could you let go of any sense of wanting security that may have been stirred up by that challenge?

Did you challenge, oppose, or threaten this person?

If so, could you now just let that go?

When you are ready, move on to the third question: *Could you allow yourself to have only a feeling of well-being, safety, and trust with this person?*

Would you allow yourself to feel that way?

Do you have only a feeling of well-being, safety, and trust for this person?

If you cannot truthfully answer "yes," cycle back through these questions again.

Then, look inside and see how you're feeling right now about this person. I think you'll notice that there has been a major shift—and it probably took you only a few minutes. Pretty exciting, huh?

A Final Thought

I recommend that you do the Cleanup Procedure twice more—on two different people—before moving ahead to the next chapter. Once you've integrated this technique into your life, you'll find all your human interactions more pleasant and relaxed. In Part Two, we'll begin applying this important tool to many different areas of your life.

Chapter 12

Putting It All Together

Congratulations, you've reached the end of Part One of the Sedona Method Course. All that's left to do is put together everything you've been learning into a single perspective. Then, you'll be even more ready than you already are to go forth and boldly incorporate releasing into every area and aspect of your life. Real life applications, of course, are addressed in Part Two of the book. This chapter will cover three main topics introduced by Lester Levenson: the Three Aspects of Mind, the "I" Diagram, and the Six Steps, each of which can enhance your depth and breadth of understanding of the Method. Once you understand why the system works as it does, it will take on new layers of helpfulness.

The Three Aspects of Mind

Most of us confuse our thoughts with our identity. We are actually more than our minds. So please don't mistake this diagram as a representation of three aspects of "you." The unlimited potential that is truly "you" is represented on this diagram

Three Aspects of Mind

aspects of mind

"I" Sense

Program Aspects

Discriminator

the programmer

sensing, recording, replaying

your ability to discriminate

by an infinity sign behind the Three Aspects of Mind; or, even more literally, by the blank paper upon which this diagram is printed. Every time we use the Method, we tap into the infinite field of potential by harnessing the mind to undo its own limited programming.

The Three Aspects of Mind include:

- *The "I" Sense:* the sense of personal identity, such as "I, Hale," "I, Mary," or "I, (your name)," which runs your program aspects.

- *The Discriminator:* the lens through which we view the world.

- *The Program Aspects:* the sensing/recording/replaying qualities of the mind, which include our five senses, our memory banks, as well as our tendencies, beliefs, decisions, attitudes, judgments, and interpretations.

The Three Aspects of Mind combine to function in a simple manner. To begin, "I" perceive what's going on in the world. My five physical senses—sight, smell, touch, hearing, and taste—relay information back to me through the lens of my discriminator. Then, based on the information that's available to "me," "I" make decisions about what to do in my life and how to handle the world.

For the sake of this book, when I refer to a *program*, I mean a combination of these three things:

1. A set of instructions
2. A belief system
3. A decision once made consciously that's now running unconsciously

In some of our Advanced Courses, we teach a system for letting go of programs. Of course, in this book, you've already learned how to release the master programs, the four basic wants: wanting control, wanting approval, wanting security, and wanting separation.

What do you think happens when the sense of discrimination shuts down? Accurate information is not received. Unfortunately, this happens to most of us quite a bit. There are a whole host of things that can shut down the sense of discrimination. Here are a few examples you may recognize:

- *Bright lights.* Why does the law mandate that drivers

switch off their bright headlights when another car is coming towards them on the highway at night? Because that light makes it difficult to see. It can and does cause accidents. A bright light closes down your sense of discrimination since you try to block it out.

- *Loud noises.* If you're surrounded by loud noise for a while, your hearing shuts down. Anyone who has ever been to a rock concert will know what I mean. When you go out into the world after a loud concert, it's hard to hear anything that's being said. Other people have to shout for you to hear them.

- *Drugs and alcohol.* Drugs and alcohol can anesthetize you to your feelings. That's why there are legal limits to the amount of intoxicants you can consume before driving, and also why many prescription and over-the-counter medications come with warnings about operating heavy equipment. People have even been known to get legal documents reversed by proving they were "under the influence" when signing.

- *Sickness:* Sickness can shut down your discriminator. It doesn't even need to be extreme. Just think back to the last time you had a cold and tried to concentrate with a stuffy head.

- *Lack of sleep.* Even lack of sleep can cause us to say and do things that we later regret, because we were not able to receive and process information accurately.

On your own, I invite you to explore what else shuts down your discriminator. Simply notice what kinds of things make you find it difficult to think straight, to see clearly, or to feel appropriately as you go about your day. Notice anything that blocks information from getting through to you. In order not to get fixated on that, also look for what supports you in perceiving clearly.

Of course, there is one thing that shuts down the ability to discriminate more than anything else, and it's something that's with us all the time: our emotions. According to their intensity, our emotions interfere to different degrees with perceiving what's actually happening in the environment. If an emotion comes up strongly enough, we lose our ability to distinguish a correct response. We go on automatic pilot. Programs in the mind take over, and we have no sense of separation from the emotion. Then, to the degree that we identify with any emotion, that emotion is running us. We're not running it.

Consider past experience. I'm sure you can remember many occasions when you were upset or bothered, and you either

"I can't begin to tell you how much the Sedona Method has helped me. I was feeling the financial pressure that all farmers are feeling this crop year, and I had managed to worry myself into quite an emotional state. After just a few days, I had released enough inner blockage to be able to work through new financial strategies that pulled me out of my slump and brought in more income than I could even hope for in a year when crop commodities are at an all-time low! Once again, I am enjoying the work that I do without considering throwing in the towel."

—Sandra Perry,
Earlimart, CA

didn't take an action, or you did something you later regretted having done. You probably have known people who were grieving, angry, or upset and accidentally injured their bodies in ways they weren't even aware of until days later. Are you also familiar with the expression "blind rage"? You may know individuals who became so upset with others that, all of a sudden, they saw a red haze in front of their eyes and attacked. Perhaps these people didn't remember anything that followed the impulse to rage until after they were pulled off their victims.

This is where the Sedona Method enters the picture. It helps us to let go of the emotions that block the sense of discrimination. One of the purposes of the questions that we use in the Method is to help us perceive more clearly. When you ask, or someone else asks you, "What are you feeling?" it reminds you that you aren't the feeling—you are merely *having* a feeling (see Chapter 3, page 102). Let's use anger as an example. You're not angry. You're *feeling* angry. As soon as you've recognized this detail, your sense of discrimination opens up a little. Take that a step further by asking, "Is that a feeling of wanting approval, control, or security?" And you recognize, "Oh! In this case, I want control." Your discrimination opens up more. Then, ask yourself the releasing question, "Could I let it go?" And when you let go, in the release of the emotion, your discrimination opens up even further.

The Method works in the present moment by helping us to process information we're receiving from the environment that's triggering our programs—especially the basic programs of wanting approval, control, security, and separation. Those programs, our reactions, produce a constant internal background noise. Now, when conditioned feelings and thoughts get triggered, instead of always automatically allowing them to put us into action or to inhibit action, we have a choice to let go and respond appropriately.

As we use the Method over time, the resting state of our discriminator begins to remain open instead of going back to a mostly closed state. We can receive and process more information in less time. We can more readily access and discern our intuition. We can feel our feelings more acutely, including pleasure and joy. We can enjoy even the simple things in life more fully.

As you learned in Chapter 6, Taking Your Releasing to a Deeper Level, human programs were originally based on what was pro-survival. As we were evolving from apes into people, the species didn't have much time to evaluate each danger as it arose. We had to know instantly when it was time to fight and when it was time to take flight. Some people refer to this reflex as our "jungle mentality." We wouldn't have had the energy or wherewithal to flee or fight if we had to remember, "Heart beat, heart beat, heart beat," all day long. Most people are still lost in a jungle of our own making. We seem to put way more into our program banks than we require for survival.

Here is a fictitious case of how programming can run amok. Let's say that, when you were a child, you had an abusive relative who just happened to be a tall, gray-haired woman. Therefore, after interacting with her often, you made an unconscious decision to the effect that all tall, gray-haired women are dangerous. The sensing/recording/replaying aspect of mind records this pertinent information, and, from that point forward, you view the world through the lens of this decision. You're always on guard to make sure you're protecting yourself from tall, gray-haired women. It becomes second nature, and

253

soon you forget that you ever made this decision. Now that it's an automatic way you respond to the world, you no longer think of it consciously. It is apparently as natural as your survival programs, such as breathing, heartbeat, and digestion.

Time passes. Many years later, you're in a job interview. It's going great: You've found the perfect position that is the right next step for you. Although a gray-haired woman is conducting the interview, she's behind a desk, and she's your height. So everything's okay. Then she says, "I'd like to hire you." You answer, "I'd like the job." You both stand up to shake hands and, all of a sudden, you realize she's a lot taller than you. You get a funny feeling in the pit of your stomach. Now the gray-haired woman wants to show you around the plant, but, as you start your tour, you are having ambivalent thoughts. "I'm not sure this job is right for me," "What if this is a mistake?" "Doesn't this place feel funny?" You may complete the tour or you may not, because inwardly you feel as though you have to do whatever you can to get out of a dangerous situation. Unfortunately, you may be running away from an ideal job opportunity for no good reason.

That's how people make decisions every day based on past programming that has nothing to do with the present. Thankfully, the Sedona Method teaches us how to take ourselves off automatic. It helps us use the sense of discrimination to become free from self-imposed limitations, and thus to function optimally in our lives.

Because the sensing/recording/replaying aspect of mind is responsible for our autonomic functions (circulation, respiration, body temperature, etc.), as well as for our response to perceived threats, our overall functioning is impaired when it's overloaded.

want to be separate

want to survive as a body

want approval

want control

A G F L A P C A P

thinking

the world

Disease occurs. Most of the threats we perceive are purely imagined; nonetheless, they burden the entire physical system, slow it down. Every time we release, we dump the excess programs and lighten the load we're placing on the autonomic nervous system.

In a nutshell, as you release your feelings and the underlying wants that motivate them, you see what's really going on more accurately, thus increasing your ability to be effective. You free yourself to be here NOW, in this moment, where you can respond accordingly to your present circumstances from a place of discrimination and knowing.

Our entire sense of limitation stems from identification with the personal "I." As we discussed in Chapter 6, when we were born, we came in with certain tendencies. However, these tendencies did not lock in and bear the sting of personal suffering until we believed we were the "me" or "I" to which everyone we knew kept referring. In truth, just as we saw in the diagram of the Three Aspects of Mind (see page 248), we start out and never leave the state of unlimited potential, of infinity, that's in the background. Any suffering we appear to go through, and all the limitations we appear to be bound by, are only superimposed on top of that which we are.

With the Method, we uncover the unlimited potential just behind our mind, which is just behind our feelings, which is just behind our troubles in life. You've probably already noticed that, as you become increasingly aware of this unlimited potential, it's more available to you moment to moment. If you recall how you felt when you first started reading this book and working with its processes, you'll observe that you feel less tied to your feelings and problems and more able to handle whatever it is that life dishes out for you. And this is just the beginning. As you keep working with the Method, you'll get even more out of it.

The other thing to notice about the "I" Diagram is something quite obvious that most people miss. If you look at the page it is printed on (see page 255), just as with the Three Aspects of Mind diagram, you'll see that, although there's some writing on the page, too, it's mostly white space. Another way to look at our unlimited potential is like how we look at the white space of this page: most of it is already shining through, uncovered. That's also true in our lives. Unlimited potential is always a lot more available to you than you may realize. As you use the Method, this will become more obvious. An analogy for what we're doing with the Method is taking an eraser to the remaining limitation that's still on the page (thoughts, feelings, wants) and gradually eroding it or taking it away. That's letting go.

The welcoming part of the Method is just allowing things to be the way they are. Even if there is still some writing on the page, the white space becomes more obvious and more operative in your life.

The diving in part of the Method begins with some of the obstruction on top—wanting approval, control, security, and separation; or apathy, grief, fear, lust, anger, or pride. As you dive into that to the very core, what you discover is the underlying paper, the white space, our unlimited potential.

Now, notice the letter "I" at the top of the page. It represents our limited sense of who we are: "I" Hale or "I" your name. If we didn't have programs attached to it, it would dissolve right back into the unlimited potential. In fact, limitation often does dissolve throughout the day. But it would not keep coming back and hooking us without our programmed thoughts, feelings, and wants.

Let us move down the chart now, item by item, to see where each fits in. As you can see, the deepest want—the desire to be separate—is the one we haven't referred to as frequently as the others in this book. Wanting to be separate comes from the sense of being an individual apart from the unlimited potential. Remember, you can directly release on this want anytime you choose (see page 175).

The other three wants, which are right below wanting separation on the diagram, are wanting to survive as a body (a.k.a. wanting security), wanting approval, and wanting to control. Wanting security is based on the assumption that we are the limited bodies we inhabit. Even if you don't have any metaphysical inclinations, I am sure you at least have a sense that there's more to life than the obvious. That's probably part of what attracted you to this book in the beginning. The body is the least of us, not the most of us. As you release, you'll discover that maybe, just maybe, the body isn't all you are. By letting go of your sense of wanting security or survival, you'll begin to feel safer.

The second deepest program is the sense of wanting survival. Underneath that is the sense of wanting approval. We believe that if everyone loves us, likes us, and cares about us, we'll be safe and able to survive. We believe that somehow we need to get love and approval from outside of ourselves. In my conception, this isn't true; and you have probably already discovered this for yourself. I am sure you've noticed that in letting go of wanting love or approval, you feel more loving, approved of, and approving.

Right underneath wanting approval is the sense of wanting to control. Sometimes people don't approve of us in exactly the right way. They don't give us the right gift, the right compliment, or they're not being nice enough to us. You get the picture. Then, we want to control them to get their approval in the way that we'd prefer. Sometimes we give up on getting approval from a particular person, or in a particular situation, or we sense an apparent threat that has nothing to do with others or with love. In cases such as these, we want to control directly—instead of for the sake of approval—in order to be safe or survive as a body. That's what the arrow connecting wanting to control with wanting to survive as a body represents.

All four wants culminate in the nine emotional states: apathy, grief, fear, lust, anger, pride, and the limited parts of courageousness, acceptance, and peace. That's why AGFLAP-CAP appears underneath wanting to control on the diagram. The feelings are what we use to try to get approval, control, and security, and to maintain a sense of separation. Our feelings also motivate our thoughts.

In *The Sedona Method*, we've been focusing more on what we feel than on what we think. We do this because it is nearly impossible to make changes in your life solely by thinking positive thoughts. If you've ever tried, you know it can be very difficult unless you deal with any apathy, grief, fear, lust, anger, and pride you may be feeling, and the underlying wants. What you've probably already noticed, however, is that your thinking naturally changes to the positive as you start to release on any topic, feeling, or want. You don't have to try to think positively. It just happens of its own accord. You don't have to effort at it. You don't have to try to do something.

When I was in my early 20's, just before I took the Sedona Method, I was extremely shy. I thought that positive affirmations would help me feel more comfortable around people. For months on end, I went around all day long repeating, "I am highly pleasing to myself in the presence of other people" without getting anywhere. It makes me laugh when I think about it now, because the only thing that changed was that I heard these sounds playing in my head like a record, over and over again, yet it made no difference in how I felt. It wasn't until soon after I started releasing that my lifelong shyness disappeared. I now feel comfortable in front of large groups of people and when I'm alone. I don't need to exert any effort to maintain this state. Based on my personal experience and the reports of many of the thousands of people with whom I've worked, I believe it's a mistake to assume that thoughts alone are responsible for your unhappiness or your lack of effectiveness in life.

Positive thinking has been popular worldwide since the 1920's, and entire systems have been created to enhance our ability to do it. You've probably heard the expression "As you think, so is your world," or some variation of it. Positive thinking assumes that negative thoughts are real and that we are the sum total of our thinking. If this were true, there would not be much we could do about this except cover the negative over with positive thoughts. Unfortunately, our subconscious is so overloaded that this would be a huge job.

In contrast, the Method is effective because, although we have thoughts, we are not our thoughts. Imagine that each of us has a barrel inside that represents the subconscious mind. This barrel has a golden lining representing our unlimited potential—our intuitive knowing—which is covered over by a bunch of rotten apples that represent apathy, grief, fear, lust, anger, pride and all the wants. Even if you covered the golden lining over with good apples (happy thoughts and happy feelings), what would eventually happen to the apples? That's right: eventually, they'd all rot. Also, placing a layer of good apples on top of the rotten apples only obstructs the golden lining further.

The Method is a means of emptying the barrel so you can discover the golden lining that's already present and available, here and now, in your life, in this moment. The only reason you can't see it is because of the covering of limiting thoughts, feelings, beliefs, and wants that you have. Remove them, and your thinking will be more positive.

It is plain to see that, to a degree, your thinking does color your perception of the world; and, if you're willing to stretch a little bit, you might even see that it colors what actually happens in your life. Here is a concrete example from sales. If you're a salesperson and have a positive attitude—you feel good about yourself and good about your product—it's easier to sell your product. Whereas, if you've had a bad day, experienced a series of rejections, or it's been a long time since you made a sale, it is difficult to make sales, because you feel progressively less positive. That is the time to release. As a result, your thinking will be increasingly positive—and so will your world.

"After years of searching and 'seeking' a spiritual path that made sense to me, I always came up empty-handed. The Sedona Method is the first path that actually showed me how simple it is to let go of everything that has kept me back in life. No other teaching showed me exactly how to do it. I'm so thankful for the life-changing tools I've been given for a happier, easier life."

—Leandra Ginevra, San Pedro, CA

261

Have you noticed that the emphasis in this book, unlike the emphasis of most self-improvement programs, has nothing to do with getting you to modify your behavior? That's because people naturally move in a positive direction through releasing. As I have already mentioned, lasting change, positive change, real change, comes from the inside out, not from trying to impose changes from the outside. Look to your past experiences to verify this point.

For instance, before you had the tools of the Method, you may have been able to quit smoking temporarily, only to have the habit reassert itself. Or perhaps you replaced smoking with overeating. Thus, in sublimating your urge, you possibly gained weight. The reason this happens is that when you push down a tendency in one spot, it usually pops up somewhere else. That is what most people and organizations do when they try to change from the outside in. It is different when you fully release a tendency. When you change from the inside out, the changes are lasting, and they're positive. Every change you make using the Method brings you more overall freedom since it uncovers more of the unlimited potential of who you are.

I encourage you to ponder the "I" Diagram. Work with it. Take it for checking. Don't believe it: prove it for yourself.

The Six Steps

The Six Steps are a distillation of the essence of the Sedona Method. They were created in 1974 by Lester Levenson to summarize the whole process of letting go. He had been working with a small group he was hoping to train as counselors—people who were helping him systematize his teachings into a do-it-yourself system—when he hit upon the Six Steps and wrote them down on the inside leaf of a book he was reading. Since then, they haven't changed dramatically.

You may find it helpful to refer to the Six Steps whenever you are using the Method. Many people have reduced the list so it fits into their wallets or purses. I know of several others who have pasted the list into their Day-Timers. You could also hang them on the wall by your desk, or create a Six Steps screensaver on your computer to keep them handy and remind yourself to practice releasing throughout the day. I would also recommend that you keep a copy of the Six Steps in front of you when you sit down to do some focused or written releasing. Then, if you get stuck at any point, you can just look back at the Six Steps, and they will help you get unstuck. As I said, they represent the core of everything that you've been doing, and will continue to be doing, as you allow your exploration of the Method to unfold.

The Six Steps

1. Allow yourself to want freedom/imperturbability (your goal) more than you want approval, control, security, and separation.

2. Decide that you can release and be free/imperturbable (achieve your goal).

3. Allow yourself to perceive that all your feelings culminate in the four wants: the want of approval, the want to control, the want of security, and the want of separation. Then allow yourself to let go of the wants.

4. Make it constant. Release wanting approval, wanting to control, wanting security, and wanting to be separate all the time, whether you're alone or with people.

5. If you are stuck, let go of wanting to control or change the stuckness.

6. Each time you release, you are lighter, happier, and more effective. If you do this continually, you will continually be lighter, happier, and more effective.

Now, let's consider each of the Six Steps in turn.

Step 1: **Allow yourself to want freedom/imperturbability (your goal) more than you want approval, control, security, and separation.**

This step is not saying that you have to want freedom more than anything else. It also doesn't mean that you won't attain your goals or start to experience freedom until you have completely eliminated any sense of wanting approval, control, security, or separation. It does mean that the more you tip your inner scales in the direction of freedom/imperturbability, the more quickly you will see results in your life from the Method and the faster you'll pull your goal into your awareness.

Interestingly, wanting freedom/imperturbability is what attracts us to this type of work. Many, if not most, people would prefer to remain unconscious. They'd literally rather not see that there's a way out, that there's an alternative. Because you have gotten this far into the process of the Sedona Method, rest assured that you're one of the lucky people on this planet who are willing to change it for the better from the inside out.

You can reinforce your desire for freedom by choosing freedom as often as possible. If you're having any doubts about whether or not to proceed with the Method, there's a question that will help you to discriminate. It is very helpful, especially if you're having difficulty letting go of an uncomfortable feeling.

- *Would I rather have this stuckness (this feeling), or would I rather be free?*

Most of the time, as soon as you ask this question, you'll notice how the energy around the stuckness is starting to shift. Very often, the question by itself will cause you to let go of whatever it is that you're holding on to in the moment.

Yes, we used the word "want" in the Step 1 statement. If you use this want to convert all your other wants into the desire for freedom, then you'll no longer need it and it will fall away of its own accord.

Step 2: **Decide that you can release and be free/imperturbable (achieve your goal).**

Every time you release, it's just a decision, a simple choice. You have that choice to make in every moment of every day. Of course, this fact doesn't indicate that you'll always choose to release from now on. But as you make that choice—as you decide to do the Method and be free—it gets easier and easier to do. The more you can recognize that freedom is easily and readily available, the more likely you are to choose it.

Step 3: **Allow yourself to perceive that all your feelings culminate in the four wants: the want of approval, the want to control, the want of security, and the want of separation. Then allow yourself to let go of the wants.**

This step is the heart of the Method. As you continue to explore releasing, you'll become more in tune with how your

265

underlying basic wants cause you to feel other than the way you would choose and to act in ways that you later regret. As you increase your attunement, you will find yourself letting go spontaneously—immediately and with greater ease.

Step 4: **Make it constant. Release wanting approval, wanting to control, wanting security, and wanting to be separate all the time, whether you're alone or with people.**

Every time there's a problem, you have an opportunity to release and turn it around. Change your whole perspective on life by recognizing that every down is an opportunity to go even higher. Making the use of releasing *constant* is not a rule about a lot of doingness—although it might seem that way in the beginning—because you're forming a new habit. It's about becoming more aware of the unlimited potential that's just behind whatever you're experiencing. Making its use constant doesn't mean that you're asking the releasing questions all the time. It means that you're relaxing into who you really are. You're being at ease and as open as you're able in order to release whatever emotion is arising in the NOW moment. You're seeing the truth.

Letting go can become as second nature and apparently automatic as suppression and expression are now for most of us. Since we're always doing something with our feelings anyway, why not just let them go?

Step 5: **If you are stuck, let go of wanting to control or change the stuckness.**

This step is so important that I devoted an entire chapter to it, Your Key to Serenity (see page 127). It is the safety valve of the Method, a single action that will set you straight, in most cases, and get you back on track when you've derailed. Specifically: When we want to change or control how we feel, we get stuck. Thus, when we let go of wanting to change or control how we feel in the NOW moment, the whole dynamic is changed.

It is so simple. Let go of wanting to change or control it if . . .

- You're feeling overwhelmed.
- You're moving away from releasing.
- You've forgotten to release.
- You feel like you just can't let go.
- You're not sure what you are feeling.
- You find there are certain patterns that you're having more difficulty letting go of than others.
- You simply want to cut to the chase and let go NOW.

Step 6: Each time you release, you are lighter, happier, and more effective. If you do this continually, you will continually be lighter, happier, and more effective.

As I mentioned in the Introduction, Lester used to call the Sedona Method the "bottoms-up method," meaning that, as you use this technique, you'll notice that what you may consider a peak experience right now will eventually become where you bottom out. It's not that there won't still be ups and downs. As you release, your highs get higher but so do your lows. You might feel your feelings more acutely, because, as you release, you become more open, more sensitized, more discriminating. But even though you're feeling your feelings more, you're also letting go of them much more easily; because of that, you'll see a rapid increase in your freedom over time.

This is the reason I encourage you to write down your gains as you work with this book. As you keep track of the positive changes in your life, you recognize, "Yes, I feel freer, I feel happier, things are getting easier, I'm becoming more effective." As you acknowledge that, you're feeding energy to the positive instead of the negative, and this will also cycle you back to Step 1. As you see that you are getting freer and happier, it strengthens your desire to have more of the same.

Explore a question that Lester used to ask himself:

Could it get any better?

If it can get any better, when you release, it will.

Especially if you have a tendency to want to understand, after reading this chapter you may feel like the Sedona Method makes more sense. It is all based on repeatable formulas that work whenever you allow them to.

Exploration: There Are No Problems

Before we move on to Part Two, I'd like to share one of the most powerful perspectives that we've been exploring in Sedona Method Advanced Courses with you: There are no problems in the present moment. I saved this piece for now, because I know this may be hard for you to accept, but—what if all the supposed problems you have right now are only memories? I challenge you to explore this question for yourself and at least entertain the possibility. If you can even partially accept this notion, and work with it as best you can in the way outlined here, it will give you another powerful tool to transform your life radically for the better.

The reason that problems appear to persist through time is that, whenever they're not here, in this moment, we go looking for them. Yes, we actually seek our problems. We tend to filter our experiences based on the belief that we have a particular problem, unconsciously censoring anything from our awareness that doesn't support that belief, including the fact that the problem is not here NOW.

I have worked with this perspective in the background of my awareness for many years; however it has only been in the last few years that I have used it in our classes and retreats. One of the first times I shared this perspective with a group was at a Seven-day Retreat a few years ago. Henry came to the retreat wearing a leg brace and feeling a lot of pain due to torn ligaments in his knee. His doctors had told him that the pain would probably persist for about six months until all the ligaments healed. So, he was quite skeptical when I told him that even pain is a memory. Yes, there were sensations in the NOW, but the pain itself was only a memory. He was so skeptical, in fact, that he spent the next 24 hours trying to prove me wrong. He was certain that if he got completely present with the sensations he was experiencing, he would still feel pain.

The next day in class, Henry shared that he was more than a little shocked that, despite the fact he had doubted what I said, every time he looked for pain in the present, he couldn't find it. He went on to explain that not only could he not find pain in the present, but there was no more pain to be found period, and his swelling had gone down about 85 percent. He also no longer needed his leg brace to walk!

I invite you to challenge your long cherished problems by embracing at least the possibility that they are only memories and allowing yourself to be open to what you discover.

To release the suffering caused by your perceptions, begin by thinking of a problem that you used to believe you had. (Notice that I have purposely phrased this sentence in the past tense.)

If you have a hard time accepting the problem as being from the past, allow yourself to include the last moment as part of the past. Most of us think of the past as at least yesterday, last year, or years ago. For the sake of understanding what I am suggesting, please view the past as anything that is not happening at this exact moment, including a second ago, or even a nanosecond ago.

Then, ask yourself this question: *Could I allow myself to remember how I used to believe I had this problem?*

The shift in consciousness that follows the question may make you laugh, it may make you tingle inside, or it may simply open the possibility in your awareness that, "Yes, even *this* is just a memory."

Next, ask yourself: *Would I like to change that from the past?*

If the answer is "yes," ask: *Could I let go of wanting to change that from the past?* Then let go as best you can.

Simply move on to the next step if the answer is "no."

The completion question in this series is: *Could I let go of wanting to believe I have that problem again?* Or: *Could I let go of the expectation of having that problem happen again?*

As always, just do your best to let go. If you find that you're still clinging to the memory of the problem in this moment, however, repeat the steps from the beginning until you can let go fully.

Super Charge Advantages and Disadvantages

I highly encourage you to use the past tense perspective when working on problems using the Advantages/ Disadvantages Process from Chapter 10. Instead of asking, "What *is* the advantage in having this particular problem?" and, "What *is* the disadvantage in having this particular problem?" ask, "What *was* the advantage . . . ?" and, "What *was* the disadvantage . . . ?" Then follow the steps as outlined in Chapter 10 (see page 225).

Doing advantages and disadvantages in the past tense allows for the possibility that the problem is just a memory and may not reoccur. This frees you to release that particular pattern in consciousness without validating a sense of limitation. As you do this, you'll find that you can cut to the core of the feeling much more quickly and let go much more fully.

As you work with this perspective more and more, you'll find it easier and easier to let go of even those problems you used to believe were long-standing, and it will help you to take everything that you've learned in Part One to a deeper level.

Take Just One Feeling or One Moment at a Time

Often, when people write a book like this one, they entreat their readers to make a commitment to themselves for a minimum of 21 days, so they can create a new habit of thought and action. To me, this seems a little contrived and forceful. Instead, I would highly recommend that you simply take one moment at a time, doing the best you can to apply what you have learned. If you forget to release in any given moment, it doesn't indicate that you've somehow failed to be diligent. It only means you have a fresh opportunity to succeed by letting go NOW. As you succeed moment by moment, you'll be inspired to keep on gaining from releasing and accepting the truth of who you are.

Stephanie: There's No Such Thing as "Wasted Time"

As we worked together on this book, my editor Stephanie began the process of learning how to do the Sedona Method. One day on the phone, as we were in the middle of a discussion about the structure of a chapter, she mentioned that she often felt peeved at the suggestion to let go of her story. "Things have happened to me in my life that affected me deeply," she said. "I don't appreciate being told that these are lies or fiction. Furthermore, even when I release my feelings about these events, they keep coming back." I encouraged her to release some more and see what would happen if she gave up planning to re-experience them. Then we went on with our regular business.

A few days later, Stephanie called me again and asked, "Do your remember me telling you how annoyed I was at being told to release my story?" I said I did. "Well, I had a shame issue that I never told you about, which has been running my life for the past couple of years. After we got off the telephone, I sat down and made a decision that I would let it go—even though I didn't really believe it was possible. As an experiment, for the next 24 to 48 hours, I would live my life freely, as though my shame was unreal.

"Right after I made that decision, I must have cried hard for about five minutes, constantly releasing and letting it all move through me. As soon as I stopped, the phone rang, and it was an acquaintance of mine from one of the Sedona classes. This seemed like a gift from the universe. So, I decided to take the opportunity to tell her my 'deep, dark secret' and find out if my shame was *really* gone.

"When I did, it was so interesting," Stephanie said, laughing. "First, I heated up from head to toe. Then I felt intensely sad for about three seconds . . . and then I was fine, absolutely fine." She was amazed at the energy pouring through her body. Her only complaint was the grief she was feeling, because, as she said, "Hale, I've wasted so much time not being happy. It was so easy to be free, and I was so committed to my pain."

If you feel that you've wasted time, like Stephanie, let me assure you as I assured her. In my conception, there's no such thing as wasted time. We are all doing exactly what we're supposed to be doing in order for our lives to function. Honestly, all the time and energy that's invested in our stories and suffering comes back to us a thousand fold when we release them. We are not wasting time.

There are no mistakes.

PART 2

REAL LIFE APPLICATIONS

In Part Two, "Real Life Applications," we'll be exploring some of the many ways you can apply the Sedona Method in your life, beyond the obvious one of feeling better NOW. Every chapter in this section could be expanded into its own book about a specific application—and it may be in the future. My current purpose, however, is to help you begin using the Method across a broad range of conditions and scenarios. My goal is to help you integrate this material into your life and make it your own. As you work with it, you'll discover ever more ways the Sedona Method can serve you in your success and freedom.

At the end of Part Two, I have devoted an entire chapter to supporting the world, if you're inclined to get involved. I invite you to join me in communicating this message of freedom throughout our often-troubled world by sharing *The Sedona Method* with the people you care about. Together, we can spread peace, joy, prosperity, and well-being worldwide.

Chapter 13

The Secret of Letting Go of Fear and Anxiety

Lester Levenson used to say, "Fear, and it will appear." He had observed that fear of any type or degree, from extreme chronic anxiety and panic attacks to run-of-the-mill worrying and fretting—even the jitters—is a sticking place in our consciousness. By placing a continual emphasis on avoiding what we fear, we call it to mind over and over again, like a perverse mantra, or a focal point for meditation, and it becomes a program limiting our happiness and freedom. Fear can prevent us from doing what we'd like or need to do, because we construct elaborate "what ifs," or expectations, around taking action. Fear also stops us from letting go of our "problems," since we can't predict what will happen when we drop our guard.

There is an acronym—FEAR equals False Evidence Appearing Real—that I often share with my students, because most people's fearful expectations are totally unfounded. Even when fears appear to have a foundation in reality, these are usually blown way out of proportion to the actual risk, if there even is any. It's clear that anything that can help us let go of fear more easily can make a tremendous difference in our lives.

So, what's the secret behind letting go of fear? It may surprise you. Nonetheless, in my experience, it's true. On some level, we subconsciously want or expect anything we're afraid of to happen. Not consciously—*sub*consciously. Once we can welcome this, we can release.

I know the idea might seem hard to believe. You may be asking, "Why would I want to have a disease?" or, "Why would I want to be audited by the IRS?" But consider it. When we see something in the world that we don't like, we think to ourselves, "I hope that doesn't happen to me," or, "I hope that never happens again." What the mind hears and pictures, of course, is the fear happening as though we'd actually had the thought, "I *want* this to happen to me." Thus, our creative energy starts flowing in that direction. For, as I mentioned in Chapter 8, the mind only creates in pictures. Since it cannot translate the words *not* or *never* or *don't* into imagery, it ignores them.

We may set reversed intentions in motion when we don't like something we've experienced, read in the newspaper, or seen on television. It may also happen when we don't want to have a particular experience, or when something tragic happens to a person we know or care about. It's common for such things to trigger our resistance. Then, because we want to change whatever it is, we say, "I hope I don't get cancer like my father," or, "I hope I never make that same dumb mistake again." Remember, this is all going on below the level of consciousness. Most of us don't consciously affirm to ourselves that we want to get sick. We don't say, "I want to lose money," or, "I want to have an accident." But we have all said the opposite. Every time we do, without realizing it, we're holding what we fear in mind.

Here is another way this operates. If we worry about something, we believe that we're somehow preparing ourselves for an inevitable outcome. If the unwanted thing happens, we want to be prepared internally and in our lives. We prefer the false sense of security that comes from preparing for what we don't want to the uncertainty that comes from not knowing what is going to happen—even if what we know is going to happen is not a positive outcome. But again, even though we may get to be right by being prepared for a disaster, we may also be bringing the disaster about through our inner and outer preparations. Whenever we worry, we're holding in mind what we don't want, and that is what we tend to get.

Now, before we work together on getting unstuck, I'd like to address a few practicalities. First, if you've been diagnosed with an anxiety disorder, understand that the information in this book is not intended to replace your work with a therapist or doctor.

"I used to wake up in the middle of the night with my head spinning with thoughts about tomorrow's workday or fears, worry, and guilt for what happened or might happen. Since using the Sedona Method, that 'night talk' has lessened incredibly, and when it does happen now, I can release and go back to sleep instead of staying awake."
—Kathleen Bell,
Oakley, IL

Please do not change your current treatment regimen without consulting your healthcare practitioner. Secondly, I would suggest that you allow yourself to remain open to the possibility that your original diagnosis may have become a self-fulfilling prophecy. As you continue reading this chapter, release on anything related to your condition with an open heart and mind, knowing that there is a possibility it can change. Thirdly, if you have a strong fear issue, it might behoove you to skip directly ahead to Chapter 18, Developing Radiant Health, after reading this chapter. The releases you'll find there complement our current topic.

Every reader should continue applying the basic releasing process to the issue of fear and anxiety. This shortcut is not intended to replace your work on letting go of the wants for control, approval, and security that underlie your individual fears and feelings. Here is a tip: Fear is almost always anchored in place by wanting security or survival, or a sense of wanting to die.

A *final note*: One of the ways that fear feelings lie to us is by telling us that if we face them directly and let them go, the worst will happen. In my experience, this could not be further from the truth. It is the unaddressed feelings lying dormant in the subconscious mind that eventually have potential to bear fruit. Every fear is always better out in the light of awareness than lurking in the darkness of the shadows.

A Shortcut for Releasing Fear

Make yourself comfortable and focus inwardly. Begin by bringing to mind something about which you feel afraid or anxious—you may want to start with something small—in order to see exactly what it is that you fear is going to happen. Give yourself a moment to notice whether there is a strong feeling of fear at the moment, or a very light hint of fear. It doesn't matter which it is—simply observe and welcome it.

Now, ask yourself: *Could you let go of wanting this to happen?*

The question may have made you laugh. "Oh, come on," you said. "I don't actually want this to happen!" Well, try asking the question again, and notice what else you discover. In fact, if you go back to that same thing now, you may already be able to discern a difference. So, focus on that same thing you're afraid of, or on something else, and we'll go through a series of questions for releasing fear in this simple way.

What is it that you're afraid will happen?

What is it you do not want to have happen?

Now, could you let go of wanting that to happen?

Once you've gotten over the shock of the fact that you somehow want a negative thing to happen, it's often very easy to let go of the fear in this way, because, consciously, it's not truly what you want.

If you get stuck on any particular fear and are having a hard time letting it go, simply switch back to using the regular releasing questions. Check to see which want is stirred up in the moment and let it go, or simply check to see if you want to change that you are having difficulty and let go of wanting to change it. Then go back to experimenting with this shortcut.

Again, focus on something that you fear. It could be the same thing, or it could be something else. Notice exactly what it is that you're afraid will happen. If you're afraid of heights, for instance, underneath it there might really be a fear of falling.

Could you let go of wanting that to happen?

Focus again on that same fear, or on something else that you do not want to have happen, on something that you worry

"For years, I have suffered from a social phobia that crippled me. Being a full-time student, I come across new faces every day, and this caused me so much anxiety that I often felt like my heart would come out of my chest—just from sitting in class! In the past ten years, I have gone through a dozen psychologists and medications, none of which helped even half as much as the Sedona Method. I would love to tell all others out there who suffer from extreme shyness or social anxieties, you are not alone! You can be free of the chains! The Method has given me my life back."

—M.H., Allentown, PA

about, or on something that makes you nervous. Maybe you have a fear of public speaking. This could include the fear of making a mistake, or of seeming like a fool in front of a roomful of people.

Whatever underlying fear you feel: *Could you let go of wanting that to happen?*

Check how you feel inside. Wasn't it easy to let go in that way? This process will help you clear out the hidden recesses of your subconscious mind. After you release something that you've subconsciously wanted to happen, you'll see a tremendous difference in your life in many areas, including how you feel. Have fun experimenting with this shortcut on your own.

Add this little trick to your toolbox of Sedona Method applications and enjoy the results. It's great for those occasions when fearful thoughts arise in your consciousness, but you don't have enough time to do an in-depth process. Whenever you become aware of yourself thinking about an unwanted outcome, simply let go of wanting it to happen by asking yourself the question: *Could you let go of wanting that to happen?*

Releasing Your Fear about Others

What kind of images do you hold in mind when you're worrying about somebody you love? If you're honest, you'll probably admit that the pictures are not very positive ones. We also promote reverse intentions when we feel concerned on behalf of other people.

If you are worrying about someone, in addition to letting go of wanting that thing to happen to them, you can ask: *Would you rather hold in mind _____ (what you worry might happen) or would you rather hold in mind _____ (the opposite)?*

This is a no-brainer, don't you agree? If your husband or wife, son, daughter, or best friend is a little late driving home from an evening appointment, would you rather hold in mind that they have slid off the road into a ditch, or would you rather hold in mind that they are merely running late? Like most of us, I'm sure you would rather experience a positive outcome. So, allow yourself to let go of expecting or wanting the opposite.

Jennifer: If Not Now, When?

Jennifer found the Method at age 58 after decades of searching for an answer to her anxiety and depression. She says, "I believe that anxiety is a habit. As a younger person, I learned anxiety and perfectionism from my mother. When I was 12 years old, I made a decision that has affected my life ever since. I did something that I thought would make my mother hate me and give me away. The only way I could see to make up for this heinous crime was to be the dutiful daughter the rest of my life."

In her 20's, Jennifer began experiencing heart palpitations and panic attacks. She went to therapy and began reading self-help books, but, as she says, "My whole history was mostly talking and telling my story. It was nice to have listeners, but there was no concrete message: 'This is how you get better and get rid of this garbage.'" At age 34, her husband died in an automobile accident, leaving her to raise their eight-year-old son on her own. She was still grieving when she remarried three years later. In the 1980's, her gynecologist put her on Prozac, thinking the anxiety was related to hormonal problems, but she didn't like it. Then she went on Xanax.

One day, Jennifer received a package in the mail with a promotional audio from Sedona Training Associates. As she says, "It spoke to my needs. I thought, 'What the heck?' and ordered the full program. I had spent so much money on counseling already that I was very skeptical. So I started and stopped releasing a few times. I had to release on the issue of releasing. But I commute, so it was easy to listen to the program in the car. Another idea kept me going: At 58, I could say to myself, 'If not now, when? In 30 years, you'll be 88, like your mother. What are you going to do for the next 30 years?'

"Releasing wasn't an instant resolution of my anxiety, yet I noticed very quickly that I was feeling better. And I would do anything not to have to take pills again. All I know is that this is a tremendous program. I fired my last therapist on July Fourth, which is both Independence Day and my birthday."

Today, when Jennifer starts feeling anxious, she may for an instant think, "Oh my God, I need an antidepressant." She worries that her emotions may spiral out of control. Then, she reminds herself, "It's just a feeling I'm having." The Sedona Method has helped her to face her anxiety and understand what it is. "The Method is a wonderful tool," she says. "I no longer feel as though I'm in a void, and I don't dwell on my anxiety. The anxiety was a ball and chain I was carrying around that's gone. Now I'm discovering who I am and learning to accept myself without it."

Putting Your Fears Behind You

Like other problems, your fears are merely patterns ingrained in your consciousness. Another effective way to let go of fears, therefore, is to refer to them as memories by phrasing your releasing questions in the past tense. Please be mindful: the past can be as recent as an instant ago.

Begin by allowing yourself to remember a fear that you used to have.

Then, ask yourself: *Could you allow yourself to remember how you used to be afraid of_____?*

Would you like to change that from the past?

If the answer is "yes," ask: *Could you let go of wanting to change that from the past?* Then let go as best you can.

Simply move on to the next step if the answer is "no."

The completion question in this series is: *Could you let go of wanting to be afraid of _____?*

As always, do your best to let go. If you find that you're still clinging to the memory of the fear in the present moment, however, keep going back and repeating the steps from the beginning until you can let go fully. This can be a powerful release.

Bob: Turning the Corner on Chronic Anxiety

At Sedona Training Associates, we regularly receive excited letters from course graduates thrilled to have broken free of their unwanted patterns of feeling, thought, and belief. Bob mailed us two such letters. Here is an excerpt from the first:

"The Sedona Method freed me from over 40 years of psychological pain that was the result of a severe case of anxiety disorder. Approximately 18 months after I began using the audio program, my paralyzing fears were nearly extinguished! I did not believe this was possible. I am so grateful for the Sedona Method and the wonderful life I am now able to enjoy."

As a result of his initial breakthrough, Bob then decided to attend a Seven-day Retreat in Sedona, Arizona, in early October, and returned home with a renewed commitment to listen to the audio programs. A few weeks later, he sent a second letter:

"I am so happy and pleased to let you know that I became totally free of my anxiety disorder at the end of October. This is all I ever hoped for when I received the first of the tapes I ordered two years ago. Anything beyond this would be something I was not cognizant of, and therefore was not seeking.

"I initially made dramatic progress, and over time continued to improve through the Sedona Method. Of late, I intensified my releasing and listening to the tapes recorded by Lester Levenson. Somehow, I felt that I was on the brink of breaking completely free. Then on Sunday, October 13, I woke up with a certain sense of calm about me. The feeling was surreal. All of a sudden, it dawned on me that this must be what Lester meant when he indicated that one must "quiet the mind." Over the next three days, I experienced incidents that would normally trigger small traces of anxiety. These would still pop up when I was not prepared for them. Now, to my surprise, the compulsive behavior was not only gone, but was replaced by feelings of confidence. By October 16, my visceral response to anxiety-causing stimuli was to expect not to have feelings of anxiety. This was significant, and I think it marked the final turning point for me in ridding myself of a problem that had plagued me practically all of my life.

"Although I have not reached what to most of us seems like the mystical perspective on the universe that Lester spoke of, I am able to identify with key elements of what he described as being free. I can feel the distinction and separation of my body from my consciousness and my thinking. My body has been de-emphasized in importance to me. It is as though I am subtly looking at things through a different prism that forgets to think about the body. I am also experiencing what Lester described as the absence of ego. *This is the most pleasurable aspect of becoming free.*

"Today, I feel a complete lack of fear and anxiety in all situations. It is as though the feelings lodged in the subconscious mind that caused the anxiety have been completely cleaned out. Fear and anxiety are no longer impediments to me. This was my problem and what I had been trying to rid myself of all these years."

Two More Quick Tips

The processes in this chapter will really help you to cut through all your fears. An idea for accelerating your freedom from anxiety is to make a list of things that you used to be afraid of, and then let go of wanting them to happen one by one.

In addition, as you go about your day, if you happen to catch yourself getting jittery about something or dreading an outcome, check to see what it is that you're actually afraid will happen. Then ask: *Could you let go of wanting it to happen?*

Chapter 14

Beyond the Tyranny of Guilt and Shame

Guilt and shame are tricky feelings that cause so much unnecessary suffering. Nearly identical in the way they work within us, guilt and shame generally form a single complex. But while it is possible to feel guilt without shame, we cannot feel shame without guilt. The way to distinguish them is this: Guilt is the feeling that follows a perceived wrongdoing: "I did wrong." Shame is the feeling that we, ourselves, are made "wrong" or "bad" for what we perceive we did. On the chart of the nine emotional states (see page 106), guilt floats between several categories. It relates to the energy of every emotion from apathy through pride. Shame, on the other hand, is a grief-related feeling.

This chapter will explore and debunk the common misunderstandings about guilt and shame—the insidious robbers of our happiness, freedom, and peace of mind. Then, it will provide a few simple strategies for releasing these self-sabotaging feelings. Since they are for most purposes interchangeable, I'll be referring to guilt and shame collectively throughout the remainder of this chapter either as "guilt" or "guilt/shame."

Lies Perpetuated in the Name of Guilt and Shame

There are three major myths about guilt/shame that often severely limit our lives and make us miserable. The first and biggest lie is that guilt can protect us from being punished. In fact, guilt is an unconscious "I owe you" for punishment. That's right. When we feel guilty, we attract punishment from the world, and we also create it for ourselves. And here's the kicker: We *never* feel as though we've been sufficiently punished.

How does self-punishment arise? First we do something, or think of doing something, that we believe we shouldn't do, or that is wrong to do. Interestingly, we often feel guilty even when we haven't followed through with an external action. Then, whether or not we'll "get away with it" in the eyes of the world, we remain aware of what we did or thought, and we won't easily let ourselves off the hook. Because we believe that punishment from the outside is inevitable, we punish ourselves in the false hope that this will enable us to prevent receiving it. But since we have no idea of what others', or even our own, sense of inner governance will determine is an appropriate degree of punishment, we invariably overdo it.

The first time I remember inflicting guilt-motivated punishment of this kind on myself was in preschool after I got angry with a fellow student and pushed him so hard that he slipped, fell, and broke a glass. I felt so bad about having hurt him, and so afraid of what my teacher and parents might do to punish me, that I picked up a piece of the glass and cut myself, inwardly hoping that the action would protect me from any impending repercussions. Of course it didn't work. I still got reprimanded and received a punishment. It was so insignificant, however, that I can't even recall what happened, except that I did get punished and also had a cut on my hand for good measure.

Pause for a moment to consider anything you feel guilty about doing or not doing, saying or not saying, or even thinking or feeling. Make a point of noticing whether you have been punishing yourself and living in fear of an impending external punishment.

When you think about the things that you've been feeling guilty about, also check to see if your guilt has actually protected you from being punished, as the feeling "promised" you it would. Like the lies that most feelings tell us, you'll usually find that your guilt produced the opposite effect. It caused you to punish yourself. And, if your actions involved others, most likely it didn't prevent you from receiving their punishment. After all, if feeling guilty truly prevented external punishment, wouldn't our prisons be a lot emptier?

A second lie perpetuated in the name of guilt is that the feeling somehow prevents us from repeating our "wrong" actions. But haven't you—or someone you've known—ever done, said, or thought anything that you felt guilty about more than once? Of course you have. We all have. Guilt frequently triggers us to do, or to continue doing, the exact same things that we believe we've already

> "The Sedona Method works on a feeling level and allows people to eliminate both their negative emotions and thoughts. It is fast and effective, because it goes directly to the heart of the problem. It is a shortcut for anyone who uses it."
> —Dr. Elliott Grumer, Phoenix, AZ

done wrong—again as self-inflicted punishment. Guilt is one of the main causes of actions that we later regret.

Consider the following example. Imagine that you're on a diet to lose weight. You slip and have a cookie or a dish of ice cream, and you feel guilty about it. So, what do you do? That's right. You punish yourself by having another cookie or another scoop of ice cream. Now you feel even guiltier. Pretty soon, as an escalating punishment for your indiscretion, you finish the entire bag of cookies or pint of ice cream. And you probably don't allow yourself to enjoy even one bite. Sound familiar? You bet. The diet industry thrives on this little-understood phenomenon that causes most dieters to fail.

It is also why the world is full of people atoning in various ways for sins that they have every intention—at least subconsciously, if not overtly—of doing again.

Now, I am not going to suggest that we all begin doing anything we want to do with reckless abandon, ignoring the guidelines of moral or disciplined behavior. However, since our guilt feelings don't stop most of us from doing things we later regret, when we willingly release our guilt/shame, the benefits are usually profound. Freedom from guilt/shame means we are free to make better, healthier, more supportive choices.

Another area in which guilt plays a significant role is being unable to move beyond early abuse. When our parents, guardians, teachers, or spiritual leaders abuse us when we are young, it is difficult for us to accept that these people could do something so wrong. When we are young, adults—especially influential ones like our parents—have a tremendous amount of power in the world compared to our own. After all, they provide our food and shelter and are supposed to protect us from the outside world. Since we cannot yet survive on our own, discovering their fallibility directly threatens our survival. We may elevate the adults in our lives to the status of gods, or at least representatives of God. Therefore, when abuse occurs, we seek to pin blame on the only other participant that we can find: ourselves. We do this as a distorted, imaginary form of self-protection.

In Sedona Method courses, I've often worked with survivors of childhood abuse. Because survivors often blame themselves for what has happened, many have been feeling guilty and punishing themselves their whole lives for the mistakes made by the adults that they trusted. Once they release their guilt feelings and stop blaming and punishing themselves for their abusers' mistakes, they are able to free themselves of the emotional, mental, and visceral patterns of trauma and shame in which they've been locked.

Annie: Setting Down Her Burdens

As you're no doubt aware, the mind and the body are intimately connected. Oftentimes, when we're working deeply to let go, we discover that the body is holding the memory of a story. It is also typical that, when we're suppressing them, our feelings will seek expression through the body.

Annie is a perfect example of the mind-body connection. She arrived at a Seven-day Retreat in Sedona, Arizona, with a severe neck and backache, saying that her shoulders felt as though they weighed ten thousand pounds. Since this kind of pain is common, when she approached me for help in the middle of the week, I asked her if she'd allow me to lead her through a five- to ten-minute release on behalf of the entire group. It honestly didn't matter to me what the story behind Annie's pain was. However, she revealed that she was worrying extensively about her 24-year-old daughter who was pregnant at the time. "Frankly, I thought I'd let go of my fears as a mother by going to therapy and using the Sedona Method. But my control issues are resurfacing now. See, my daughter began having grand mal seizures at age 13. The first time it happened I was sure that she was dying. In the years that followed, I'd often relive the horror of that experience when I looked at her. Even though she's been seizure-free for two years, I'm afraid that she's on so much medication it might impact the baby. I feel responsible."

First, I led Annie through a general release on her physical pain. In the middle of it, she reported feeling like Atlas, saying it was her role to hold the world upon her shoulders. I asked her if she could let it go, and she agreed that she would put the world down. This released some of her pain, but we didn't stop there. An even deeper release occurred while using the following sequence of questions: *Have you punished yourself enough? Could you let go of wanting to punish yourself? And, could you let go of feeling guilty?* When she fully released, her pain was gone and did not return, except for a twinge when her daughter picked her up at the airport. She quickly released again, and it evaporated.

Here's how Annie describes her significant release: "It unlocked so much for me. I had been literally carrying around the guilt of having a child who was less than perfect for 24 years. This was the burden that came off my shoulders. Now I understand on the deepest level that my daughter's epilepsy wasn't related to anything I did or didn't do. In addition, I am not responsible for her path or her journey. She's not 'mine,' she's her own. And she's going to take care of what needs to be done. I no longer feel as though I have to control the world so it's better for her. I just need to stay present to what's going on right now. None of what I have feared has happened in the moment, so it was easy to let go. The power of the universe knows the way for her, her unborn child, and me."

Four Brief Processes for Releasing Feelings of Guilt/Shame

Okay, now that we've turned a few cherished beliefs on their heads, let's look at some practical ways to eliminate the tyranny of guilt/shame. These are designed to augment, rather than supplant, the various releasing processes you learned in Part One of this book.

1. *Release Your Underlying Wants*

As part of the self-punishment/imagined protection syndrome described above, we try to use our guilty, shameful feelings to gain approval, control, or security. So, this simple series of releasing questions may be helpful to you:

Am I using this guilt/shame to gain approval, control, or security?

Could I let go of wanting approval, control, or security?

Or you may substitute: *Could I let go of wanting to use guilt/shame in that way?*

The word "using" may help you to take responsibility for having the emotion of guilt/shame and subsequently to let it go more easily.

2. *Decide that You Have Been Punished Enough*

Another powerful way to release guilt/shame is to decide that you have been punished enough, and then to let go of wanting to punish yourself. You can use these questions:

Could I allow myself to decide that I have been punished enough?

Could I let go of wanting to punish myself?

Could I stop planning to punish myself again in the future?

If you are having any difficulty letting go of guilt/shame in this way, simply stick with the basics until you can answer "yes" to all the questions.

3. *Evaluate the Advantages and Disadvantages*

In conjunction with the process just mentioned, the Advantages/Disadvantages Process is an excellent tool for making a decision about continuing to punish or blame yourself for what happened. Remember, it is best to phrase your questions in the past tense to allow for the freedom to be NOW. This also increases the possibility that any release can be the last release needed on this topic. Alternate between asking the following two questions:

- *What was the advantage to me in punishing myself?*
- *What was the disadvantage to me in punishing myself?*

4. *Embrace Your True Feelings about What Happened*

Guilt also gets sticky when we sometimes pretend

to feel guilty even though we secretly feel, "I did it. I'm glad I did it. And I'd do it again." This is where guilt differs from shame. If you ever fall into this trap, acknowledging the truth of your feelings will release much of your guilt. The balance of the guilt can then be released by asking:

* *Could I let go of wanting to do it again?*

Breathe a Deep Sigh of Relief

Not only will seeing guilt and shame from a fresh perspective open up new possibilities in your life, I am sure you'll now find these oppressive emotions much easier to deal with and release. Please use the tools you've learned in this chapter to encourage yourself to shift in that direction. After all, guilt and shame are just feelings. They are not you, and you can let them go. So, breathe a deep sigh of relief, and move on when you're ready.

Chapter 15

Breaking those Nasty Habits

One of the key applications of the Sedona Method is breaking unwanted habits. It is not that all habits are bad. It's just that we habitually do certain things that we know are not good for us. For most people, habits are not easy to break. They're like deep grooves or ruts in our thinking, feeling, and behavior patterns. In addition, because we've often invested a lot of time and energy in first creating and then fighting these patterns, we sometimes resist the process of letting them go even after we know how.

Think of the things that you believe you do habitually. You may be a smoker. You might feel like you eat too little or too much. You might be addicted to the television, movies, sex, or alcohol. Not all addictions or habits are that obvious. Some habits are subtler. Do you feel like you *have to* be right? Do you feel that you *have to* be felt, heard, or seen? Do you feel like you can't stop judging yourself or others? These are also addictions. Even wanting approval, control, security, and separation are addictions. There are many things that we feel addicted to, or that we habitually do, no matter how hard we try to stop. If you've ever tried to stop indulging a habit, you know it can be very difficult.

My purpose in this chapter, as in the entire book, is to show you how to change from the inside out by teaching you to unhook from the inner motivators that cause you to act in ways you later regret. You have probably noticed by now that I haven't tried to tell you what to do in other chapters. I am not a believer in giving out lists of new behaviors to follow, because behaviors imposed from the outside often just become new limiting habits.

By the way, I have watched even seriously chemically dependent people—and those who had been diagnosed with an organic chemical imbalance—break the different types of habits caused by these chemicals. If you experience a medical condition of this nature, you will surely benefit from this chapter, as well as from reading the material in Chapter 18, Developing Radiant Health.

Before we go any further, I would like to point out that I am not suggesting that you discontinue what you're already doing if you participate in a support group like Alcoholics Anonymous, or you are under treatment for any kind of chemical or even emotional dependence. Use everything in this chapter to support what you are already doing, and do not make any changes to your treatment regimen without first consulting your medical practitioner. If you're in a 12-step program, do not divert from the step you are currently on without the permission of your sponsor. In our work with the recovery community, we've determined that releasing is a tremendous aid in following through on the discipline necessary to become substance-free, as well as in coping with and preventing relapses.

A Different Approach to Breaking Habits

If there's a habit in your life, or an addiction, that you want to modify or be free of, there is a very simple way of doing so. As an example, imagine that you have a tendency to eat an extra dessert after dinner, or to eat dessert more often than you should. In this situation a lot of us would decide, "Oh, I'm not going to eat dessert anymore." That stringent commitment may last a couple of days, or, if we're really strong, a couple of weeks, and then we're back eating desserts again—maybe even more than before.

Here is another way to approach the dilemma when

"I have despaired—for decades—of ever being able to let go of smoking. Now that I've got the Method, for certain I am smoking less without any effort at all. I was shocked a couple of days ago to realize I had spent the entire evening and never even thought about smoking. Today, another first: I stayed in the building during lunch hour, ate in the lunchroom, and did not feel deprived at all when I started working again without having smoked. For the first time since I started smoking (45 years ago!), it felt natural not to smoke. I am astonished."

—M.L., Carbondale, FL

you're interested in having a dessert. Rather than saying, "I'm *never* going to do it again," make a pact, "Look. You can have it if you want it, but release first." The reason to release first is that all habit patterns are locked in by patterns of feeling. Certain feelings come up in our awareness, and the way we compensate for them is by taking a particular action, such as overeating. So when you release, you let go of the underlying cause or motivation for that particular habit.

Caution: If you are addicted to a controlled substance, prescription, or if you are addicted to alcohol, please bear in mind that this instruction—"to let yourself have it"—may not be appropriate for you. So, simply release the feelings that cause you to crave the substance to which you're addicted as they arise, and stick with your discipline.

To go back to our example, let's say you're interested in having a piece of pie. If you tell yourself you can't have it, you just get into a push-pull situation. You miss it and obsess over your missed piece of pie. You feel deprived. You do the boy-would-a-piece-of-pie-taste-good mantra—holding your desire in mind—and this merely builds up inner pressure. Then you end up having the pie anyway, or two days later you break down and eat two pieces of pie instead of the original one. But if you first release whatever feeling is making you feel like you need to eat the pie, and then you let yourself have it if you still want it, it's easier. This creates the space to get into releasing around the habit, and you'll soon notice the habit drop away.

An actress I know thought it was very important for obvious reasons because of her trade to be a certain weight. At the time of this story, she'd been trying to lose 20 pounds for over 20 years and could never reach what she considered her ideal size. She tried every diet imaginable. She exercised like a fiend. In fact, she was running so much that she destroyed her knees and couldn't run anymore. She had to find another aerobic exercise to do. We used to teach the Sedona Method over two weekends—now we teach it over one weekend—and the instructor suggested to her that, during the week in between, she try the little trick I described above: to let herself eat whatever she wanted as long as she released first. This helped her have a breakthrough.

About two days later, she went out and had the first hot fudge sundae she'd had in years, and she actually enjoyed it and felt satisfied. However, because she was releasing before she reached for the food every time she ate that week, she lost five pounds in only five days. Within about six months, she had lost 20 pounds. It is now many years later, and the last time I saw her she was still maintaining her ideal weight.

If it's possible for this actress and the thousands of other people who have used this technique effectively, it's possible for you. And it's not complicated. Rather than trying to fix or change your habit, make a pact with yourself that the next time you want to reach for a cigarette, the next time you want to turn on the television, the next time you want to reach for a dessert, you can do it if you still want to after you release. You will notice that the habit will fall away gradually, or very quickly. I've literally seen hundreds of people stop smoking this way. So, experiment with it on your own, and you'll see that it's a very effective way of applying the Method.

Now that we've discussed the principles of breaking habits and going beyond addiction, let's get into some practical applications.

Letting Go of the Memory of the Habit

A very powerful way of breaking habits is to use the perspective, which we discussed at the end of Chapter 12, that there are no problems (see page 268). This is because habits, like any other problems, are merely patterns in consciousness that have become customary. I have seen whole habits drop away very quickly and easily when an individual caught this tendency of expectation and let it go.

The one disagreement I have with various 12-step programs is the continual affirmation and reaffirmation by people speaking in their meetings of: "I am a _____ (insert your particular addiction, e.g., alcoholic, sex addict, or overeater)." This may be extremely helpful in the beginning to break through denial, but after someone has completed the steps of the program, and kicked his or her particular habit, it would be much better to affirm: "Hi, I am _____ (insert your name) and I *used to be* a _____ (insert the particular addiction)."

I had a friend who'd learned the Method and was also very involved with 12-step programs, and he fought me on this point. But he had gotten really stuck in his life and was unable to let go no matter how hard he tried, because he kept going back into agreement with his past problems. One day, I finally insisted that he at least give the perspective that problems are only memories a try. After only ten minutes of working like this, his 18-month stuckness completely dropped away, and his life totally turned around.

If you can allow for the possibility that the past does not have to dictate the future, the results you'll experience may be miraculous.

Begin by allowing yourself to remember a habit that you used to believe you had. Notice that I have purposely phrased this question in the past tense.

Then, ask yourself: *Could I allow myself to remember how I used to believe I had this habit?*

Next, ask: *Would I like to change that from the past?*

If the answer is "yes," ask: *Could I let go of wanting to change that from the past?* Then let go as best you can.

Simply move on to the next step if the answer is "no."

The completion question in this series is: *Could I let go of wanting to believe I have that habit again?* Or, *Could I let go of wanting to have that habit again?*

As always, just do your best to let go. If you find that you're still clinging to the memory of the habit in this moment, however, repeat the steps from the beginning until you can let go fully.

> "I was addicted to sleeping pills and booze. Every night for three years, I took a sleeping pill after five to six drinks to blot out life and sleep, never realizing the lengths to which I was going to avoid growth. I had terrible colitis from stress—would spend days in bed with a heating pad. At the end of the course, never another sleeping pill and no more booze. After a year, I finally can choose to have an occasional glass of wine— never any more colitis."
>
> —S.D., Phoenix, AZ

Advantages/Disadvantages and Likes/Dislikes

The Advantages/Disadvantages Process and the Likes/Dislikes Process are great tools for working on a habit. If you've been trying unsuccessfully to change a habit, understand that there is usually at least one hidden advantage or liking for that particular behavior just below your conscious awareness. If you can elevate this perceived benefit into your conscious awareness and let it go, you'll find that the habit drops away by itself. Remember, if you're working directly on a habit, work on it in the past tense. Give yourself the possibility that it may not reoccur.

Immediately after attending a Seven-day Retreat in Sedona, Steve decided to apply the Method to his shopping addiction. He loves quality men's clothing so much that he even published a book about finding good deals, which he was researching at the time. "I tend to be extreme about everything I do," he says. "When I got to the stores, it was as though they were lobbing things at me to say 'yes' to. Technically, I could afford them, but did I really need to allocate my resources that way? There must have been five or six times as much stuff as the items I finally bought that I initially wanted to purchase.

"Using the principles I'd learned, I told myself that if I still wanted something after releasing on it, I could have it. When I came across an excellent shirt at an outlet place, I released and set up a few caveats, too. The advantages were that a) the item fit; b) I would be able to wear it that season, instead of merely adding it to my wardrobe; c) I had already bought a tie, which it matched perfectly; and d) it was 80 percent off. As these outweighed the disadvantages, I bought it. But, later in the day, I used the same technique, and there was a bunch of other stuff that I didn't buy. So I know it works."

Releasing Your Habits

Although it's ideal to release on a habit before you indulge it, you often won't catch yourself in time to make a different, preferred choice. In retrospect, you'll know you could have released first, but you didn't. Now you've "gone and done it again," and you have some feelings about it—guilt, shame, anger, sadness, etc.

No need to be concerned. Releasing after the fact can also be a powerful way to break habits. Each time you release on the feelings related to a habit or an addiction— before, during, or after—you weaken the pull in that particular direction. Eventually, the process of releasing will help you change your behavior completely. You will incorporate it into your everyday life.

Remember, it is our patterns of feeling that create our patterns of behavior. As we break our patterns of feeling, the behaviors drop away effortlessly, too.

Begin by making yourself comfortable. Then think of a specific habit from which you would like to be free. It could be an addiction to alcohol, cigarettes, drugs, sex, overeating, watching TV, or anything else that makes you stuck. Once you have a habit in mind, focus inwardly, and get in touch with your NOW feeling about it.

Could you welcome the feeling and allow it to be present?

Notice what it feels like to have this particular addiction. Also notice how you disapprove of yourself for this recurring behavior. And, again, focus on your NOW feeling about the addiction.

Would you allow yourself to dig a little deeper and see whether that feeling comes from a sense of wanting approval, control, or security?

Could you let go of whichever want it is?

Repeat the above steps as many times as you need to begin feeling lighter, more spacious, and relaxed. As you release your feelings about the habit, your goal is to release to the point that it feels okay either way—whether you do it or you don't. Understandably, this may seem like a stretch. However, if you can release to the point where it feels entirely as acceptable to you to keep the habit as it would be to let it go, you will take away the fight. It will then be a lot easier to become free of your habit or addiction.

Focus again on how you feel about the addiction. Just let yourself feel the feeling you have about that habit.

Does the feeling come from wanting approval, control, or safety?

Could you let the want go?

Repeat the steps above a few more times.

Now, recall a specific time when the habit was in operation, a time when you indulged that particular behavior. Perhaps you reached for a drink or a cigarette. Maybe you ate an extra cookie. Whatever time you're focusing on, allow yourself to get in touch with the feelings that were present right before you took that particular action.

Could you welcome that feeling?

Can you identify the want that underlies and motivates the feeling?

Could you let it go?

Focus again on that same time, and see how you felt right before you did it. Was there another feeling that pushed you in the direction of your habit? This could have been hunger, anger, sadness, a sense of emptiness, or a feeling of compulsion. It may have been subtle or it may have been strong.

Very often we use addictive behaviors to anesthetize ourselves to our feelings. So it may not be easy at first to get in touch with them. Please stick with the process, however. The more you do this work, the more obvious your feelings will become.

Whatever your feeling was before you did the habitual

behavior, let yourself experience it again now, as best you can.

Check to see if it comes from wanting approval, control, or security.

Could you let it go?

Next, see how you felt when you were actually doing that particular behavior: eating the cookie, drinking the drink, smoking the cigarette, or whatever it is that you're focusing on. Pay close attention to any artificial good feeling that you were getting from doing it, as well as to any other feelings you had at the time. Maybe there was also a struggle going on within you.

Could you welcome how you feel as you picture yourself right in the middle of doing the action?

Which want is stirred up in this moment?

Could you let it go?

Very often there's a sense of relief or misappropriated enjoyment from habituated behaviors. But as we let that go, we feel enjoyment directly without the behavior, since good feelings are always available to us in every moment. Remember, all limiting feelings—even so-called positive ones—are releasable.

Focus again on that same specific time when you were engaged in this particular behavior. Identify and welcome the feelings that motivated you to do it. Allow them.

Is there an underlying want?

Could you let it go?

Now, remember how you felt immediately after doing that particular behavior. When you were done, did you feel any guilt, regret, disgust, or any other feeling? Perhaps you thought: *Oh my god, I did it again!* See if there was a sense of disapproval or being out of control. *Could you do your best to become aware of that feeling now?*

Remember, these feelings are only feelings.

Underneath them, is there a sense of wanting approval, control, or security?

Could you let it go?

Repeat the steps above several more times.

Take a moment to notice how your overall feeling has already shifted in relationship to this particular habit or addiction. It may only be a small shift, or it may be a major shift. However much the shift is, it indicates that you've begun to move in a positive direction.

Now, tune in to how you feel about breaking the habit. People frequently have residual feelings from previous attempts to change habits. These could be times when you said, "I'm going to stop," but you weren't able. If you have a residual feeling or doubt about changing this habit, simply welcome that feeling into your awareness.

Is there an underlying sense of wanting approval, control, or security?

Could you let it go?

Take another inward look and allow yourself to feel however you feel right now about going beyond the addiction or habit. Could you embrace the feeling?

Do you want approval, control, or security?

Could you let it go?

Rick: No Longer Ruled by Chocolate

Rick used to be addicted to peanut M&Ms. In his own words, "I was a candy monster. There was no day that could go by without them. Some nights, I had to run out at 10 P.M. to get them. Ninety percent of the reason I went to the movies was to indulge myself with a big bag of them. I honestly didn't care what was playing." But now he doesn't crave them. What helped him was releasing on the feeling of needing M&Ms— really welcoming that want into his awareness. He still enjoys them occasionally, but they gradually became less than the primary focus of his activities. "The truth is that we all let ourselves be controlled by things in our lives. When we release on them, it frees up our power. Although I used to jump through hoops for M&Ms, I don't have to anymore. The greatest gift of this process was how it freed me up to enjoy the present moment. To be there when I'm there. I'm more in the NOW than ever before."

A Couple of Extra Points

I suggest that you use the focused releasing process often (see page 306). Every time that you do it, you'll get more out of it. But, just as importantly, keep releasing on your unwanted habit while you're doing it, before you're doing it, and after you do it.

Also, unless you're under medical supervision, or it runs contrary to the rules of the 12-step program you're working, experiment with making a pact with yourself that it's okay to indulge your habit after releasing the feelings that are motivating you to do it. In making it okay, it will become more and more okay to *not* do it—and the habit will drop away.

Chapter 16

Your Wealth Builder

Welcome to your mini-course on financial freedom and abundance. In this chapter, we'll explore several exercises that will help you to apply the Sedona Method to increasing your prosperity. Each exercise is designed for frequent and repeated use, so that you can gain increasingly more from it. The exercises build on the foundation of the material in Part One, so if you haven't completed Part One of this book yet, please return to this chapter once you have, even if this is a key area of interest for you.

Increased wealth is one of the most commonly reported benefits we hear about from our seminar participants and those who listen to our audio programs. As we release on any area in life, we naturally become more positive and therefore tend to attract more abundance into our lives. Of course, abundance is not only financial. But the world runs—maybe a little too much—around money, so most of us feel varying degrees of intensity around the topic of our finances. When we begin to let go of our beliefs in this area, we find it easier to receive, have, and even save more money.

Like many people, I used to believe that it was somehow unspiritual to possess money. So, I had a tendency to spend what I did receive, and I wouldn't allow myself to earn what I deserved. Since I began using the Method to let go of this belief, I have experienced increasing abundance in every area of my life, not solely financially.

Bank in the Bank, Not in Your Head

Lust is an emotional state in which we hold ourselves back from having what we want, often without even realizing it. As described in the Introduction, when I was selling real estate, I was "head banking" instead of banking in the bank. When I ultimately allowed myself to let go of the lust that was causing me to fantasize about how great it was going to be to make sales, and just went about the business of making sales, I closed many more deals. Salespersons, marketers, entrepreneurs, and managers are very prone to head banking. However, they are definitely not the only ones. Another notorious place many people tend to slip into head banking is in the area of investing.

You may have heard an expression referring to investing: "The bulls and the bears make money, but the pigs get slaughtered." A secret lies behind this maxim, with which you may have direct experience. Most investment decisions are emotionally based, as opposed to being based on solid facts and clear intuition. Unsuccessful investors, and even some successful ones, often begin counting their gains and losses before a transaction is actually closed. They count their paper profits and spend them mentally before the actual results come in. They also tend to stay in a transaction longer than they should, because it might get better. Both of these actions are due to lust and its inherent substitution of fantasy for what is. If you are this type of investor, you can let go of your lust instantaneously by determining which want is involved in it: approval, control, or security. As you do, you'll make wiser investment decisions.

Fear is also part of the problem of emotional investing. People often don't act on what they intuitively know is correct in the market, because they're afraid of making mistakes. Or fear paralyzes them and prevents them from taking their profits or cutting their losses. So, if you find that you are getting caught in fear-based investing, allow yourself to let it go directly, or see it as one of the wants and let it go in that way.

A third big way that many investors fool themselves into believing that they are more in control than they are is to call the moves after the fact and tell themselves that they knew what was going to happen. They can often be much better "paper traders" than real ones. They make the wrong decisions when they are actually using cash. Again, it's the emotions coloring our perceptions that cause us to do things we regret later.

> "Without reservation, I can state that the Sedona Method works! I originally set a goal of organizing my finances. After releasing it, I found that my real goal was to allow myself to know my own value. In the next three weeks, I did more about my finances than I had in the previous eight months."
>
> —Noel Kelly, Broomall, PA

If you allow yourself to release before you enter or leave a business deal or stock transaction, you will find that your timing improves. If you also let go before you act when you have a hunch, you will be able to tell the difference between intuition and fear or greed. The more you use the Method in your investment activities, the more you will find yourself following fact instead of fancy, and intuition rather than lust and fear.

Releasing on Your Parents' Financial Activities

In considering abundance and financial freedom, one of the areas where most people get stuck is resisting or wanting to change how their parents viewed and handled money. Now, this might seem obvious, or it might come as a surprise to you. Most of us either strongly model ourselves after our parents' financial viewpoint—whether it worked for them or not—or we live in resistance to it. Either way, it totally obscures our own power to create what we want in life. It also holds us back from having what we want.

A Sedona Method student named Nancy made a major discovery in this regard one day when she was listening to my audiotape program on financial freedom. As she says, "A pirate has downloaded some software into my operating system. It's a continuous loop that keeps repeating the message: 'Money is scarce.' I hadn't realized before how deeply I'd adopted my parents attitudes about money. So much so that I recreate them in my life.

"My mother is financially set, yet she worries constantly that she won't have enough. Of course, her attitude goes back further, to my grandparents. It's a farmer's mentality. There's secrecy about money. You must act poor even if you're not poor. You are not supposed to 'brag' about being successful. So I work on commission, and it's either feast or famine. I can see now that I've created a pattern on purpose of almost succeeding and then pulling back. I'm feeling freer though, now that I release on it."

So, consider your parents' attitudes about money, how they treated you in relationship to money, and how they treated each other.

Then ask: *Is there anything about your parents' attitudes and their actions with money that you would either like to change or which you're resisting?*

Could you let go of wanting to change or resist the way they were, or they are?

Find something else that you resist about the way your parents handled money or their attitudes about money.

Could you let go of that resistance now? Could you just allow it to dissolve?

Now, think of something else that you'd like to change about how your parents handled money, what happened to them in relationship to money, or how they treated you in relationship to money.

Could you let go of wanting to change it?

Repeat the questions above a few more times before moving on.

Did your parents have a negative pattern related to money that you've imitated without even realizing it—a pattern you've adopted in your own life?

If so, could you welcome that attitude, belief, or habitual pattern?

Does it come from wanting approval, control, or security?

Whichever want it is: *Could you allow yourself to let it go?*

Is there any other way that you've modeled your finances after your parents' that you don't like and would like to change?

Just for now, could you simply welcome it?

Could you let go of wanting to change it? Could you let go of wanting to imitate your parents?

As I mentioned in the chapter on guilt and shame, during the first few years of our lives—and as we're growing up—our parents are like gods to us. They feed us, house us, and clothe us, and we unconsciously model ourselves after them, even if what they are doing doesn't work well.

Check now to see if you've become aware of that kind of past unconscious modeling right now.

If so, could you just allow it to be?

Is there a sense of wanting approval, control, or security?

If so, could you allow that want to release?

Now, check again to see whether there is any way that you're resisting your parents' attitudes about money and want to change them. Or are you modeling yourself after your parents in some regard?

Could you just allow that to be, to welcome it?

Does it come from wanting approval, control, or security?

Could you allow yourself to let that go?

Take a moment to notice how you feel right now after releasing. This is an incredibly valuable topic for additional exploration. Furthermore, it's entirely possible to become free of the beliefs and attitudes your parents had about money that are holding you back. You can be the way you choose now. You don't have to be the way they wanted you to be anymore, and you do not need to live in resistance to the way they were. The key is to let go of your resistance (the sense of wanting to change what was or what is), and to let go of wanting to be like your parents in order to be safe or to get their approval.

Releasing Fear about Money

Another area in which we get stuck in relationship to money—actually in relationship to everything—is the area of fear. If you remember from Chapter 13, The Secret of Letting Go of Fear and Anxiety, anything of which we're afraid we subconsciously want to have happen. There is a pull in that negative direction without us purposely wanting or being aware of it. Consider your personal fears about money. Most of us have had things happen to us in the past that we didn't like, or to those we know, in relationship to money. We therefore want to avoid or prevent these experiences from happening again, which, of course, means that we're holding them in mind. Since I am sure you would prefer to let that whole expectation go out of your consciousness, rather than pulling it into your experience, let's explore the issues together.

My parents grew up during the Depression, and my father saw his family lose their house. My mother tried to persuade my father to own real estate with little success. As a real estate broker, he earned a good living off commissions and made other people millions of dollars on their deals. But he passed up many real estate purchases that he could have made for himself, which would have returned him millions of dollars on very small investments. In fact, he sometimes rented our homes, even though he could have afforded to buy them and could have sold them soon afterwards for a considerable profit. Without realizing it, I modeled after my father in this area. My wife Amy actually had to cajole me for a few years before I realized what was happening, and I released my fear of owning real estate. We then bought a townhouse in Phoenix that we sold at a profit. Now we own a beautiful home in Sedona,

Arizona. I know this wouldn't have been possible for us if I hadn't let go of the fear of owning real estate that I'd inherited from my father.

What is something that you're afraid will happen if you have a lot of money, or if you have financial freedom? Perhaps you fear being audited by the IRS, paying higher taxes, or making bad investments.

Whatever fear it is: *Could you, just for now, let go of wanting that to happen?* I know it is a funny notion, but, as we've seen in other chapters, it does work.

What else are you afraid might happen if you have a lot of money in the bank?

Might you take it for granted?

Are you afraid it will damage your relationships?

Check to see what your fears are about having lots of money or having financial freedom, and pick any one of them.

Could you let go of wanting that to happen?

Find something else that you're afraid will happen if you have complete financial freedom and abundance. Maybe you're afraid that you won't handle money responsibly.

Could you let go of wanting that to happen?

> "The gains I've received and continue to receive seem to be increasing without any additional effort, like hitting a critical mass! Before taking the course, I never received production bonus money at work. Upon completion, I received my first bonus. Then they continued every month, including three awards for being the top producer. Then the managers were asking me how to motivate others to do the same!"
>
> —Peter Piezzo,
> St. Augustine, FL

Repeat the questions above several more times, allowing your fears to dissipate.

In addition to using the shortcut of letting go of wanting your fear to become real, you could also make a list of your fears about money, abundance, and financial freedom and release on them directly using the wanting approval, control, and security questions. Either way, as you eliminate the fear, you'll be freer to move forward and create exactly the kind of abundance you want in your life.

Likes and Dislikes about Money

Our beliefs and attitudes about money frequently block us from having financial freedom and abundance. Many of these are like the air we breathe: we're totally unaware of them and the attachments and aversions hidden beneath them. Using the Likes/Dislikes Process (see Chapter 9) helps bring these layers into full awareness where we can release them.

As you work on your beliefs and attitudes, I'll ask you to do it in two stages. Begin with your current financial situation. Think how you are right now in relationship to money. Remember, it's important to release on your likes as well as your dislikes.

What is something that you like about your current financial situation?

Does that come from wanting approval, control, or security/survival?

Whichever want it is: *Could you just let it go?*

It might be hard to think of things you like, especially if your financial situation isn't the way you'd like it to be. But if it is stuck in that place, then you can be assured that some subconscious wants or feelings are preventing you from letting go and moving on. So just be as open as you can be, allowing yourself to become aware of and to accept the first thought or feeling that comes to mind as you go through the following questions.

What is something that you dislike about your current financial situation?

See if that's coming from wanting approval, control, or security.

Whichever want it is: *Could you let it go?*

What's something that you like about your current financial situation?

Does it come from wanting approval, control, or security?

Could you allow yourself to let it go?

What is something that you dislike about your current financial situation?

Does that come from wanting approval, control, or security?

Feel free to continue this line of questioning on your own, doing approximately nine repetitions on each paired layer of like and dislike.

When you're ready, let's switch gears.

Could you just allow yourself to embrace or welcome the way it is right now in your life in relationship to money? Even if it isn't the way that you'd necessarily choose or that you'd want to end up, if you can just embrace it the way it is, you've got a good platform for moving forward.

So, for the moment, could you allow yourself to embrace the way it is right now?

Let it be here? Know that it's okay?

The more you are free to allow yourself to accept it the

way it is, the more you can also move into action to have it be the way you choose.

Look at that again. *Could you just allow yourself to embrace, welcome, or let be however things are in your life in relationship to money at present?*

Your thoughts, your feelings, your attitudes, and your actions: *Could you, just for a moment, allow them to be the way they are, welcome them?*

Now, take a few moments to notice how differently you feel after doing the above three processes. Play with incorporating them into your daily life. For instance, when you notice that you're doing something the way your mother or father used to do it, and it's not the way you'd like to do it, let go of resisting it or wanting to change it, and see what happens. If you happen to notice a fear or a fleeting worry pass through your awareness, release it using the questions about approval, control, or security. Or simply let go of wanting the fear to happen. You can also do some focused work on likes and dislikes.

Finally, just allow yourself to welcome your financial situation the way it is. The more welcoming you can be, the more freedom you'll have to change it.

Cleaning Up on Money

Let's continue exploring the obstacles to you having what you want in life, the obstacles to having financial freedom. The Cleanup Procedure is an excellent tool for achieving resolution and equanimity with people; yet, it's also a very powerful means of improving your financial and business interactions.

Keep a few of things in mind. First, when you use this process, some of your releasing will happen spontaneously. Secondly, releasing is always just a choice, such as allowing the situation to be the way it is, is merely a choice. Thirdly, welcome whatever comes into your awareness as you work through this process. If you're ready, begin.

Have you ever felt that money tried to control you? Now this might seem to be a silly question, because money is an inanimate object, but you might feel that way.

Could you welcome your sense of wanting to control money back?

Then, could you let that go?

Did you try to control money? Most of us want to control money all the time. So, that's an easy one.

For right now, could you let go of wanting to control money?

Did money try to control you? Or did you ever feel controlled by money?

If so, could you let go of wanting to control it back?

Did you try to control money?

If so, could you let go of wanting to control money?

Did money try to control you, or did it feel that way? Have you ever felt victimized by, or at the mercy of, money?

Could you let go of wanting to control money?

Did you try to control money in any way?

If so, could you now let go of wanting to control money?

Could you grant money the right for money to be the way money is?

Remember, this last question is simply a decision, and, in

deciding to grant money the right to be the way it is, you'll be powerfully shifting your relationship to money.

Would you grant money the right to be the way money is, just for now?

Do you now grant money the right for money to be the way money is?

If you are able to do that, even a little, notice how much better you feel inside. If you answer "no," you obviously feel that there is more releasing to be done on the issue of control. Keep repeating the questions above until you let go. If you answer "yes," feel free to move on to the next section on approval.

Did you dislike or disapprove of anything in money, or anything about money?

If so, could you let go of withholding your approval for money?

Could you let go of that dislike or disapproval for it?

Did you feel somehow that money disliked or disapproved of anything in you? Now, I know that's a little bit of a stretch, but you might feel that way.

Could you let go of wanting approval from money?

Did you dislike or disapprove of anything in money?

Could you, just for now, let go of your dislike or disapproval for it?

Did it feel somehow that money disliked or disapproved of you, or was withholding in relationship to you? I know this might not make sense, but the feelings might be there, anyway.

Could you let go of wanting approval from money?

Did you dislike or disapprove of anything in money, anything about money?

Could you let go of wanting to withhold your approval for money?

Did it feel somehow that money disliked or disapproved of anything in you?

Could you let go of wanting approval?

Just for now, could you allow yourself to have only love and acceptance feelings towards money? Just could you?

Would you allow yourself to have only a sense of love and acceptance towards money?

Do you have only a feeling of love and acceptance towards money?

Remember this last question is a decision or choice. Again, notice how this little bit of releasing on approval in relationship to money has shifted your awareness some more. You may continue doing the approval questions if you need to, or move on and explore wanting security in relationship to money.

Did you somehow feel that money challenged, opposed, or threatened you in any way, or that anything about money did that?

If so, could you let go of wanting security or survival?

Did you challenge, oppose, or threaten money in any way?
Now, again, since money isn't a person, even though we do anthropomorphize it, this might be a little bit of a stretch. But, on a feeling level, you might feel that way.

Could you let go of wanting to challenge, oppose, or threaten money?

Did money challenge, oppose, or threaten you? Or did it feel that way?

If so, could you let go of wanting the security or survival that the feeling pulls up into your awareness?

Did you in some way challenge, oppose, or threaten money?

Could you let go of wanting to do that?

Did money challenge, oppose, or threaten you? Or did it feel that way?

If so, could you let go of wanting security or survival?

Did you challenge, oppose, or threaten money? Or did you want to? Could you simply allow that to release?

Could you allow yourself to have only a feeling of well-being, safety, and trust with money?

Would you allow yourself to have only a feeling of well-being, safety, and trust with money?

Do you have only a feeling of well-being, safety, and trust with money?

You may cycle back through these questions as much as you need to, until you can say "yes" to all three questions at the end. If you are able to do that, you'll see your whole feeling relationship to money shift. Even though money is an object and not a person, in our awareness, we feel in relationship to it. Releasing feelings about it in this way can really clear up a lot of static.

Julia: Freedom to Deserve the Best

Julia found the Method when she immigrated to Canada from Romania approximately ten years ago. It was a difficult transition. She was a single mother, had no money, and needed to learn two languages, since she was living in Quebec, both French and English. She also had financial problems. Her income doing manicures was about $900 a month, and her expenses equaled it. There was hardly any money left over for food, much less anything else. "With all my worries and suffering, it wasn't freedom," she says. "So, I was amazed once I started to learn the Sedona Method, as it was so easy and worked so fast. Four days after I let go of my resistance to my lack of abundance, I got a new customer from an Orthodox Jewish community. She found a tiny ad I'd placed in the phonebook. She sent me her mother, grandmother, nieces, and friends. In a month and a half, my business tripled. I was earning $2,000, and I didn't do anything but release."

Julia realized that her poverty consciousness was inherited from the attitudes people lived with in her native country. She subconsciously had a fear of becoming rich. *What are the advantages of being poor and being wealthy?* she'd ask. She noticed that when she spent money, it made her feel funny inside. She decided to reverse her habit of always buying the cheaper item on the store shelf. She kept releasing on deserving better, using questions such as: *Can I allow myself to remember the belief that I had no money?* and: *Can I remember how I used to believe that I couldn't have money?* She also saw that her attachment to money was based on wanting security/survival.

"Before releasing, we are chained and don't know it," says Julia. "After learning to release, we know that we are chained, and it's painful unless we let go. In my resistance, my solar plexus would hurt. But slowly it dissolved as I worked on my goals about financial security. Now, I feel peaceful, and my income is dependable."

The Advantages and Disadvantages of Money

Now, you're going to use the Advantages/Disadvantages Process to focus on having what you want in life. Remember to let go of both the advantages and the disadvantages. Releasing on both sides of the equation will pull the goal of financial freedom and abundance into your conscious awareness.

What is an advantage to you in having financial freedom or abundance?

Does that come from wanting approval, control, or security/survival?

Whichever want it is: *Could you allow yourself to let it go?*

What's a disadvantage to you in having financial freedom or abundance?

If none comes up, release on that. Then, determine if there's any sense of wanting approval, control, or security underneath it.

Whichever want it is: *Could you allow it to release?*

Remember, if you don't feel like you have financial freedom or abundance in your life now, there are probably hidden disadvantages to having financial freedom or abundance. So, stay as open to this process as you can, and allow yourself to focus on whatever thought or feeling first comes to mind. Then release it. Until you uncover the hidden disadvantages, they'll keep running your life.

What's an advantage to you in having financial freedom or abundance?

Does that come from wanting approval, control, or security?

Could you allow yourself to let it go?

What's a disadvantage to you in having financial freedom and abundance?

Check to see if it pertains to wanting approval, control, or security.

Could you just set the want free?

Repeat the advantages and disadvantages questions in alternation a minimum of nine times before stopping, making sure to

"I had worked for Fortune 500 companies for 25 years, and felt that I lost myself. I had always wanted to go into business for myself, cut the umbilical cord from the Mother Ship, so to speak. Someone gave me a Sedona Method tape set, which I threw into my car and listened to for a year. During this time, I went out on my own and wasn't afraid to do it. I simply believed that prosperity would come to me, and it has—miraculously. I can't explain it. I'm working less hard and making more money, and I'm more at peace, while doing things I love to do. I credit it to the Method, because nothing else has changed in my life."

—Rick Forrest,
Claremont, CA

release on every layer. As I have already mentioned, I have sometimes done advantages and disadvantages on a single topic for more than an hour at a sitting. In fact, many times even longer than that. Because each advantage and disadvantage together form a whole layer of feeling about that particular topic, as you let them go, you will be getting closer to having the financial freedom and abundance that you've always wanted.

Visualizing Your Ideal Finances

Allow yourself to visualize what your life would be like if you achieved total financial freedom and abundance. Remember to engage all your senses on every level. Your "picture" may be visual, kinesthetic, or auditory. But paint a vivid picture of having all the money that you've always wanted, complete financial freedom, and phenomenal abundance. Really experience it deeply and fully.

Then check to see if there is anything inside of you right now that's saying, "No, I can't have it." "I shouldn't have it." "It's not here." "It's not possible." Or any other thought or feeling contrary to your imagery.

Underneath that opposition, do you want approval, control, or security?

Could you release the want, just for now?

Go back to allowing yourself to picture having abundance NOW, having financial freedom NOW. Imagine it in this moment. See what that looks like, feel what that feels like, and hear what that sounds like.

Check to see if there are any thoughts or feelings to the contrary.

Then see if there is a sense of wanting approval, control, or security in association with those thoughts or feelings.

Then, could you let that go?

Again, allow yourself to visualize having financial freedom and abundance.

What is your life like now that you have it?

See if that comes from wanting approval, wanting control, or wanting security.

Could you let that go?

See if there is any wanting in the picture itself.

If there is, could you just allow that to be released?

Again, allow yourself to picture financial freedom and abundance in your life now. Check to see if there is anything inside you that's still holding back or resisting the image, or saying you "can't" or "shouldn't" have it.

If there is, does it come from wanting approval, control, or security?

Whichever want it is: *Could you allow yourself to let it go?*

Again, allow yourself to picture financial freedom and

abundance NOW. Know that it's okay to have it.

Could you just allow yourself to welcome that picture fully into your awareness? Embrace it, nurture it, and let it be here.

Allow yourself to rest in the knowing that it's okay to have this, and that it is NOW. Simply allow yourself to accept financial freedom and abundance into your life, knowing that you deserve it.

Setting Goals and Taking Action Steps

I highly recommend that you write a goal statement for what you'd like to create in the area of wealth. The Goal Process will liberate you by helping you hold in mind what you truly desire while letting go of all your feelings that are contrary to it. As always, please remember to keep working with releasing as you begin taking action steps to attain your financial goals. As you release on the activities that you may take, or those you actually do take, you'll find that you create results much more easily than before. (More details about this process appear in Chapter 8, Setting and Attaining Your Goals.)

A Final Idea

Reread this chapter often. The more you work with this material, the more you'll get out of it. As you begin to accept deeply that you're entitled to have financial freedom and security, the more you'll naturally move into a positive attitude about your abundance.

Chapter 17

Relationship Magic

Have you ever wondered why some intimate relationships work and others don't? Why so many of us seem to have the same relationships with a series of different people? Why some people can easily find a mate while others struggle? The answer to these and other frequently asked questions are contained in this mini-course on intimate relationships. The exercises, perspectives, and processes in this chapter can and will accelerate the process of you uncovering and living your natural loving nature.

The explanation for most vexing relationship questions is actually quite simple. The majority of our relationships, as well as our patterns of relating in general, are based on need rather than love. This is probably no surprise to you. However, it may surprise you that there is something you can do about it—and you already know what that is: release. Every feeling except love is a non-love feeling. Because your basic nature is the love that you seek in and from others, each time you let go using the Sedona Method, you're freeing yourself of non-love feelings and becoming more outwardly and inwardly loving. The more loving you are, the more successful your relationships can be—and the more attractive you will be to the perfect partner. It is that simple. All the releasing you're already doing, and will do in this chapter, will improve your current and future relationships.

Stop Looking for Love in All the Wrong Places

Most of us are on a quest for love that amounts to trying to fill a leaky cup. Every time we appear to get love from an external source, especially from another person, it merely reinforces the belief that love can be found outside us. So, the feeling of receiving love or approval inherently has "leakage." Common leaks include the fear of losing love, resentment towards the people we feel we need to get it from, and the simple act of looking away from the love that we, by nature, already are.

Good news. You can turn each of these dilemmas around simply by letting go of wanting love or approval. You can also hasten the process by looking for mutual ways to love—as opposed to getting it—and mutual ways to give love, in addition to receiving it. If you're in any kind of an intimate relationship—with a life partner, friend, or family member—and you can reach the point where you simply love the other person as he or she is, as best you can, then both of you can relax and be authentic with each other. This promotes much healthier, more satisfactory interactions.

There are a few important keys to improving relationships that are often overlooked. One is mutuality. If you are doing something internally or externally that is not mutual with your partner, it will only frustrate you both. Here is a simple example taken from my relationship with my wife. I used to enjoy only seeing "guy flicks," and Amy only wanted to see "chick flicks." It caused a dilemma with our TV watching and movie-going. Instead of trying to impose our will on each other, or assuming that one of us had to sacrifice for the other, which wouldn't have been a mutual solution, we openly discussed the issue, released our feelings about it, and began to identify movies that we both could enjoy. In fact, because we released to gain mutuality, we both are now more open to the other's tastes in movies and rarely disagree about our choices. When we do disagree, we simply go to see the movie our partner chose, if we feel mutual, or we go alone or with another friend. Either way, we're both a lot happier. I even enjoy most chick flicks now as much as I enjoy guy flicks. Amy likewise enjoys some guy flicks.

To be truly nurturing and supportive, love must also come without strings. The more you can give of yourself and give your caring without wanting anything in return, the happier you will be. Instead, what most of us do in relationship is barter. "I'll do this for you, if you do that for me." In commerce, bartering can be great; however, true love is much more than a business deal.

True love or caring should always be supportive of both partners. If one is giving to the other at personal expense, it is not giving. Such situations can turn codependent or even abusive. So, when you give, make sure you're giving something that is wanted as well as something that you also enjoy giving. Now, this doesn't mean that you must always do what the other partner wants; neither does it mean that you must only do what you want. It means that you allow yourselves to explore ways of relating that are mutually beneficial.

You will be way ahead of the game if you follow these few guidelines in your intimate relationships.

What If Your Partner Is Already Perfect?

If you've ever been in a romantic relationship, you probably experienced what most people call the "honeymoon phase." Unless your relationship is brand-new, the kind of love, caring, and enjoyment that you experienced during that phase is probably only a memory by now. So, what's the difference between what you may be longingly looking back to as your honeymoon and what you are experiencing now? Simple: in the beginning of the relationship, you loved and accepted your partner *as your partner was.* You may even have loved your partner because he or she was a certain way, even if that way—or those certain qualities—now drives you crazy.

Where a relationship can sour is at a point when your partner says or does something, or behaves in a particular way that you inwardly refuse to accept. You then start resisting that particular behavior or trait, while at the same time expecting the person to exhibit it again. As I mentioned in Chapter 8, we start these informal internal lists of the things we want to change—or resist—about our partner, and then we start comparing everything they do to that internal list. If it matches, we add an inner check mark and resist it even more. Once we start this list, we are also constantly looking for items to add to it. This whole process usually spirals out of control and ends in separation, divorce, or in simply putting up with a relationship that is no longer supportive of both partners.

There is a simple way to break this pattern and extend your honeymoon for the rest of your lives. First of all, burn your list. Unless you're determined to destroy your current relationship, continuing to add to and tweak your list is merely asking for trouble. Get into the habit of looking for what you can love and appreciate about your partner, rather than how they need to change or be fixed, and it will change the whole dynamic of your relationship. This is not a substitute for loving communication about things that your partner does that you would prefer he or she not do. Nor is it an excuse to allow your partner or you to continue indulging in obviously destructive behaviors. It is merely a way to start to tip the balance back to the way it was when you were enjoying your honeymoon. The Like/Dislikes Process is also an excellent "list burner."

Let me describe how this has worked in my marriage. As I mentioned, we all tend to create inner lists of what our partner has done wrong or has done to offend us. We then expect our partner to keep making the same mistake, and we, of course, get to be right when they do it again. After a while, it becomes more important to us to cling to the false security of being right than to nurture the love that attracted our partner to us in the first place. The difference between this pattern, which most of us fall into, and the "honeymoon" stage of a relationship in which our partner seems to do no wrong is simply what we are focusing on and expecting.

What's happened over the past eleven years of being with my wife is that the lists of offenses and wrongs just keep dissolving. Yes, Amy has tendencies that I don't like at times, and I have character traits that she doesn't like, but neither one of us holds that against the other. We're simply right in the moment with each other, finding ways to be with each other as we are now, releasing our hurts and expectations. We share unlimited possibilities for loving each other. I love Amy even more now than I did in the "honeymoon stage" of our relationship.

The Disagreement Dissolver

Several years ago, Amy and I facilitated a couples' course at a resort in Jamaica. The following exercise was one of the more powerful tools we used there to help couples dissolve their disagreements and come to a place of greater mutuality. It is based on the principle of seeing an issue from the other person's point of view, of "walking in your partner's shoes." When you get even a glimpse of your partner's point of view in any particular disagreement, it becomes very difficult to maintain the conflict. The following exercise is a quick, fun way to do just that.

The guidelines for this exercise are simple. Do it full out, without censoring, and without doing anything that is either physically or emotionally hurtful to your partner. Pick a topic that you both have been struggling with and would like to resolve.

Step 1: Both partners argue full out for their own points of view. Do this with as much feeling and import as possible. However, there is one important qualifier: you may only use the word "blah." Do not use any other words. Simply argue the way you usually do—even exaggerate a little—yet avoid actual language.

Keep arguing until you both feel you have gotten your point across to the best of your abilities. Then, take a few

moments to release whatever this activity has stirred up
before going to Step 2.

Step 2: Now, both partners argue each other's points of
view. This time use words and allow yourself to step into your
partner's shoes as much as possible. Argue as thoroughly for
your partner's point of view as you argued for your own. As
best you can, feel and express your partner's emotions—even
use your partner's mannerisms.

Keep arguing like this until you have both run out of
things to say. Then take a few moments to release whatever
this activity has stirred up.

Step 3: Share what you've discovered with your partner.
Take as much time as you need to talk through and release
together on any feelings, thoughts, insights, and beliefs that
arose during this exercise. I promise that if you're like the people who were on this couples course, the many others who
have successfully worked with this exercise since then, and my
wife and me, you'll be amazed and delighted by the results you
can achieve from doing this exercise whenever you are stuck in
opposing points of view.

Releasing to Support Relationships

In the remainder of this chapter, we're going to apply the
principles and processes described in Part One of this book to
issues pertaining to our intimate relationships. As you work
through the following exercises, you can focus on a relationship that you'd like to improve, a past relationship that you'd
like to complete, or on having a new relationship that's truly

appropriate for you. Even if you only explore a few of the activities described in this chapter, you will easily join the ranks of thousands of people who've already improved relationships by releasing.

Going Beyond Your Parents

In addition to the area of money, our parents color the way we view the act of relationship. They're our earliest models, due both to the way they related to each other (if they weren't single parents) and to how they related to you. So, to begin achieving complete freedom in your relationships, start by focusing on your relationship with your parents, or on theirs with each other.

Is there anything about it that you're resisting or want to change, or anything about it that you've used as a model for yourself?

Does that stir up wanting approval, control, or security?

Whichever want it is: *Could you allow yourself to let it go?*

Find something about your relationship, either with both of your parents, or one parent, or in their relationship with each other that you'd like to change.

Could you let go of wanting to change it?

Is there something else about your relationship with your parents, or with their relationship to each other, that you'd like to change?

If so, could you let go of wanting to change it?

Look at that again. See if there is something about either your relationship with one of your parents or their relationship with each other that you didn't like, or you don't like, and that you'd like to change.

340

Could you let go of wanting to change it?

Now, is anything else about your relationship with your parents, or their relationship with each other, that has somehow colored all your relationships in this lifetime? Keep in mind that you're either living in resistance to those early relationships, or you've modeled yourself after them—even if they didn't work.

Of course, you may have had a very healthy relationship with your parents. So doing some releasing on it now can only make it better.

See what your overall feeling is about your relationship with your parents and about their relationship with each other. *Underneath, does that come from wanting approval, control, or security?*

Whichever want it is: *Could you allow yourself to let it go?*

Now, also check to see if there's anything about your early relationships with your peers, your first friends, that you don't like or that you would like change.

If so, could you let go of wanting to change it?

Is there anything else about your early relationships with your peers that you'd like to change? Maybe you felt shy, or it was difficult to relate to the children with whom you grew up. *Perhaps there was something else about your early relationships with your peers that you resist now?*

Is there any sense of wanting approval, control, or security now about it?

If so, could you allow yourself to let it go?

I highly recommend that you continue releasing on your relationship with your parents, their relationship with each other, and on the early relationships you had with your peers.

These first relationships are where most of our adult patterns were initiated. By doing some clean up now, everything in your experience can shift.

Claire: Creating Safety in Her Relationship

"A lot of people have serial relationships with the same guy with a different face," says Claire. "For me, it was a projection of my father—an imagined person from the past. He kept showing up for me in my relationships." The Sedona Method helped her enormously in forgiving him and feeling safe with him. As a result, she was able to begin truly being with the man she was actually with instead of reacting to her father's specter. Once she let go of wanting approval, control, and security—and especially wanting to change what was— she took a tremendous leap forward.

"Now I have a love that I never thought I could have, because I could never perceive people's love for me. Both my partner and I use the Sedona Method, and it has helped tremendously in moving through the issues that came up for us at the beginning. Once I practiced deep forgiveness with myself and with others, I started loving myself more and was not as self-destructive."

Going from Fear to Love

Fear is also something that holds us back in the area of relationship. We might be afraid to commit, afraid of intimacy, or afraid of being hurt. But if you dig a little deeper, when you release on that fear, you'll see that you are liberated to be fully present in the relationships that you're in now, or to find and have that perfect someone. Remember that there's a secret way of letting go of fear, a shortcut that you can use in addition to letting go of wanting approval, control, and security (see Chapter 13, The Secret of Letting Go of Fear and Anxiety). So, let's do some focused releasing on fear now.

What is something you fear might happen, either in this current relationship or in your ideal relationship?

What are you afraid of about relationships, or in this relationship?

Could you let go of wanting that to happen?

Find something else that you're afraid will happen either in this current relationship or in relationships in general.

Could you let go of wanting that to happen?

Repeat these questions four or five more times, welcoming

"I have taken other courses that left me feeling confused and threatened in some ways, but the Sedona Method did more for me than any of those. I became aware of how I was sabotaging my relationships by wanting control, wanting approval, and wanting security. I shared the course with a very close friend who listened to the tapes and then took the Seven-day Retreat. The growth I've experienced myself, and the growth that I've witnessed in him, has changed our lives. We continually get closer and help each other."

—Chari Paulson,
Houston, TX

any fears that come up and releasing on them. This is an area that you can continue releasing on during the day. When you notice that you're afraid something might happen in your current relationship, or in the relationship you are considering, catch it in the moment. See if you can just let go of wanting that fear to be manifested.

Please understand that your fear may not be something that you desire consciously. But, as subconscious fears are "I owe you's" for those things to happen, it really behooves you to let go of any fears you may have about relationship.

The Likes/Dislikes Process

Let's explore the various attachments and aversions that may be keeping a particular relationship stuck, or keeping you stuck in general about forming satisfying relationships. There are two points to remember about likes and dislikes. First, alternately release on both sides of the equation. Do one like followed by one dislike, and so on. Secondly, if you can't think of something you like or dislike in the moment, release on your feelings about that and keep going. Each pair of likes and dislikes forms a whole layer of limitation that you're dissolving about that particular topic.

So, what's something that you like about relationship, either the one you're in right now, one from the past, or one that you're anticipating?

Does that stir up a sense of wanting approval, control, or security?

Whichever want it is: *Could you allow yourself to let it go?*

Think of something that you dislike about your current relationship, a past relationship, or an anticipated future relationship.

Does that stir up wanting approval, control, or security?

Whichever want it is: *Could you just set it free?*

What do you like about relationship?

Is that about wanting approval, control, or security?

344

Could you allow yourself to let it go?

What do you dislike about relationship?

Does that come from wanting approval, control, or security?

Could you allow yourself to let it go?

Repeat the questions above four or five more times, releasing as you go. This process is a powerful way of dissolving the attachments and aversions that prevent you from having your ideal relationship.

Accepting What Is

As I have already mentioned, accepting your partner just as your partner is will help you to open to the love you've been seeking.

Could you simply allow yourself to welcome your current relationship if you have one? Could you embrace what's happened in the past and also whatever might come in your future?

Can you allow yourself to embrace what is now? Just let it be here?

The most dynamic source from which to create anything you want in your life is the sense that everything is perfectly okay the way it is right now. This doesn't mean that you might not choose something different were you given a choice. But when you can welcome, accept, embrace, or allow what is in this moment, it gives you tremendous power to shift the energy of your relationship both to being in love with it as it is, and to open yourself to an even more positive relationship.

So, could you allow yourself to embrace what is right now in your relationship?

Could you allow it to be the way it is?

Know that it's okay as it is—in that knowingness lies the possibility for something even better.

Could you allow yourself to relax in this moment, knowing that all is well?

Not only will you feel better the more you can relax and just be in this moment, you'll also be in a much better place for relationship. I'm sure you've noticed that the people you like to be around are relaxed inside. They're not tense or uptight. The more you can relax and be your authentic self in every moment throughout the day, the more you will improve your relationships. Being relaxed and at ease is natural, and it's always available to you just below the surface every time you let go.

Take a moment to notice how much better you feel now about relationships than you did only a few minutes ago, and how much better you feel about any specific relationship that you were working on.

The Cleanup Procedure

The Cleanup Procedure is one of the most powerful tools I know for improving relationships. It can help you transform even the most difficult situations by bringing you back to a place of loving equilibrium.

I have modified the process that follows from the process taught to you in Chapter 11 by adding a fourth series of questions on separation. These are specifically designed to help you get closer to the people that you care about.

You need to remember a few things when you're working. First, welcome the feelings that are stirred up in your awareness when I ask such questions as: *Did this person try to control you?*

Notice that the sense of wanting control simply dissolves when welcomed. Secondly, the third question in each set of questions is just a decision. Thirdly, you're doing the release for you. You're not doing it for your partner or potential partner. The Cleanup Procedure is a tool to help you achieve the freedom you desire in relationship.

Begin by making yourself comfortable and focusing inwardly. Select a person to clean up on. This could be someone with whom you're currently in a relationship, someone from the past, a potential mate, or even one of your parents. As I already mentioned in Chapter 11, one of the most significant ways I supported my developing freedom was doing the Cleanup Procedure on my mother. We had a pretty good relationship by then, but we didn't have such a great history. When I did this process on my mother, it not only changed my relationship with her and everyone else, it also changed my relationship with my feelings about myself.

So, think of the person that you'd like to do some releasing on right now, someone with whom you'd like to improve your relationship. Or, if you're not in a relationship right now, clean up on a difficult relationship from the past. Allow yourself to picture this individual. See them in your mind's eye, using your dominant senses. You could feel them, see them, or possibly hear a narration about them.

Did this person try to control you?

If so, could you let go of wanting to control them back?

Did you try to control this person?

If so, could you now let go of wanting to control them?

Repeat as many times as needed, and then, when you are ready, move on to the third question in this series: *Could you grant this person the right to be the way this person is? Just could you?*

Would you grant this person the right to be the way this person is?

Do you now grant this person the right to be the way this person is?

Remember, this is just a decision. It is choosing freedom.

Did you dislike or disapprove of anything in this person?

If so, could you let go of withholding your love from this person?

Did this person dislike or disapprove of anything in you?

If so, could you let go of wanting them to approve of you?

Repeat the approval questions above as many times as needed. Then, when you are ready, move on to the third question: *Could you have only love or acceptance feelings for this person? Just could you?*

Would you allow yourself to accept or love him/her? Again, remember that it's just a choice.

Do you now have only love feelings for this person?

If the answer is "yes," move on.

Did this person challenge, oppose, or threaten you?

Does this stir up any sense of wanting security or survival within you?

If it did, see if you can just let it go.

Did you challenge, oppose, or threaten this person?

If so, could you let go of wanting to challenge, oppose, or threaten him/her?

Did this person challenge, oppose or threaten you?

If so, could you let go of the wanting security or survival it may have stirred up?

Did you challenge, oppose, or threaten this person?

If so, could you let go of wanting to protect yourself in that way?

Cycle through these questions as many times as needed. When you're ready, move on to the third question in the series: *Could you allow yourself to have only a feeling of well-being, a feeling of safety and trust with this person? Just could you?*

Would you allow yourself to have only a feeling of well-being, safety, and trust with this person?

Do you now have only a feeling of well-being, safety, and trust with this person?

If the answer to this question is "yes," please move on.

Did this person reject you, cut off from you, push you away, or in any way try to be separate from you?

If so, could you let go of wanting to be one with him/her?

Did you reject, cut off, push away, or in any way try to be separate from this person?

If so, could you let go of rejecting him/her and wanting to be separate?

Cycle through these questions as many times as needed. When you're ready, move on to the third question in the series: *Now, could you allow yourself to have a feeling of oneness with this person, a feeling of "you are me"? Just could you?*

Would you allow yourself to have only a feeling of oneness, a feeling of "you are me" with this person?

Do you have only a feeling of oneness, a feeling of "you are me" with this person?

Remember, this is merely a choice. If the answer is "yes," you can rest. If you're not sure, you may want to do some more releasing before stopping.

Advantages and Disadvantages

The Advantages/Disadvantages Process is another powerful way of releasing on your relationships. Use this technique if:

- You are happily relating to your partner, as this can make you feel even better.
- You have the possibility for a relationship, but you're not absolutely sure whether or not to pursue the connection.
- You want to gain resolution about a past relationship.

Let's work through some advantages and disadvantages now.

Begin by focusing on a current relationship, a past relationship, or on having the ideal relationship. Ask: *What is the advantage to you in this relationship?*

Underneath, is there a sense of wanting approval, control, or security/survival?

Whichever want it is: *Could you set it free?*

What's a disadvantage to you in this relationship?

Is there a sense of wanting approval, control, or security/survival?

Whichever want it is: *Could you set it free?*

What is the advantage to you in having the relationship be this way?

Does this stir up wanting approval, control, or security?

Could you just let it go?

What's a disadvantage to you in having the relationship be this way?

Does this stir up wanting approval, control, or security?

Could you simply release it?

Repeat this series of questions and releases at least nine

times before stopping to get beyond the obvious answers and reveal new insights. Then, I encourage you to continue working on the Advantages/Disadvantages Process in the near future. It truly has the power to transform any area of a relationship where you're feeling stuck or would like to experience more freedom.

The Oneness-Separation Paradigm

The desire to be separate, and its opposite, wanting to be one, are great points of release in the area of relationship. For, in a relationship, there's usually one person who always wants to get closer, and there's one person who's pushing away. Sometimes couples trade off, but, no matter which side you're on in your relationship, you can release. You can let go of wanting to be closer and, as a result, you'll find yourself closer. You can let go of wanting to be separate, and you'll find yourself being comfortable the way it is.

"The greatest gift of the Method is to be there when I'm there. I'm more in the NOW than ever before. I've discovered that my wants fall mostly into the categories of approval and security, which is a holdover from childhood. To let that go—my God, that's terrific! My sex life has improved, because I don't have to be a performer. It is so much better. That's worth the price of admission right there. My wife got happy, and I didn't know why. Boy, that's a blinding flash of the obvious."

—R.F., California

Be on the lookout for the sense of wanting to be one, and the sense of wanting to be separate, in your relationships.

You'll discover that consistent releasing on this issue changes your relationships for the better.

William: Nothing Seems All that Serious Anymore

William and his wife Emily have been together for six years and, as he jokes, "We both seem to be pretty good at fighting." Before they learned the Sedona Method, they'd get embroiled in ugly energy for days and even weeks. They'd get invested in it and become blinded to what was going on. But the more they released, the more they were able to recognize that they were like two kids acting out by being angry, upset, and unresponsive. Once they'd mutually realized it, a few times they actually started to fight and burst out laughing almost immediately. It seemed so ridiculous.

"At the last Seven-day Retreat we went on, we were leaving our hotel and driving to the course one morning and got involved in a disagreement," William reports. "As we drove, both of us simultaneously got to the point where we were almost out of our bodies and looking at the person (ourselves) engaged in the argument." They broke out in laughter together at that moment.

"You see," says William, "nothing is all that serious. All the stuff that used to be subject matter for huge fights that engaged us for hours, days, and weeks doesn't have the same impact anymore."

Picturing Your Ideal Relationship

Make yourself comfortable and begin focusing on what your ideal relationship looks like. Remember, when you "visualize" anything, as best you can, use all your senses. Combine mental pictures with physical sensations and sounds, and even include aromas if that helps to enhance your imagery.

So, how would the relationship that you're in right now be, if it were perfect? Or, what would be your ideal relationship in general? Allow yourself to picture what that looks like, engaging as many of your senses as you can.

What does your ideal relationship look like, feel like, and sound like?

Now, is there anything inside of you that says, "No, you can't or shouldn't have it," or, "You don't have it"?

Does that come from wanting approval, control, or security/survival?

Whichever want it is: *Could you let it go?*

Again, picture having your ideal relationship here and now. *What does it look like, feel like, and sound like?* Engage all your senses. Make the image as vivid as you can.

This time, see if an idea, thought, or belief arises that says, "You can't have that," or, "You shouldn't have that," or, "You'll never have that," or, "It's not possible."

Does the thought come from a sense of wanting approval, control, or security?

Could you set it free?

Now, picture your ideal relationship again. *Could you just allow it to be?* Know that it's okay to have the ideal relationship and, at the same time, embrace however it is in this moment in the relationship. Allow yourself to relax and be at ease with relationship. Let it be okay here and now.

If you feel any holdbacks to having the ideal relationship, could you just set them free and know that you are okay right now?

In addition to visualization, you will benefit from doing the Goals Process on your relationship issues (see Chapter 8).

Releasing Improves All Kinds of Relationships

The techniques you've just seen applied in this chapter to romantic relationships are equally useful in relating to your children, parents, friends, colleagues, and anyone else. Consider how you might begin to incorporate these forms of releasing into all of your human interactions. I promise that every relationship—including the one you have with yourself—will be vastly improved and become a source of joy and comfort.

Chapter 18

Developing Radiant Health

In the mid 1970's, when the Sedona Method was first being taught, it wasn't generally recognized that illness is often aggravated or directly caused by suppressed emotions and stress. Today, the mind/body connection is so widely accepted by healthcare professionals that many commonly prescribed treatment regimens include a level of emotional support. Although my associates and I would never attempt to treat, diagnose, cure, or even advise people about their specific health issues, developing more radiant health and physical well-being is one of the most frequently reported gains from using the Sedona Method.

Most of the suffering, if not all, that accompanies physical disease derives from our emotional reactions to what our bodies are experiencing. For instance, have you ever had physical pain and found that you were not affected by it on one occasion, but, under similar circumstances on a separate occasion, the same type or amount of pain caused you extreme distress? If you are like most of us, you probably answered "yes." Why does this happen? Our term for illness contains a clue: dis-ease.

Too often, we do not feel at ease inside our bodies. We often make judgments about a specific physical problem we have. Perhaps we've even heard from others that we somehow caused it, and we've interpreted the problem as personally generated. Or maybe we believe we're being punished for "wrong" behavior. In these ways, we cause ourselves unnecessary suffering based on the condition of the body.

There is a bittersweet joke in consciousness raising circles (mind-over-matter groups), which sheds light on the kinds of beliefs mentioned above. "Somehow it is noble to die . . . but God forbid you should get sick." Sickness indicates that you have somehow failed.

I do not subscribe to this philosophy.

Even the bodies of saints, sages, and those who are emotionally healthy get sick and die. So, why give ourselves such a hard time? If you have an illness, don't add to it by judging yourself poorly for having that particular condition. Yes, due to the mind/body link, the healthier you are on an emotional level, the less likely you are to experience disease in the body. However, there are no guarantees that emotional wellness will enhance your physical health. Sometimes physical pain can be released by using the Sedona Method, and we'll explore several ways to do so later in this chapter. Nonetheless, even when our pain or other symptoms persist, it is always possible to let go of our emotional reactions to them, and therefore ease our suffering.

This chapter, which is a mini-course on physical well-being, is divided into two major sections: the first describes a five-step process for coping with illness and discomfort; and the second shows how to use techniques such as

356

Likes/Dislikes, Advantages/Disadvantages, the Cleanup Procedure, and Visualization for releasing on health in general and the body.

If you are currently undergoing treatment for a physical ailment, please do not change your regimen without first consulting your physician, therapist, or other medical practitioner. The processes described here are intended only as emotional support. In addition, if you believe you could have a physical condition that requires professional assistance, it is important to consult a healthcare practitioner before you begin working on the following material.

Now, let's proceed.

Five Steps for Coping with Illness and Discomfort

This five-step process is useful for releasing on issues such as those pertaining to illness, injury, appearance, and weight loss, to name only a few. In fact, these steps are effective with almost anything you would consider a problem. As mentioned in Chapter 13, you can also adapt these steps very easily and effectively to cover psychological conditions for which you may be receiving clinical treatment, such as depression, panic disorder, bipolar disorder, etc. The techniques are inclusive and aimed at helping you love and accept yourself as a whole body/mind/spirit, no matter what you've "got."

1. Be Open to the Possibility of Healing

As I've already stated, the Sedona Method does not promise a cure for any physical ailment. That being said, be as open as you can to the possibility that shifting your thoughts and emotions can bring about positive shifts on a physical level.

Such results are well documented. In other words: To change your body, change your mind. Before I work with anyone on a physical issue in one of our classes, the first thing I do is check whether they're open to this possibility, or whether they have doubts about it.

You do the same now. Take a moment to check within yourself and find out if you are open to the possibility that releasing your emotions can improve your physical health. If you are, great! Simply read on. If you are not open—if there is any doubt in your mind at all—check in again to determine which sense of wanting the doubt comes from (approval, control, or safety). Then, let it go.

Believe it or not, this step can make an enormous impact on your releasing process, as it cuts through resistance like a warm knife through butter. I have seen people let go of long-standing issues just in the process of accepting that it was possible.

2. Love Yourself as You Are

When you see that you are giving yourself a hard time for having a physical problem, do a brief exercise.

First, notice the disapproval, and then simply ask yourself: *Could I let go of disapproving of myself?* Then, let go of disapproving of yourself as best you can. Continue until you have released your disapproval. Afterwards, take the process a step further by giving yourself approval *for no reason.*

When you catch yourself disapproving of the part of your body that is causing you distress, ask yourself: *Could I let go of disapproving of my*_____ *(body part)?* Then, shower the body part with as much love as you can in that moment. This extremely simple technique works wonders, I assure you.

The more you let go of disapproving of yourself and your body, and the more you get in the habit of giving yourself approval for no reason, the happier and more alive you will feel, which will also definitely help you in any healing process.

3. Going from Why's to Wise

Often, a physical problem persists because we get lost in trying to figure out why we have the problem or what it is. As I have already mentioned, the only reason we ever truly want to understand "why" about any type of problem is that we're planning to experience it again in the future. The future could be tomorrow, next week, or five minutes from now. We suffer less when we let go of planning ahead to feel poorly.

Of course, I am not suggesting that you ignore a medical condition. If you have an issue that could require medical attention, please get it promptly.

Allow yourself to go beyond obsessing about your condition by asking: *Would you rather understand why you feel sick or just feel better?* If you would rather "just feel better," then let go of wanting to figure it out. Leave that to the experts.

Now, some people also have a fear of doctors and other people resist asking for help in any form, both of which can interfere with receiving appropriate health care.

If you do have a fear of doctors or medical procedures, you can simply release on this by asking yourself: *How do I feel about doctors, hospitals, and medical procedures?* Allow yourself to welcome whatever thoughts, feelings, or pictures arise in consciousness in response to the question.

Then ask yourself: *Does that come from wanting approval, wanting to control, or wanting security or survival?*

Whichever want it is, ask: *Could I let it go?*

Keep cycling through these questions until you feel freer about doctors, hospitals, medical procedures, and nurturing or support in general. In and of itself, this can promote healing and promote clearer communication between you and your health care professionals and others that care about and for you.

4. Going Beyond the Diagnosis

Another area where people often get stuck when working on a physical or psychological problem (see Chapter 13) is the diagnosis itself. Once we hear from an expert that we have a particular diagnosis, such as cancer, heart disease, or anxiety disorder, to name only a few, these diagnoses can become self-fulfilling predictions. After all, we've paid professionals, experts, to give us their best idea of what is wrong with us, and what to do about it, so it makes sense to accept and go along with them, doesn't it?

I highly encourage you to follow your physician's advice, yet simultaneously remain open to the possibility that your condition can change for the better, above and beyond whatever your professional can do for you. For too many of us, a diagnosis can become an obsession. We then use our expectation of recurring symptoms as a mantra for a new fear-based meditation.

A great way to facilitate releasing your expectations for further problems and suffering is to see the problem as a memory, as described in Chapter 12, Putting It All Together (see page 268). Here's how to do this:

First, ask: *Could I allow myself to remember how I used to believe I had _____ (your diagnosis)?*

This question may shift your consciousness and make you laugh. It may make you tingle inside. Or it may simply open the possibility in your awareness that, "Yes, even *this* is just a memory."

Next ask: *Would I like to change that from the past?*

If the answer is "yes," ask: *Could I let go of wanting to change that from the past?* And let go to the best of your ability.

Even if the answer is "no," move on to the next step.

The completion question in this series is: *Could I let go of wanting to believe I have _____ (your diagnosis)?*

Then do your best to let the belief go.

Check in with yourself emotionally again. If you are still clinging slightly to the memory of the problem in the NOW, repeat the steps from the beginning until you can fully let go.

As you work from this perspective more and more, you'll find it easier and easier to let go, even of what once seemed to be immutable physical or emotional issues.

5. Letting Go of Your Physical Pain and Symptoms

Now that you've taken the first four steps to relieve your suffering (you've opened up to the possibility of the problem changing, you've given yourself approval instead of disapproval, you've let go of wanting to figure out your condition, and you've let go of believing in your illness or discomfort), there may be nothing left. Just in case there is, and so that you'll know how to handle any physical issues that arise in the future, let's explore two easy ways of working directly on symptoms.

The first effective way to work on a physical symptom is to use the basic process of the Method. First, simply notice how you feel about having this particular problem. Then, identify whether the feeling comes from wanting approval, control, or security. Finally, allow yourself to let it go. Very often, it's our feelings about our symptoms that lock them into place. As you've already learned, it's also our feelings about our symptoms (the condition of the body) that cause our suffering. So, even if a symptom or pain persists after you've released on it, you'll still feel a lot better inside.

Another powerful way to let go of a physical symptom is to alternate between feeling it fully and then feeling the emptiness or space that surrounds and interpenetrates it. I have seen people let go of even the most intense and long-standing symptom just by practicing this simple technique. In one of our Seven-day Retreats, a man who'd been on morphine for over two years to manage severe back pain had it clear up completely after only a few minutes—no more than five or six—of this type of letting go.

As with embracing our emotions, being willing to feel a symptom as much as you do can provide you a lot of relief. Part of why our symptoms persist and seem to get magnified is that we resist having them. Welcoming our feelings and sensations is always a powerful first step. We can then take the process a step further by becoming aware of the underlying stillness or beingness that allows for all positive and negative experience. By acknowledging this underlying spaciousness, we tend to dissolve whatever emotions and symptoms appear on the surface of our awareness.

So, simply switch back and forth between welcoming the sensations associated with your symptom and then feeling and acknowledging the space that surrounds and interpenetrates it. As you do this, you'll watch pain and other symptoms quickly and effortlessly dissolve.

Duke: Freedom from Seeking Sympathy

Duke had been suffering from chronic fatigue syndrome for six years before he learned the Sedona Method. The main symptom of his disease, beside a deep exhaustion, was a nearly constant aching in his arms, feet, and legs. As you can imagine, he took a lot of painkillers during this period, but there wasn't much else medicine could do to give him relief. He was excited to learn that the Method could possibly reduce his pain.

"After I took the Basic Course, every time I had another pain, I would release on it," Duke says. "I'd sit down and focus my attention on the actual pain itself, and go through a process first of allowing it to be there. Then I'd release it. Automatically resisting the pain and trying to get rid of it had always made me feel upset in the past. Now, just allowing the pain to be present usually had the effect of reducing it, and sometimes I let go of the aching sensation right on the spot."

After a year or so, most of Duke's pain was gone for good, but he still didn't feel as well as he hoped to be. He phoned me one day while soaking in his hot tub, and I led him through a release beginning on the question: *Could you allow yourself to let go of wanting to have the illness?* This session had a major impact on him. In his words: "It was a significant turnaround for me. I realized that, for some reason and at a very deep level, I must have wanted to be sick. Maybe it was to get attention and sympathy, or possibly to get out of working. I don't really know why—and it doesn't really matter. What matters is that I could immediately sense an improvement in the various aspects of my illness. It was an amazing experience."

Releasing on Your General Health and Well-being

Now that we have explored specific ways to work with physical problems, let's do some releasing on our general health and well-being. These techniques, which are applications of the principles discussed in Part One of this book, can be used to boost your self-esteem, to accept the signs of transformation that accompany aging, and to support yourself when you're on a weight loss program or undergoing a detox, as well as for coping with symptoms of illness and pain. Everyone benefits from letting go on the body.

Embracing What Is

Simply welcoming the body as it is can boost its ability to heal; it helps you to feel okay in this moment no matter what the body does or does not do. Read the following questions silently to yourself or have a releasing partner ask them of you.

See if, just for now, you can fully allow your body to be as it is.

Could you welcome it, being the way it is?

Could you relax even more into that sense of welcoming or allowing your body to be the way it is? After all, the body is the way it is right now. Resisting it, wanting to change it, or any other feelings you have in opposition to the way it is, only makes you feel worse. So, let your body be okay as it is, as best you can. Welcome however it is, and however you feel about it.

Now, could you do that even more?

Is there something about the way the body looks or the way it feels that you've been resisting?

Just for now, could you let go of resisting it, and allow it to be the way it is? It is the way it is right now. Your resistance and wanting to change it do nothing to help.

So could you embrace the body as it is?

Could you relax into that sense of welcoming or allowing?

And even more?

And more still?

Allow yourself to experiment with embracing things as they are. Even if you are releasing on something that you strongly dislike about your body, such as a serious illness or a physical flaw, your sense of wanting to change it or resistance to it only makes you feel worse. If you can allow the body to be the way it is, even for a brief moment, you'll feel a lot better—and it opens up the possibility of change.

Going Beyond Your Parents

As I've already mentioned, we model ourselves after our parents from a very young age, either through directly copying what they're doing or through resisting what they're like. Both instances dramatically color how we experience life and how we feel. Therefore, releasing on our parents is a powerful tool in cultivating peace about the body.

Begin by focusing on one or both of your parents. *What were their overall feelings about their bodies and their appearance, and also about your body and appearance?*

Is there anything about that which you would like to change?

If so, could you let go of wanting to change it?

Find something else about your parents' attitudes towards their bodies, or their attitudes about yours that you'd like to change.

Then, could you let go of wanting to change it?

Repeat this series of questions several more times before you move on.

Now, is there anything about your parents' attitudes towards their bodies or your body that you resist?

Could you let go of that resistance?

Find something else about your parents' attitudes toward their bodies or your body that you resist.

Then, could you allow that resistance to dissolve?

Did one or both of your parents think of themselves as too fat, or unhealthy, or awkward in their bodies? Can you clearly see how you've either adopted that belief for yourself without even wanting to, or how you are living in resistance to it?

Either way, notice if you would like to change that.

Could you let go of wanting to change it?

Find something else about your parents' bodies, how they related to them, or how they related to your body that makes you feel uncomfortable, that you don't like, and that you want to change.

Then, could you let go of wanting to change that?

Is there anything else about your parents' relationship to their own bodies or your own body that you're resisting?

Could you let go of resisting that?

Is there anything about your parents' attitudes towards their bodies, or their attitude towards yours, that you've subconsciously taken on as your own?

If it is not something you like, notice whether you want to change it. Then, could you let go of wanting to change it?

See if there's anything else about your parents' attitudes about their bodies or their attitude about yours that you've adopted as your own.

Would you like to change that you adopted it?

Could you let go of wanting to change that you adopted it?

Is there anything at all about your own attitude about your body that you'd like to change?

Could you let go of wanting to change it?

Is there anything else about your body that you'd like to change?

If so, could you let go of wanting to change it?

Remember that there's nothing wrong with taking appropriate action. However, the desire to change the way the body is can freeze us in stuckness and prevent us from doing what's necessary. Sometimes, there is nothing we can do about the body and wanting to change it only causes us unnecessary suffering. For instance, we obsess about the fact that it ages. But that's what all bodies do.

Letting go of the attitudes that we have adopted from our parents about health and appearance is a very powerful place for releasing on the body. I highly recommend that you release on this topic on a regular basis for a few weeks, or whenever you get

"My gains include being more relaxed. My blood pressure has gone down to within normal limits. I am more comfortable with me, and not running from myself. I find myself using the Method whenever my negative self-talk begins. I am more centered and my concentration is slowly increasing. I am also working on releasing my sleep apnea. The physical methods I've tried have not worked. Somehow I know, on a higher level, that I must release what causes me to stop breathing while I sleep."

—Dr. Michael Shapiro, Bronx, NY

the chance. Each time you do, you'll uncover and let go of deeper layers of limitation.

Going Beyond the Fears that Make You Sick

As we explored in Chapter 13, The Secret of Letting Go of Fear and Anxiety, on a subconscious level we actually want the things that we're afraid of to happen. Not consciously, of course, but below our awareness. When we release on a particular fear, we drop it as a possibility in our awareness. As a result, we're creating a better picture for our lives, and we feel a lot better, more relaxed and at ease in our bodies.

Here's a releasing process for fear related to the body:

What are some of your fears about the body, fears about its condition, or the condition it might be in? What exactly is it that you're afraid might happen?

Could you let go of wanting that to happen?

Find something else that you're afraid of in relationship to your body. *Do you fear that as it gets older it might become wrinkled, or that you'll gain weight or be sick?* Whichever fear you feel, allow a picture of it to come into your awareness, as best you can, so you can let it go. Really embrace what you're afraid will happen.

Could you let go of wanting that to happen?

Find something else that you're afraid will happen to your body, something you're consciously hoping doesn't happen.

Are you afraid of getting hurt?

Are you afraid of falling?

Are you afraid of a particular disease?

Whatever it is: *Could you let go of wanting that to happen?*

What else are you afraid might happen to your body?

368

Could you let go of wanting that to happen?

Repeat this series of questions as many times as necessary to alleviate your fear. Remember, you can always release on fear directly like this. Or you can check to see if there's a sense of wanting approval, control, or security underneath the fear and release on the want. Either technique is a very powerful way of releasing the fear.

George: Loving His Body in Every Condition

Four years ago, George noticed that his prostate gland felt slightly swollen, so he went to the doctor. Since the doctor was acting worried during his examination and wanted to take some tests, George's mind immediately jumped to the worst outcome. *Prostate cancer! But I'm only 37!* He was glad he had the Sedona Method to rely on in confronting fear.

"We have lots of choices about what happens to our physical bodies, and ideas about what the body can and cannot do that relate to our emotions," he says. "When I went to take my test, I released the whole time. I released on the fear of death and the fear of being sick. There were waves of fear. When I got home, I kept on releasing, and focused on sending love and appreciation to that part of my body."

The results of George's blood work that day showed he was fine. When he went back for a follow-up test a few months later, the doctor told him everything was completely normal. He reports, "My symptoms from that time occasionally recur, and when they come back I simply release. Letting go helped me not make my condition seem like something it wasn't on an emotional level, and I believe it improved the physical aspect. In my experience, releasing takes away the contraction of energy in the body that causes a lot of physical problems."

He adds, "The body does what it does. Releasing to control it won't work. We all want good outcomes, yet we release on outcomes so we can feel calm. Allowing what's going to happen to happen and loving myself where I am makes it easier to accept."

What If Your Body Is Okay as It Is?

Now let's apply the Likes/Dislikes Process (see Chapter 9) to the body. As you let go of your likes and dislikes, you'll begin to feel more accepting of the body as it is, which will cause you to feel better immediately. In addition, whenever you're in the high-energy state of acceptance, you're going to have much more ability to take positive action than you would if you were caught in one of the more limited emotional states.

Begin by finding something about your body that you like. See if that stirs up any sense of wanting approval, control, or security.

If so, could you let it go?

Next, find something that you dislike about your body.

Does that stir up wanting approval, control, or security?

Whichever want it is: *Could you let that go?*

Find something else about your body that you like. *Is there an underlying want?*

Whichever want it is: *Could you just set it free, let it go?*

What is something that you dislike about your body?

Does that stir up a sense of wanting approval, control, or security?

Could you allow whichever want it is to release?

Repeat this series of alternating questions at least nine times, focusing either on your body in general or on a specific symptom or condition that you want to clear up. If you're addressing feelings about a health challenge, I recommend that you phrase the releasing questions in the past tense, specifically:

- *What did I like about having _____ (the condition)?*
- *What did I dislike about having _____ (the condition)?*

Cleaning Up on Your Body

The Cleanup Procedure was designed to work on our feelings about people. But you can also work on your feelings about an object, such as your body. In fact, most of us have a relationship with our body that's almost like a relationship with another person. So these questions should make sense. Just do your best with the images and feelings that arise, without trying to figure it out. This process is very powerful. As you work with it on the body, you'll probably start to see profound results.

Did your body try to control you? Or did it feel that way?

If so, could you let go of wanting to control it back?

Did you try to control your body?

If so, could you let go of wanting to control your body?

Repeat four or five times, and then ask: *Could you now grant your body the right to be the way it is? Just could you?*

Would you grant your body the right to be the way it is?

Do you now grant your body the right to be the way it is? Remember, this third question is a choice or decision.

Repeat these last three questions a few times on your own until you can say "yes" to granting your body the right to be the way it is. Then, whenever you feel ready, move on to the next set of questions.

Did you dislike or disapprove of anything in your body?

Could you let go of that dislike or disapproval you have for it? Just for now?

Did you feel like your body disliked or disapproved of anything in you?

If so, could you let go of wanting your body's approval? Just for now?

Repeat the preceding four questions four or five times and then ask: *Now, could you allow yourself to have only love or acceptance feelings for your body? Just could you?*

Would you allow yourself to have only love or acceptance feelings for your body, even for the moment?

Do you now have only love feelings, only acceptance feelings for your body?

If the answer is "no," do some more releasing on this series before you move on to the next set of questions. If the answer is "yes," move on.

Did it feel like your body challenged, opposed, or threatened you in any way?

If so, see if that stirred up a sense of wanting security or survival. Ask: *Could you let that go?*

Did you challenge, oppose, or threaten your body, or did it seem so?

Could you let go of wanting to challenge, oppose, or threaten your body?

Did it seem like your body challenged, opposed, or threatened you?

If so, could you let go of wanting to challenge, oppose,

or threaten it back to protect yourself from it?

Did you challenge, oppose, or threaten your body, or did it seem that way?

If so, could you let go of wanting to do that?

Did your body challenge, oppose, or threaten you?

If so, could you allow your insecurity to release?

Did you challenge, oppose, or threaten your body?

If you did, or it seemed like you did, could you now let go of wanting to do that?

Now, could you have only a feeling of well-being, safety, and trust about your body?

Would you allow yourself to have only a feeling of well-being, safety, and trust with your body?

Do you have only a feeling of well-being, safety, and trust for your body?

If the answer is "yes," that's great! If the answer is "no," do some more releasing on this issue before you move on.

"I arrived at the Retreat with daily, chronic, debilitating migraine headaches. They had become so significant that I hadn't worked in a year and a half. I had a major concern that I wouldn't be able to participate in much of the course, because of the pain. During the Retreat, I experienced only three minor 'head sensations' that disappeared in less than an hour. The learning associated with my 'past headaches' is invaluable. I recognize that everything I was doing to get rid of them was causing them to remain. How do you say thank you for getting your life back? What a great experience."

—Dr. Sharon Crain,
Scottsdale, AZ

Advantages and Disadvantages

You can use the Advantages/Disadvantages Process to release on any area of physical stuckness, such as a plateau during a period of weight loss, while quitting smoking, or on any physical condition with which you're feeling stuck. Done with an open mind and heart, this exercise is often able to unhook us from whatever it is in our consciousness that was holding the problem in place.

As with the Likes/Dislikes Process, I recommend phrasing the questions in the past tense when you are working on a specific condition. For the purpose of learning this process, however, you'll be releasing on your body being the way you want it to be.

What is the advantage in having your body the way you want it to be?

Does that stir up a sense of wanting approval, control, or security?

Whichever want it is: *Could you allow it to release?*

What is the disadvantage in having your body the way you want it to be?

Does that stir up a sense of wanting approval, control, or security?

Whichever want it is: *Could you allow yourself to let it go? Just set it free?*

Repeat the above six questions approximately nine times. The more you release, the better you'll feel overall. Furthermore, I encourage you to do the Advantages/Disadvantages Process on your body regularly for a couple of weeks, as this will help you move through many layers of subconscious programming—like a student of mine did.

Dhiresha had been using the Sedona Method to attain a personal goal: "I allow myself to easily achieve and maintain my ideal bodyweight." In the past, she hadn't found dieting easy. She had a history of losing and then regaining weight even when she'd participated in a weight loss program. This time, however, she'd been more successful by combining releasing with going to Weight Watchers for its structure.

She reports, "At first, the restrictedness was a big problem for me. Overeating is a hard cycle to break. Even if you're on a diet or change the way you eat, you have a mentality that recreates the weight. There are tons of beliefs to let go about what it means if I'm not my ideal weight. I had loaded up the issue with 'I'm not spiritually advanced,' 'I'm not a good person,' 'I'm lazy,' 'It's not fair that I can't have what I want,' 'I need to eat at night,' and 'I have to lose weight quickly.'"

Dhiresha found doing the Advantages/Disadvantages Process on overeating an exceedingly helpful tool. She released on her advantages, which included not having to worry about men feeling attracted to her, not thinking about how she looked, being certain that people liked her for her character rather than her appearance, and maintaining her belief that she could have whatever she wanted to eat. She also released on her disadvantages, which included that she might keep gaining weight forever, she didn't like how she looked or felt in clothes, she was always thinking about food, and, because food controlled her, she didn't feel like a "good" person. Interestingly, she discovered that the last disadvantage was also an advantage, since it took the pressure off her to be "perfect."

"I had to create space to see things from a different perspective," she concludes. "I had to get to a place where I don't care whether I change or I don't: hootlessness. The Method truly helps with that. When I release, I feel it in my body; tension builds up in my solar plexus, and then it's gone, and I feel peaceful. It has changed the way I lead life. In addition, I am gradually and easily continuing to drop my excess weight."

Picturing What You Want:
Combining Imagery and Releasing

Throughout the United States, many healthcare clinics have successfully employed visualization, or guided imagery, as a healing aid. Cancer survivors and patients with heart disease have used it, as well as others. In combination with releasing, visualization is an incredibly effective way to support your body to heal and function optimally. It is also a good accompaniment to any weight loss program or detoxification plan.

In a way, the visualization process resembles the Goal Process that we explored in Chapter 8. For, as we create images in our minds about health and the ideal body, different feelings and beliefs come into consciousness in opposition and support of those imaginings. When we release on these feelings and beliefs, we move into a state of greater courage, acceptance, and peace, and thus we free energy for action.

Remember, when you "visualize" anything, as best you can, use all your senses. Combine mental pictures with physical sensations and sounds, and even include aromas if that helps to enhance your imagery. Let's proceed.

Begin by allowing yourself to picture your ideal body. *What does it look like? What does it feel like? What is its level of health?*

376

Notice how you feel about having your body be that way. In addition, notice whether there is any sense of wanting approval, control, or security connected with that picture.

If there is, whichever want it is: *Could you just let it go?*

Return to picturing the healthy body, or the body exactly the way you want it to be. Imagine it as vividly as possible. Then again, check to see if the picture originates from a sense of wanting approval, control, or security.

Whichever want it is: *Could you simply allow it to release?*

Now, picture your ideal body again. Make the image as vivid as you can. This time, see if an idea, thought, or belief arises that says, "You can't have that," or, "You shouldn't have that," "You'll never have that," or, "It's not possible."

Does the thought come from a sense of wanting approval, control, or security?

Whichever want it is: *Could you just let it go?*

Go back again to picturing your body being exactly the way you want it to be. Remember to engage all your senses. *Is there any opposition or resistance, or any other feeling about the image?*

Could you just welcome whatever that feeling is?

Is it coming from a sense of wanting approval, control, or security?

Could you let it go, at least for now?

Repeat the series of questions above a few more times, allowing whatever wants and resistances are stirred up to be let go. When you're ready, move on.

Now, picture your body being exactly the way you want it to be. Give yourself fully to the picture. Engage yourself in it

377

as completely as you can. Ask: *Could you welcome the picture into your full awareness and embrace it completely?*

And even more?

Could you just let it be?

Could you truly accept the ideal image as it is?

Now, as you allow the image to come into your full awareness, understand that it's okay to have your ideal body. Also know, at the same time, that it's okay for your body to be the way it is. There really is no conflict between the two. Just allow yourself to sense how all is well with your body, as best you can.

Rest in self-acceptance for the moment.

A Final Word

The more you work with the exercises in this chapter, the better you will feel in, and about, your body; it may even lead to improved health. I encourage you to use these exercises to boost your well-being, as best you can, before you move on to the next chapter, Organizational Freedom and Effectiveness.

Chapter 19

Organizational Freedom and Effectiveness

If you have been enjoying this book, I'm sure that you've already begun to see many ways that the Sedona Method can positively impact any organization with which you are involved. Sedona Training Associates is often called upon to design customized training programs for managers, teams, and corporations that help them to handle the specific challenges they face and more easily meet their goals and objectives. Even if you are not the primary decision maker for your company or group, consider handing a copy of this book to the person in charge. The more people in your organization who begin using the Sedona Method, the more profoundly these techniques will affect the whole.

When you try to fix any system by changing behaviors from the outside, or solely by moving around the parts, it tends not to produce a lasting effect. Although such restructuring creates momentary gains in productivity, it is well documented that these benefits are temporary. Entropy soon develops unless change goes deeper than merely shifting environmental factors or intellectual points of view. Productivity tends to go back to exactly, or nearly, where it was before.

Good news. As you and other people in your organization begin using the Sedona Method to release, you are letting go of the inner attitudes that lead to failure. You are changing your organization from the inside out, one person at a time. This has been proven to produce lasting transformation. As I explained in the Introduction, when the insurance company Mutual of New York did a pilot study with their field under-writers (a euphemism for insurance salespeople), the results were extraordinary. The group that learned the Sedona Method outperformed the control group by an average of 33 percent. By itself, this was an impressive outcome. But it was even more impressive that gains increased the longer it lasted. The study was broken into two three-month segments. During the first period, sales went up 23 percent. During the second period, sales increased 43 percent.

As you and your team members learn to tap your natural ability to let go of any uncomfortable, unwanted, or limiting emotions, thoughts, or beliefs on the spot, your organization will easily move into a much higher level of efficiency and pro-ductivity, while increasing each team member's sense of well-being and job satisfaction.

As you release, you'll free yourself to think more clearly, act more decisively, and feel calm and in control, no matter what business or personal challenges you're facing. The Sedona Method will help motivate you to make the important changes that are needed in order to have the career and the personal life that you choose. It will show you how to let go of the habitual patterns of thought, feeling, and behavior that prevent you from achieving your goals and enjoying the process. By enabling you to be alert and effective in every moment, even when you're under pressure, the Method will free you to have a more productive, pleasurable life.

By the way, although it's great when lots of people use ongoing releasing in an organization, it is not required. You can completely shift your experience of work and your effectiveness just by doing the releasing processes yourself. Letting go can often shift an entire work environment, even when you're the only one consciously releasing.

Emotional Intelligence/Emotional Mastery

There is a growing consensus that emotional intelligence (EI) is just as important, if not more important, than IQ in predicting someone's level of success and life satisfaction. This idea is helping us to redefine, as a culture, what it means to be smart and effective. Research consistently shows, for instance, that differences between average performers and outstanding performers in a given organization are about 90 percent attributable to their EI and only about 10 percent attributable to their technical skills. Nothing is more effective at quickly building EI than the Sedona Method. But what exactly is EI, and how does the Sedona Method help us to enhance it?

In his book *Emotional Intelligence*, Daniel Goleman, who coined the phrase, defines five critical skills that make up emotional intelligence. These include:

1. *Self-awareness:* Goleman defines this as "recognizing a feeling as it happens." The Sedona Method helps us monitor our emotions in the moment and gives us a

roadmap to navigate through different emotional terrains. In business, having heightened self-awareness enables us to make better decisions.

2. *Managing emotions:* Instead of allowing ourselves to be run by emotional attachments and aversions, the Sedona Method gives us effective tools to handle painful and limiting emotions appropriately. Letting go reduces stress, increases energy, and helps us bounce back from life's inevitable setbacks and challenges. In business, this translates into being able to perform at our best.

3. *Self-motivation:* As Goleman says, "Marshaling emotions in service to a goal is essential for paying attention, for self-motivation and mastery, and for creativity." The tools of the Sedona Method easily eliminate the feelings that prevent us from achieving what we want in life. As we eliminate thoughts and feelings that say, "I can't," "I don't know how," "I don't deserve it," or, "I can't handle it," we uncover the innate sense of "I can" that naturally catapults us to greater success. Consistent releasing results in greater access to the state of effortlessness and flow we all seek.

4. *Empathy:* As we use the Sedona Method, we not only become more aware of our own emotions, we're also more able to recognize the emotions of others and the impact that emotions have in our behavior towards them, as well as in theirs towards us.

5. *Handling relationships:* "The art of relationships is, in large part, skill in managing the emotions of others," according to Goleman. When we use the Sedona Method to let go of emotional baggage, we naturally begin to develop an ability to relate better to others. Furthermore, people enjoy relating to us more and giving us what we want, which smoothes the flow of business exchanges inside the workplace, among colleagues, and outside it, with clients or customers.

Sedona Method instructors have been assisting individuals and organizations to develop emotional intelligence, and go beyond it to emotional mastery, since 1974. In the remainder of this chapter, you'll learn more about how and why we use the Method to build the emotional skills shown on the short list above for the benefit of organizations.

Moving Beyond the Control Paradigm

Most organizations are built around an overarching need to control both their internal and external environments. But poor decisions are often made when an organization is dominated by a management team that wants to control outcomes. No matter how much they plan, their plans usually get derailed whenever they plan from a sense of lack (wanting to control). Do you recall this statement from Chapter 4, "Resistance is pushing against the world so that it will push back"? A controlling management style creates an unnecessary pushback both from the environment and from within organizational ranks.

As individuals and entire groups begin to shed even a portion of their desire for control, they experience a marked increase in the harmony and efficiency within their organizations and an increase in their effectiveness in the marketplace. If you are part of the management of an organization that is lost in wanting to control, please understand that you can do your part in many ways, including just by doing your own personal releasing. As you let go of wanting to control your staff, you'll stop assuming that you need to micromanage your team, and you'll find yourself more easily delegating responsibilities. You will also actually let go of the tasks that you delegate, which allows them to get done. In addition, you'll be willing to empower your teammates, as opposed to feeling you need to dominate them. Empowered teams get more done with less effort.

If you have any difficulty delegating, simply ask yourself the basic series of releasing questions that you learned in Part One, until you can feel truly comfortable turning the task over to someone else. As you do this, also release on any negative expectations that the person to whom you delegate a task will not do the job properly. Go back to the releasing questions whenever you find yourself worrying about performance.

Please recognize that I am not suggesting you turn over responsibility to people whose competency is in question. Unless you have truly let go of both your need to control and your doubts about the ability of the person to whom you are delegating, keep letting go until the choice is unforced. Too many managers have heard of the need to delegate and feel pressured into doing it. Without truly letting go, they end up delegating out of desperation, which only adds to their overall burdens instead of lightening them.

If you are a team member, one of the best ways that you

can contribute to the ease and flow of your organization and your own job is to let go of your resistance. Repetitive tasks that we do not fully enjoy doing often need to be done on a daily basis.

Simply ask: *Could I let go of resisting doing this particular task?*

Could I let go of resisting not doing it?

If you go back and forth with these questions a few times on any occasion that you feel resistance rising in your awareness, you'll find yourself letting the resistance go and getting things done with more ease, joy, and alacrity.

Of course, any general releasing that you do will also make your whole job easier. You will feel better and have a positive effect on the people around you.

Building and Leading a Cohesive Team

The true leaders in any organization are the people who others trust to do the right thing. It is apparent that they have in mind the best interests both of their organizations and of the team members with whom they're working, not just their own. Genuine commitment such as this cannot be faked, no matter how hard you try. But it can be developed. The more you let

"The Sedona Method is a very powerful business tool, especially when negotiating from a position of 'weakness.' It dissolves resistance, is mutually respectful, and is great fun to use! I have never encountered a technique that was so easy, so all-encompassing, and yet so utterly simple to apply."
—Ben Jansz,
Buckingham, England

go, the more you'll seek the greatest good for everyone involved with your organization. You will also be more aware of others' points of view and relate more openly. As you reveal and express your authentic self, people will naturally choose to follow your lead.

In many organizations, team building is a matter of forced bonding through attendance at offsite events or artificial interventions. Although these interventions can be helpful, and even fun, they often only produce the short-term results I mentioned earlier in the chapter. Be assured, however, that coworkers will spontaneously bond without forcing when they begin to release.

James: Releasing for Workplace Success

James has been using the Sedona Method since 1983. He first learned it through a live seminar where we only taught the Method as far as letting go of wanting approval and control. He later purchased the Sedona Method Course audio program, which is more complete and includes letting go of wanting security. Here is the story of how the Method has contributed to the trajectory of his career, told in his words:

"When I first took the Sedona Method live seminar, I was angry with a lot of things in my life. I was a computer programmer in Silicon Valley and only earned about $25,000 a year. I was mad at my boss because I didn't like the way he defined my job, and I felt constrained. Among other things, he wanted me to work nine-to-five, and I wanted flexible hours. After I started releasing, the first thing I noticed was that I was free of my anger. Once I was done with that—no longer a victim—I began looking for other jobs.

"I ended up moving to Pacifica, southwest of San Francisco, and went from $25,000 to $35,000 in my next job. The course was in April and that was in June. Then I made job contacts and an agency called me about a position in New Jersey and a position in Seattle both paying $75,000. As they seemed to need me more in Seattle, I took that job. This was in October of the same year. Other things in my life were changing, too. I met and fell in love with my wife. My health was improving. Change came rapidly.

"Several years later, after going to graduate school and working overseas, I returned to Seattle and took a big pay cut to work at one of the giant computer software companies. I really wanted to work there. But now our family had three kids in diapers, and my wife and I were faced with the financial issues of paying off a mortgage, a car, and student loans. There was a temptation to rely on credit cards. My new manager wasn't supportive, but combative. She attacked me in every conversation, often with a smile on her face. Work wasn't going properly, and I wanted approval and control. But I didn't feel as though I could stand up to my boss, because of my financial insecurity.

"I was reminded of the value of releasing when I purchased the Sedona Method Course audio program explaining the process of letting go of the sense of wanting security. I stayed up all night releasing energy for safety. I let go of feelings about monetary issues and feelings about verbal attacks. From then on, I no longer cowered when my manager yelled at me, and I stood my ground in the next couple of meetings. After that she stopped meeting with me, and I hardly saw her anymore. The good part of this was that she wasn't interfering with my work,

387

and I could do it properly. The bad part was that there was no communication. We even did my performance review by email. For a while, I wanted to quit; then I tried to transfer within the company, and she blocked it. But, ultimately, she promoted me to be the director of a software testing team.

"As a manager, I spent a lot of time thinking about how to apply the Method to work situations. I looked at my history with it. Initially, all I'd wanted was to get rid of my anger and move up to a state of pride. I aimed there before being a group leader, because it made me feel happier. Although this was good so long as I was an individual contributor, it wasn't great for management. People are put off by the emotional energy of superiority. I knew I needed to move into courage.

"From then on, when I noticed that I was feeling 'better than' others, I'd let go of wanting to put them down until I felt like we were equals, both members of a team, children of God working towards a common goal. Whenever I noticed that I was thinking someone was being 'stupid,' I'd let go on the spot. I could do it while we were conversing. I could listen and release. I didn't want to put artificial limits on what people would do. By letting go, I'd get upside surprises. They'd prove themselves more capable, or, if they were on another team and we were at loggerheads, they'd be more amenable to my suggestions or come up with a compromise. There never was a war in my department, even though the corporate culture was often adversarial. As an outcome of my ability to get teams together, I ended up being the top test manager in the company for a few years. The people who worked for me felt at ease and therefore used more creative out-of-the-box thinking than others did.

We got the job done. I owe this success to the Method.

"I love the feeling of releasing. Typically, it's as though energy is directly leaving the midsection of my body, my abdomen and thorax. It feels like plods of dirt are falling away from me, and something that's been trapped by them is rushing out. When I let go, I usually feel a tingling or crunching sensation, and sometimes hear an auditory explosion. I know there are emotions imprisoned inside of me, and these are signs that the blocks of the prison walls are moving."

De-stressing Stress

If you are interested in contributing to a stress-free work environment, adopt a simple principle: Ask, don't tell. You may recall reading about this in Chapter 4. Using this approach, you'll notice a marked increase in the level of cooperation you receive from those who report to you, and you'll be lightening both their stress and your own.

Another powerful way to reduce stress in your work environment is to stop pushing yourself and others to do what needs to be accomplished. As I've already mentioned elsewhere, any pushing—even of one's self—causes equal pushing back from that which, or whoever, is being pushed. So, if you catch yourself pushing yourself or others, simply let go and sit back, while inside taking on the attitude, *as best you can,* of watching the show unfold. Accept that all is well and unfolding as it should be.

Does this mean that you won't give orders anymore? Of course not. Does it mean that you won't discipline yourself? No, it doesn't mean that, either. All that happens, as you let go of the feelings and wants that are creating stress, is that you create the room that's necessary for things to get done with greater ease and efficiency.

Even when the feelings and situations that you and your coworkers are releasing do not pertain specifically to the work environment, that releasing will enhance the well-being of the organization as a whole and of anyone who works for it. Currently stressful work conditions can therefore become less stressful in relatively short order.

Working Under Time Deadlines

Most organizations treat time as a precious commodity in short supply. Yes, time is precious, but it's only scarce if you believe it is. In most cases, when you rush or feel pressured because of a deadline, this causes your efficiency to go down, not up, and the results show it. I first found that out in my own company. When I became willing to plan ahead, knowing that the plans might or might not happen on schedule, I found my employees and myself rushing less and making fewer mistakes at the same time. Taking our time enabled us to work at a much higher level of efficiency.

So, whenever you find yourself rushing, simply let go of the pressure, as best you can, by adopting the attitude that you have all the time in the world.

As I mentioned in Chapter 2, there's another way to say this: Do what you do when you're doing it, and don't do what you're not doing when you're not doing it. Most of us spend time thinking about what we are not doing and beat ourselves up for not doing it. Or we keep looking forward to doing something particular that we consider fun, recreational, or just more productive. Both kinds of mental activity prevent us from being present with the job at hand. So, by actually becoming present, time seems to expand. Then, we enjoy a clearer focus and get our tasks done more easily and effectively.

As you go through each day, let go of your feelings about how you're spending that day. Perhaps you feel frustrated about how long certain things take or what you are not getting done. Whatever your feelings may be about how you're currently using your time, allow yourself to let them go. You may find, for instance, that your open door policy is based on wanting the approval of your employees, even though it wastes your time. Or that your desire for security makes you feel the need to talk to people whenever they want, even when it will be an interruption. Letting go of the feelings and wants related to your use of time will make it easier to change your currently unproductive patterns.

If you are managing your time using a specific time management system, simply insert releasing into it in whatever way seems appropriate. You may benefit from reviewing the abbreviated forms of both the Goal Process and the Action Steps Process in Chapter 8. A small investment of time and effort to incorporate releasing into your daily routine is likely to pay off many times over in both saved and found time.

Effective Selling

In every interaction, we are selling our ideas and ourselves. The more we can let go and look to find mutuality rather than imposing our will on others, the more they will come our way. Therefore, do your best to see the interaction from the other's point of view. Rather than wanting agreement and wanting to close the sale, let go. See if you can find a way to connect with the human being that is also part of your transaction.

As you release your needs, you'll find them met much more easily. You will also notice that there are actually others here, and you will genuinely care about what they need. People are much more likely to want you to win if they sense you care about them.

Releasing results in sales, and it also helps all relational activities to flow more smoothly. By using the Sedona Method, you will naturally go from "win-lose" to "win-win" scenarios when you are engaged in communicating important ideas to others.

Goal Mastery

Using the Sedona Method, you can take the stress, pressure, and disappointment out of the process of setting goals, while still easily—even effortlessly—achieving them. Simply follow the guidelines in Chapter 8, Setting and Attaining Your Goals, and watch your goals come into fruition with greater ease and speed.

Groups can work on common goals when everyone is using the Sedona Method. If you are a group leader, simply have the members of your team release individually on the same goal. One way to set this process up is to write the goal on a flip chart or a white board and then have individuals share and release their considerations and feelings about the goal. By having everyone release together on each issue that's brought up, the whole team can move quickly to a much more positive inner attitude about the goal.

I led the process I just described during an intervention with a technical research and development group composed of scientists and engineers, and the results were profound. Before we did the work, they'd been racing another company to get a particular product to market, knowing that whoever brought it to market first would win the lion's share of an emerging business. They had been working on its development for over three years, had less than six months available to design a working prototype, and were hitting one road block after another both in the creation and in bringing in appropriate outside partners to move the project into completion. The group was in a state of despair and expressed that they felt that the task would be impossible even if they had twice the time.

Before we worked together on the goal, we worked through the initial resistance of approaching the goal in this way. Then the general attitude shifted, and we were able to work on the goal itself. Although we only focused on it once, as part of a two-day intervention, what happened next amazed both the group and me. They went from feeling and believing that the task was impossible to getting it done ahead of schedule!

Power Decision-making

As managers and members of teams in your organization, especially in today's atmosphere of rapid change, it is critical to be able to make appropriate decisions, and to follow through with appropriate actions, on the go. As you let go using the Sedona Method, you'll generally find yourself uncovering your intuition, your innate knowing.

I highly recommend that you use the Advantages/ Disadvantages Process mentioned in Chapter 10. Whenever you're not sure of a correct course of action or what decision to make, the small amount of time you invest in using this process will save you a tremendous amount of time, energy, and frustration. You will find yourself making choices with greater confidence, which, of course, will translate into more positive action for your team and you.

Working with Difficult People

Almost everyone in business has worked for a difficult boss, supervised a difficult employee, or struggled to get along with a difficult coworker at one time or another. These interactions can really sour our work lives, unless we let go of wanting approval, control, and security in regard to these individuals. Therefore, I highly recommend that you—and everyone else in your organization—begin regularly using the Cleanup Procedure described in Chapter 11 (see page 236). It is a terrific practice to institute before and after internal meetings, as well as before and after sales calls or other interactions with customers, clients, and outside vendors.

As a rule of thumb, suggest that your staff do the Cleanup Procedure any time there has been a difficulty, or whenever they're anticipating difficulty. This one process alone can bring harmony to all the areas of relationship I just mentioned, as well as many others too numerous to mention.

A Final Thought

I hope that you've found this chapter helpful in bringing the tools of the Sedona Method into your organization. As more people in your workplace embrace and master the principles and processes contained in this book, I promise that your whole organizational system will begin to operate at progressively higher levels of efficiency and productivity. Of equal importance, you and they will feel freer, happier, more connected, and fulfilled.

Chapter 20

Supporting Our World

From my perspective, you've already been supporting our world by releasing to correct your problems and achieve your goals. Every time you release a feeling, thought, or belief about anything or anyone, you uncover more of your basic loving nature. As Lester Levenson used to say: "One person with only love in his or her heart could do more to right the problems of the world than all the people who are actively trying to fix it." You have love in your heart just beneath the imagined limitations that you're peeling away when you release. Furthermore, from my perspective, every time you let go, you are dissolving limitations in the mass consciousness as well as your own consciousness.

In the mid-1970's, when the Sedona Method was first being taught, some people wondered if it would be possible for anyone to use it to become more destructive to the world. In my experience through the years, no matter where people appear to be in their lives, when they begin using the Method and uncovering their natural courageousness, acceptance, and peace, they only have a tendency to become more constructive.

The motivation to take actions that most of us would consider destructive simply dissolves.

Releasing to Support Our World

Beyond the natural occurrence of becoming more peaceful, loving, and constructive as you release, there are other ways you can apply the Sedona Method to support the whole. Let's consider a few of these now.

Hold the Best in Mind

When we think about the world, most of us don't experience particularly positive images. All you have to do is watch the news on TV, listen to it on the radio, or read a newspaper to recognize what I mean. In fact, many people have told me that the news is a significant part of their daily stress. Yet, many of us feel compelled to watch, read, or listen to the news so we can know what's going on. Other people stop watching the news altogether, in order not to be influenced by what they view as its negativity. Although I don't recommend obsessing over the news, I also don't recommend cutting off from it. Instead, when you see, hear, or read news, allow yourself to let go as follows.

To let go of any feelings that news reports stir up in you, such as anger, anxiety, and resistance, allow yourself to picture the world in the way you would prefer it to be. Then, release any contrary feelings or thoughts that indicate that it *cannot* or *will not* happen.

At the same time, do your best to accept the world as it is by letting go of wanting to change it (see Chapter 5, Your Key to Serenity). The more you can accept the world exactly as it is, the more you'll be able to project love and perfection to the world.

By releasing while you stay informed about the news, you are contributing to the world even if you don't take any outward action—or if you are going to take action.

Be for the Solution

Many people, even those of us with the best intentions, find ourselves being "anti" what we don't like in the world. Yet, if we are anti-something, we are still holding it in mind—sometimes even more strongly then those who are for it. All the anti-war sentiment in the US during the Vietnam War, for instance, did not bring about a quick end to the conflict. We're sending energy to anything we hold in mind, and supporting its creation.

Here are some practical ways to reframe your concerns: Instead of being against pollution, be pro-environment. Instead of being against discrimination, be pro-equality. Instead of being against war, be pro-peace. As with the Goal Process (see page 201), hold in mind the solution as opposed to the problem, and you'll get a lot more done with a lot less effort, while naturally being more constructive in the process.

Support Your Leaders

This is a difficult one for most of us, especially if we have different political views. Our leaders tend to become lightning rods for what we do not like in our world. But political leaders merely represent the mass consciousness of the region or country that they are representing. Be part of the legislative process and vote for the candidate of your choice, but allow yourself to support the winner, even if you don't agree with him or her.

If you send political leaders hate as opposed to love, you're being part of the problem instead of the solution. If they say or do things with which you don't agree, let them know (write a letter, send an email, make a phone call, vote them out of office), while also releasing the inner reactions you have to the outcome. When you make your voice heard, make it count by being as positive an influence as you can be.

A great process to use in this regard is the Cleanup Procedure (see Chapter 11). If we all did the Cleanup Procedure on our leaders, it wouldn't take very long for the energy dynamic of the world to shift dramatically for the better. Imagine what the world would be like if we all granted our leaders the right to be the way they are and loved them as they are. That alone would make a huge difference, because then our leaders could focus on correcting the problems at hand rather than protecting themselves from our negativity.

Practice Loving-kindness

As I mentioned in Chapter 17, Relationship Magic, giving without wanting anything in return is a great way to support your relationships with others. It is also an effective way to support the world. So, find ways to give to your community, your house of worship, and your country. In short, anyone you meet could potentially benefit from your support.

Always give according to your means, however. You can give through service, knowledge, or simply sharing kindness and respect. Money isn't the only way—or even necessarily the best way—to give in every circumstance. In addition, be sure that you're not giving at your own expense. Your life, and the lives of those you care about, shouldn't suffer as a result of your givingness. Unnecessary sacrifice and suffering doesn't support you or those people and organizations you're trying to support.

There are two keys for truly being supportive to others and the world:

1. Give without wanting anything in return, not even recognition or acknowledgement.
2. Allow yourself to see those whom you're supporting as already being whole and perfect as they are, and completely equal to you. Allow them to be who they are— grant them their Beingness—as opposed to seeing them as imperfect and needing to be fixed or helped.

The only way to enact these two keys effectively is to release. Release your desire for recognition or getting anything back in exchange for giving. Release any judgments that you may have towards the ones you are assisting.

Loving-kindness not only supports the world, it also supports you. The more you give from a released perspective, the better you will feel, and your personal world will reflect your inner goodness.

Share this Message with People Who Are Open to It

If you've read this far, I hope you agree that the message and processes in this book can truly help the world. Imagine a world where people are letting go of the past and living and loving in the present moment. Imagine a world where conflicts are resolved through discussion and releasing, as opposed to violence and aggression. Imagine a world where everyone lets go of their non-love feelings and uncovers their true loving nature. Imagine a world that supports people in being themselves. This is the world I envision as an increasing number of people learn to release and love what is.

If you support this vision, I encourage you to share this book with anyone you think can benefit from the message it contains. In a sudden rush of enthusiasm, however, please don't be like the youths in the following story. In a Boy Scout meeting, two teenage friends are reporting their good deeds for the week to their scoutmaster. First one gets up and reports that he's helped an old lady across the street. Then the next gets up and reports that he's helped the same old lady across the street. The scoutmaster looks puzzled and asks them, "Why did it take both of you to help the same old lady across the street? In unison they reply, "That's because she didn't want to go."

When many of us feel enthusiastic about a particular concept, we can become a little overzealous about sharing it. Please do not cram this down anyone's throat. Allow yourself to share releasing only with those people who are open and interested. On the other hand, people may be more interested than you might credit them with being at first.

One of the most liberating and eye-opening discoveries that I made when I first started teaching live Sedona Method Courses was about the diversity of people who were attracted to and positively impacted by this work. From my direct experience, I now believe that anyone who has a sincere desire to change or improve his or her life, and has even a little willingness to do something about it, can benefit from the Sedona Method. I invite you to join me in sharing a message of possibility and freedom with the world.

Holistic Releasing

The fourth way of letting go is called Holistic Releasing.

Holistic Releasing is based on the premise that everything the mind experiences, whether real or imagined, arises in pairs. With this perception of duality, if we have *in*, we also have *out*. If we have *right*, we also have *wrong*. If we have *good*, we also have *bad*. If we have *pain*, we also have *pleasure*.

Most of us live life as though we can hold onto the good and get rid of the bad, but, in so doing, we miss the obvious. Think about it. When you try to hold onto something good, it always slips away. Whenever you try to clutch onto what you judge as good, or that which you prefer, it is elusive and tends to move through your awareness. And then think about the inverse of this. What happens when you resist or try to hold away what you don't like? That's right. It persists or appears to gets even bigger. So, in effect, what most of us have been doing is pulling what we don't like towards us and pushing what we do like away!

We also spend a lot of time and energy keeping these polarities of opposites alive by trying to keep what we like *as far away as possible* from what we don't like. This takes an enormous amount of energy and creates that which we call "problems." The perception of duality also ignores the underlying unity which is here before the mind and is unaffected by all the pairs of opposites.

Holistic Releasing is very simple. You simply focus on or welcome both sides of the polarity by going back and forth between them. For instance, a very simple polarity has to do with happiness. Most of us are either feeling relatively happy or unhappy from moment to moment, but we tend to see only one and not the other. So let's just do a little experiment. Ask yourself:

Could I allow myself to feel as unhappy as I do in this moment?

And then, could I allow myself to feel as happy as I do in this moment?

And as unhappy as I do in this moment?
And as happy as I do in this moment?

And as unhappy as I do in this moment?
And as happy as I do in this moment?

As you continually move back and forth on the different sides of any particular polarity several times in a row, notice what is happening inside. You may have even noticed it just in doing this exercise: the polarities will actually dissolve each other. And you're left with greater and greater awareness of the freedom and presence that you are. You may also see the underlying unity beneath the duality and separation of the polarities. You may experience it as an energetic shift. You may feel it as a dissolving or a clearing or a lightness. You may have greater clarity and understanding within your own self.

When you bring the two sides of a polarity together, it's like bringing matter and antimatter together or positive and negative energy. They neutralize each other, and you're left with a much greater awareness of freedom, presence, and greater access to your intuitive knowingness. You see solutions, not problems. You feel more open, more alive and more at peace. As you work with Holistic Releasing, you'll discover that this effect expands over time. You'll start to see more possibilities and see things more clearly. Each time you practice releasing in this way, you'll get more out of it—more access to your own truth.

Approach this form of releasing the same way you have been approaching the other three. The following are some guidelines and reminders. Holistic Releasing can be done with statements and questions. When we use questions we are merely asking you if it is possible to take this action. "Yes" or "no" are both acceptable answers. You will often let go even if you say "No." As best you can, answer the question that you chose with a minimum of thought, staying away from second-guessing yourself or getting into a debate with yourself about the merits of this action or its consequences. All the questions used in this process are deliberately simple. They are not important in and of themselves, but are designed to point you to the experience of letting go.

The following is a list of generic questions that you can use to work on your own issues and polarities. When doing the process, simply say the statements or ask the questions, repeatedly switching back and forth between the two sides at your own rate. You will also discover the unique polarities that are limiting you as you apply this process in your life. Allow yourself to structure your own polarities using the examples that follow as a guide.

Could I allow myself to resist _____ as much as I do?

Could I allow myself to welcome (allow) _____ as much as I do?

Could I allow myself to reject _____ as much as I do?

Could I allow myself to accept _____ as much as I do?

Could I allow myself to dislike _____ as much as I do?

Could I allow myself to like _____ as much as I do?

Could I allow myself to hate _____ as much as I do?

Could I allow myself to love _____ as much as I do?

Could I allow myself to want to change _____ as much as I do?

Could I allow myself to let go of wanting to change _____ as best I can?

Could I allow myself to say no to _____ as best I can?

Could I allow myself to say yes to _____ as best I can?

Could I allow myself to be as open to _____ as I am?

Could I allow myself to be as closed to _____ as I am?

Let It Do You

The way to get the most out of this process is to merely stay as open as you can, moment to moment, as you learn and practice it. You can pretend you're asking the questions of yourself or you can repeat them to yourself. Do your best to lead with your heart, with your feeling sense. Even better, try to do this by not doing anything at all, except to stay open on every level. Let it do you. This process actually does itself. By simply switching back and forth in your mind between the two unique points of view that make up each polarity, they dissolve each other. As you work with the polarities, simply engage with an open mind and heart, being as attentive as you can. Allow whatever thoughts, feelings and limiting beliefs or pictures that arise in your consciousness to just be there— welcome them as fully as you can. You do not even need to try and let them go. They will naturally dissolve each other.

Wealth and Success Polarities:

Could you allow yourself to resist having money as much as you do?

Could you welcome having money as best you can?

Could you allow yourself to feel as much scarcity as you do?

Could you allow yourself to feel you have abundance as best you can?

Could you allow yourself to hate money as much as you do?

Could you allow yourself to love money as much as you do?

Money is evil.
Money is good.

I am a failure.
I am a success.

I never have enough.
I always have enough.

Relationship Polarities:

Could I allow myself to resist this person as much as I do?
Could I allow myself to accept this person as much as I do?

Could I allow myself to mistrust this person as much as I do?
Could I allow myself to trust this person as much as I do?

Could I allow myself to be as dependent on this person as I am?
Could I allow myself to be as independent of this person as I am?

Relationships are hard.
Relationships are easy.

There are no good men (women).
There are only good men (women).

Health and Well-being Polarities:

Could you allow your body to be as uncomfortable as it is?
Could you allow your body to be as comfortable as it is?

Could you allow yourself to be as addicted as you are?
Could you allow yourself to be as free of addiction as you are?

Could you allow yourself to want to change your body as much as you do?

Could you allow yourself to love your body as it is as best you can?

I have trouble sleeping.
I sleep great.

I am fat.
I am thin.

I am unhealthy.
I am healthy.

As you work with Holistic Releasing, you may reach a point where you feel like you've had enough. If this does happen, you can either allow yourself to relax even more into the process or just simply take a break. Go for a walk, stand up and stretch, open your eyes and look around the room. Do something to break the pattern of the moment, and then come back to several more rounds if you do not yet feel complete.

There may also be questions or statements that you don't resonate with the first time you use them. If this happens, just relax and allow the polarities to work on you subtly. Very often they will grow on you over time and may even become some of your biggest points of letting go. You can also simply tweak the wording until you feel a much more obvious release as you go back and forth.

The initial results from working with any polarity may be subtle. But as you work with a polarity, the results will become more and more profound. And if you're persistent, you'll reach a place of neutrality or a place of great expansion inside as you've dissolved the sense of limitation. Know that this can happen very quickly. Simply going back and forth a few times between two polarities can often dissolve them completely, leaving you at rest as that which you are.

Using Holistic Releasing in Everyday Life

Holistic Releasing has two purposes: it's a way of deepening the work that you're already doing with the first three methods of releasing and it's a way to deepen and open your understanding of the whole process of letting go. This process will help you to collapse, or dissolve, or let go of whatever sense of inner limitation you may be experiencing in your life. As you work with Holistic Releasing, you'll find yourself spontaneously practicing this process in life—noticing more possibilities, seeing alternatives. You will feel more flexible, more open, and much more capable of handling whatever life dishes out to you.

To use Holistic Releasing in your everyday life, do your best to start noticing how you create artificial polarities in life, and begin to bring the two sides of these polarities together. Even in just noticing them, they will start to dissolve, leaving you with greater and greater openness to the freedom that you are.

Anytime you find yourself either internally or externally being able to perceive only one possibility, there is a high likelihood that you are missing at least one or many more possibilities. Develop the habit of looking for alternatives and then doing this process to gain more inner clarity.

If you find yourself judging yourself or others, you can simply allow yourself to switch back and forth between the judgment you have and its opposite.

If you find yourself judging yourself stuck in any way, allow yourself to be as stuck as you are and as unstuck as you are.

Allow yourself to be creative as you work with this process, and you will find yourself seeing more and more possibilities and opening to having it all.

Holistic Releasing is a tool that will help you to free yourself from all of your unwanted patterns of behavior, thought and feeling. It will free you to have, be or do whatever you will or desire by showing you how to let go of whatever is inside of you that says you can't have it, shouldn't have it or don't deserve it . . . all the negative self-talk and limiting feelings and limiting beliefs that hold you back. All that it requires from you is your being as open as you can to the process. It will

I met a very attractive woman in my yoga class who I spent 4 amazing months with. As magically as it started, it ended. She actually left me without even giving me a reason why. I tried to contact her for a couple weeks to find out why she pulled away. No answer! I was in agony. I did the Holistic Releasing. Could I allow myself to hate her as much as I do . . . Could I allow myself to love her as much as I do. I was filled with the most intense bliss and peace of my life after releasing all that emotional pain. It reminded me that all the love I felt for her shouldn't end. That the love I felt was mine. I am so thankful for having loved her, and the imperturbability I now feel in relationships.

—Kurt Wagner, NJ

free you to access clearer thinking, yet it is not a thinking process. It will help you to access heightened creativity, although you don't need to be particularly creative to be effective at doing this. Once you inner negative motivators are removed, you are free to have it all.

The 5th Way of Releasing

Part of the power of The Sedona Method is that it is natural, based on what happens in us when we live life without resistance and self-obstruction as the presence-awareness that we are. Because of this, I spend a good part of my time studying what is here and now in order to unlock new ways to help us all more easily recognize and rest as the truth of who we are.

The Method is based on the premise that feelings are just feelings. They are not facts and they are not you, and you can let them go. On our retreats, we also spend time working to help each other remember that what we think we are is not us. In other words, "I" and "me" are just thoughts. They are not who we are. When that is recognized, it has a profound influence on the way life is experienced. It is very hard to take our supposed problems seriously or to cling to them when we realize that they are not, and, in fact, nothing is, actually personal.

Recognizing What You Are Not

Many times on retreats, when someone is looking to discover who he or she is or he or she is lost in "their" story—the false reference point of me—I have asked, "In this moment, if you do not go into memory, can you actually find this 'me' that you are talking about?"

I have yet to have anyone find a "me" in this moment. For most people, this brings their minds to a complete stop, and they are left resting as the presence that they have always been. Many people, rather than allow themselves to remain at rest, re-identify with the false reference point of "me" after some time of enjoying this rest. Most also find that the sense of ease and rest never fully leaves, even when it appears that presence is being obstructed by the re-emergence of this false reference point of "me."

Either way, when you examine the truth of who you are in this way, know that what you are never comes or goes, and what does come and go cannot be who you are by its very nature. If the false reference point does reappear, this does not mean that you have missed something; it only means the habit has not completely dropped away. You can always continue to remind yourself of what is actually here now or use any of the other tools that we call The Sedona Method.

In my experience, the presence-that-you-are is always here and now, and has always been. This presence is the background on or in which all experiencing appears.

Presence can also be called knowingness because it is the "cognizing" emptiness that allows for all experiencing. This knowingness that we are is closely associated with thinking. Thinking, when colored by the belief in the false reference point of "me" is limited, but as that dissolves, what is revealed is the direct knowingness that is always here and now. Thinking also gets quieter and more aligned with our natural knowingness. This shines through the mind as clear reason and intuitive knowing and infuses the body with a sense of energy and aliveness.

From time to time I add, "If there is no 'me' in this moment, is it possible that there has never been one?" And "What is here now?"

Here is how you can explore this in relationship to your feelings and problems.

When you are lost in a feeling or a story from the past or you simply would like to see through the illusion of "me," ask yourself: *Whose feeling, thought, or story is this?*

If you are identified with the false center, the answer will be "mine." If you are not identified with the false sense of "me," which may happen at any time, there may be an experience of no one and no thing taking delivery or claiming ownership of what is being experienced. If this happens, just rest as that and know that no further questioning is required.

If the answer is "mine," then ask: *In this moment, if you do not go into memory, can you actually find this "me"?*

You can also follow it up with, *If there is no me in this moment, is it possible that there has never been one?*

Allow Yourself to Also Notice What Is Here Now.

You can ask yourself: *What is actually here now?* Keep asking this simple question until you notice that all mind-generated answers dissolve. Then check to see if it is possible that the Beingness or presence of knowingness that is more obvious in this moment has always been here. In my experience, what we are is always present, but sometimes ignored.

You can also ask yourself *Are You?* And simply rest as the answer to that simple question. Then ask yourself *Could you allow that to be enough?* Keep asking these questions until you find that the mind no longer feels the need to answer and you are at rest as that which you are.

Allow this to happen naturally without forcing, and do this from your direct experience as opposed to from memory or what you think should be experienced. Also, know that this is really not a technique, but a direct looking through the illusion of separation to the ever present presence that is shining as the love and beauty that you are.

The bottom line is that when you look with an open mind and heart into what is actually being experienced here and now, two things become obvious: First, that the separate "me" with its story of suffering isn't, and what is here is simply the Beingness, presence–awareness, the knowing emptiness that allows for all experiencing.

This is like cutting the head off your problem; and if you do this with an open mind and heart as best you can, you will find that it not only causes your suffering of the moment to release, but will cause huge chunks, if not all, of your attachment to suffering to dissolve as well.

The Next Steps

Congratulations on completing *The Sedona Method*. As you apply what you've learned to your quest for having whatever it is you choose in life—including the ultimate understanding—you'll find your apparent problems dropping away and your natural freedom shining through more and more. As you incorporate releasing into your life, it will get progressively easier, as will your use of these techniques. Even what you used to consider some of your most unattainable goals will come to you with greater ease. This progression will continue until you are at rest in every moment as the Beingness that you have always been, and you see the exquisite perfection of All That Is.

The following suggestions are designed to help you get the maximum benefit from the material in this book on an ongoing basis:

1. Allow yourself to use the material in every part of your life. If you only thought about and explored freedom and letting go for a few minutes a day, you would gain tremendous benefits. However, if you allow releasing to be in your mind and heart throughout the day, your results will increase exponentially. Like everything else, the more energy you put into the process, the more you get out of it.

2. Review the material often. Every time you reread and work with the ideas in this book, you'll get more out of them. As you grow internally, you'll understand and be able to apply what you learn on deeper levels. Treat each review as though it were your first reading. Explore all the exercises with as fresh eyes as you can.

3. Join the Worldwide Releasing Community by visiting www.Sedona.com and clicking on the link that says Worldwide Releasing Community. Take advantage of the features on this site:

   • Find out about upcoming classes, free support calls, and online chats with Hale
   • Connect with a releasing partner and download releasing processes to use
   • Locate or start a releasing group in your area
   • Find a Sedona Method coach
   • Share your gains, read Hale's blog, or ask Hale a question
   • Post a job or find a job, post an ad, and check out the personals
   • Win a free retreat for your referrals
   • Peruse our complete product catalogue and find out what's on special

4. Share what you have learned. Communicating these ideas and practices with your friends, relatives, and acquaintances should stretch you and deepen your own understanding. Additional benefits come from surrounding yourself with like-minded people who are

also interested in deepening their freedom and letting go of their pain. However, please share this material only with those who are truly interested in hearing about it. Grant those you know their Beingness—see them as already perfect—whether or not they share your interest.

5. Start or join a *Sedona Method* support group. An energetic lift comes "when two or more are gathered in thy name." The larger the group, the more this energetic lift is magnified. Lester Levenson used to say that the energy in groups is "squared." In other words, two people have the power of two times two, three people have the power of three times three, and so on. Another benefit of participating in a group is seeing the material from perspectives other than your own. This can deepen your understanding. (See page 409, Guidelines for *Sedona Method* Support Groups)

6. Read the book I coauthored with Lester Levenson, *Happiness Is Free and It's Easier than You Think*. It will teach you the Holistic Releasing Process™ as well as provide you with some of the spiritual underpinnings of The Sedona Method. In the book, Lester's powerful talks and aphorisms are accompanied by my commentary and exercises.

7. Deepen your understanding of The Sedona Method® by attending live seminars or through the audio and online programs presented by Sedona Training Associates. In

this book, I've done my best to impart the entire Method in an accessible and easy-to-apply way. For many people, however, reading a book is not an adequate substitute for the experiential understanding that comes from learning the Method in a more interactive way. All these learning approaches support the others.

8. If you are part of an organization or a group that would like to implement these ideas system-wide, please feel free to contact us about our customized Sedona Method Programs.

Sedona Training Associates
60 Tortilla Drive
Sedona, AZ. 86336
(928) 282-3522 or (888) 282-5656
info@sedona.com
www.sedona.com

You are the key to your own happiness, health, well-being, and success. All you need to do is use this key to unlock the secrets of freedom and happiness that are waiting to be discovered right within your own heart.

Guidelines for
The Sedona Method
Support Groups

To find an existing Sedona Method support group or to start one, please visit The Worldwide Releasing Community (go to www.sedona.com and click on the link for the Worldwide Releasing Community), and then click on the Releasing Groups button. The goal of a group should be to support each participant in gaining the most that they can from their use of *The Sedona Method*. It is important that a safe space be created in order for everyone to feel free to participate, yet never to feel pressured to do so. Such environments are best created when a different group member is given the opportunity to be the leader each time the group meets—if they chose to do so. This policy helps prevent one individual from dominating the group. It also allows participants to stretch themselves in the direction of helping others.

Anyone who brings up an emotional or physical issue that would usually be handled by a trained medical professional should be encouraged to seek professional care. Support groups should never be used as a substitute for competent medical attention, rather as an aid to each participant's personal and spiritual growth.

Please have group participants agree amongst themselves to keep anything of a personal nature that's shared during the meeting within the group. This allows everyone who attends to have the maximum feeling of safety and comfort. This agreement can be revisited every time the group gets together.

To provide the maximum support, it is helpful to have a group meet once a week. If that frequency seems difficult, meeting once a month is still sufficient and helpful.

Especially if you are using private residences for your meetings, it is helpful to rotate locations so that the burden for hosting the support group is not borne by one person alone. However, if you can identify a centrally located, free public location, we encourage you to use that on an ongoing basis instead.

The following instructions are for the leader of the support group.

Welcome Everyone

Read the following releasing questions aloud for group participants. Then, allow a few minutes of silence in order to give everyone an opportunity to become centered and present in the room. Do your best to create a safe space for everyone attending.

Group Releasing Questions for the Beginning of a Support Group

These questions are designed as a guideline. Please get comfortable using them before you add any of the others from the book. Alternatively, if someone in your group has a set of The Sedona Method Audio Program, you may play a release from the tapes, which you can then also use as the basis for the exercises in that support group meeting.

420

Allow yourself to sit back and make yourself comfortable as you focus inside. You may close your eyes or keep them open, whichever you prefer.

Take a deep breath and allow yourself to release any tension in your body as you exhale.

Scan your body for any other tension or holding on. (Pause) If there is any tension in your body: *Could you let go of wanting to control it and allow it to release?*

Check your body again and see if any part of it is pulling at your attention. (Pause) If it is: *Could you let go of wanting to control that?*

Now, review the last 24 hours and see if there is anything about those 24 hours that you would like to change or control. (Pause) If so: *Could you let go of wanting to change or control that?*

Is there a person or situation in your life right now that is stirring up a sense of wanting approval? (Pause) If so: *Could you let go of wanting approval?*

Is there anything that you said or did recently that stirred up a sense of wanting approval? (Pause) If so: *Could you let go of that wanting approval?*

Find something in the last 24 hours that still concerns you. Is the person or situation you just thought of stirring up a sense of wanting approval, wanting to control, or wanting security or survival? (Pause) If so: *Could you allow that want to release?* (Repeat if needed.)

Is there anything about being here this evening that is stirring up any want within you? (Pause) If so, check to see if it's a sense of wanting approval, wanting to control, or wanting security or survival. (Pause) Whichever want it is:

Could you allow it to release?

Check to see if there is anything about me, as the support group leader, that stirs up a want within you. *Is it a sense of wanting approval, wanting to control, or wanting security or survival?* Whichever want it is: *Could you allow it to release?* (Repeat if needed.)

If you came with a specific issue to work on tonight, see what your NOW want is about that topic. (Pause) *Is it a sense of wanting approval, wanting to control, or wanting security or survival?* (Pause) Whichever want it is: *Could you let it go?* (Repeat if needed.)

Now, focus on whatever you want in the moment: approval, control, or security or survival. (Pause) Whatever you want: *Could you let it go?*

Focus again on your NOW want. (Pause) *Could you allow it to release?*

Take one more look inside and allow yourself to become aware of your NOW want. Whichever want it is: *Could you allow yourself to let it go?*

Gradually bring your awareness to a more external focus, and, whenever you are ready, if you haven't already, allow your eyelids to open.

Ice Breaker

Have group participants share their names and a gain that they have each experienced so far from using *The Sedona Method*.

Partner Work

Have each person in the group find a partner so they

may support each other in doing an exercise from *The Sedona Method*. Select an appropriate exercise from the book, such as general releasing, the Advantages/Disadvantages Process, the Likes/Dislikes Process, and the Cleanup Procedure. Spend approximately 30 minutes on the exercise. Either have the partners switch back and forth, taking turns facilitating each other, or time it so that each participant has about 15 minutes to do an exploration with the support of the other partner.

Ask each partner to open their copy of *The Sedona Method* to the exercise being explored, so they can remember the appropriate phrasing of the processes. Then, before breaking into partnerships, read the following statement aloud:

Instructions for Partner Work

Be there with, and for, your partners as best you can. Grant your partners their Beingness by allowing them to have their own explorations. As you facilitate your partners in releasing, also do your best to let go. You will find that this happens naturally if you are open to it. Refrain from leading your partners, judging their responses, or giving them advice. Also refrain from discussing the explorations until you have both completed them, and you have spent a few minutes in silence. Be sure to validate your partner's points of view, even if these do not agree with your own.

Please refrain from playing the role of counselor or therapist, even if you are a trained counselor or therapist. If your partner brings up a medical condition that would ordinarily require the care of a trained medical professional, recommend that he or she get whatever professional support is needed in this area. If you are not sure whether or not your partner truly needs medical support, you can recommend that he or she seek professional medical attention, just to be sure.

Have Group Share

Have volunteers from the group share what they got from doing the exercise. Make sure that the group validates their perspectives, and support them in letting go and moving up into greater freedom.

Sharing Gains

Give the group another opportunity to share gains if they choose.

Optional Release

If time allows, either read the same group releasing questions (see page 410) that were read at the beginning of the meeting—substituting the timeframe of however long the meeting lasted for the preceding 24-hour period—or play another process from The Sedona Method Audio Program.

Silence

Have the group spend a few minutes allowing their Beingness to be in silence.

Thank Everyone for Coming

Thank everyone for coming, and encourage the group to maintain the silence within as they go home or go about their day. Remind them of the date, time, and location of the next meeting and suggest that they invite their friends.

Gains from *The Sedona Method:*

Please use the space on this page and the next to share your gains from working with this material. If you would prefer, you can use a separate sheet of paper or e-mail us at info@sedona.com to send us your gains.

Gains from *The Sedona Method continued*

_____

_____

_____

_____

_____

_____

_____

_____

_____

_____

_____

_____

_____

_____

I give Sedona Training Associates permission to quote me in your publications, materials and web site. I understand that in exchange I am entitled to receive a discount on my order of Sedona Method® audio products.

Signature

Name

Address

City, State   Postal Code

Phone

E-mail Address

WE ARE HERE FOR YOU

Sedona Training Associates is dedicated to helping you liberate your true nature and to have, be, and do all that you choose. Our products have been created for this purpose. To accelerate your progress, we highly encourage you to attend one of our live seminars or purchase an audio program. The following are some of our offerings.

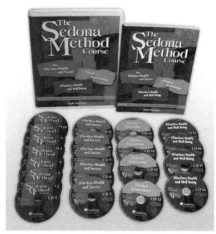

The Sedona Method Course
Plus Effortless Wealth and Success,
Effortless Relationships, and Effortless
Health and Well-being

The Harvard Medical School-studied Sedona Method will enable you to quickly and easily let go of anything holding you back from financial abundance, emotional wellness, improved relationships and radiant health.

This audio program is actually four courses in one and includes 20 CDs: 7 on mastering The Sedona Method, 5 on Effortless Wealth and Success, 4 on Effortless Relationships, and 4 on Effortless Health and Well-being. It also includes a 198-page workbook to assist you in integrating the Method into your life.

In fact it is 100% guaranteed to help you create the life that you choose for yourself NOW. This means you will literally be free to have, be and do whatever you will or desire. This process is backed by a mountain of scientific research, celebrity endorsements and the success of hundreds of thousands of people just like you who have achieved amazing breakthrough results in EVERY area of their lives.

Here is just some of what you can expect to achieve:
- Higher Self-esteem and Self-confidence
- Much Greater Relaxation and Clarity in Action and at Rest
- Freedom from the Debilitating Effects of Anger, Anxiety, Depression, Stress, Tension, Grief and Fear

- The Freedom to Live Life Fully, Happily, and Joyously every Moment
- Unshakable Inner Peace, Contentment and Satisfaction

Effortless Wealth and Success

Most of us desire to have more wealth and success in our lives. Even if we feel like we have enough, we often do not allow ourselves to create what we choose with ease. This course is dedicated to showing you how to dissolve the blocks to creating, maintaining, and enjoying effortless wealth and success.

You will gain all of this and more:
- Make More Money with Less Effort
- Access your Intuitive Knowing and Clear Reason and Make Better Investment and Life Decisions
- Free Yourself of Fear, Worry and Anxiety including Fear of Failure and Success
- Work Smarter not Harder
- Boost your Self-confidence and Flexibility
- Dissolve all the Inner Barriers to Lasting Effortless Wealth and Success

Effortless Relationships

In this course you will discover that both your personal and business relationships can be a lot more effortless, fun, loving, and mutually rewarding. This course will teach you some applications of The Sedona Method that are particularly suited to improving relationships in addition to their other applications. You will also explore and release some of the major blocks to having effortless relationships.

Here is just some of what you will gain:
- Fall in Love with Your Self and Your Partner again
- Deal with Difficult People with Grace and Ease
- Have more Open, Honest, Natural Communication
- Understand Your Partner Better and Have Them Understand You
- Take Responsibility for Your own Experience in Relationships
- Bring the Feeling of "I Am Enough" into Your Life and Your Relationships

Effortless Health and Well-being

This course will help you take the lack of ease, the "dis," out of dis-ease. Medical science now agrees that most illness has at least some psychological component and that is what this course can help you dissolve. As you let go of your stress, tension, anxiety, and frustration about whatever emotional, mental health, or physical challenges you are facing, you find that you feel better, discover the right actions to take much more easily, and support the body's natural healing process.

You will gain all of the following and more:
- Have Your Ideal Body and Feel More Love for the Body You Have
- Free Yourself from Past Traumas and Recurring Stories
- Free Yourself from the Tyranny of Guilt and Shame
- Lose Weight, Quit Smoking and Free Yourself from all Addictions
- Experience Deep Relaxation
- End Pain and Discomfort
- Feel and Look Younger and Slow or Reverse the Aging Process

Effortless Creation: The Ultimate Course on Manifesting Your Goals

With this course you will harness the excitement of our New York and San Francisco live events and propel yourself effortlessly to achieve and be whatever your heart truly desires.
- Use these unique applications of The Goals Process to create with ease.
- Exercises designed to help you to free yourself to act with effortlessness.
- Uncover your heart's desire and find your life's purpose.
- Have, be and do what you truly desire, beyond your "shoulds."
- Free yourself from the pain of lack and allow yourself to have it all.

Effortless Creation will help you to get clear on what you truly want and to let go of everything else. You will find your resistance melting away and being replaced by true happiness and the peace of being.

Effortless Creation will allow you to release all rules that are conflicting with each other or with your goal. It is very liberating to simply move beyond the world of rules, which you will do: effortlessly.

Effortless Creation helps you release all the attractions and repulsions that are preventing you from achieving your goals. Once free, you finally can have it all and simply be.

The Holistic Releasing Set: This audio set uses the fourth method of releasing known as Holistic Releasing™ exclusively. It contains two separate collections, Absolute Freedom and Practical Freedom. Absolute Freedom helps you to easily recognize and dissolve the barriers that you imagine are keeping you from perceiving your true nature. These recordings will help you to discover the natural state of Beingness that has always been available to you here and now. You will discover that who you are has only appeared to be hidden by your self-imposed sense of limitation. You have been absolutely free. Practical Freedom is designed to help you to rediscover the freedom to have, be, or do whatever you choose as an alive and practical part of your everyday life. It will help free you to perform at your best in every situation, and live your life with greater ease and clarity. As you apply Holistic Releasing™, you will find that even longstanding challenges dissolve and are replaced by a greater sense of mastery.

About the Author

HALE DWOSKIN is the CEO and Director of Training of Sedona Training Associates, an organization that teaches courses based on the emotional releasing techniques originated by his mentor, Lester Levenson. Dwoskin is the New York Times bestselling author of The Sedona Method and an international speaker. He is also one of the 24 featured teachers of the book and movie phenomenon, The Secret, and a founding member of The Transformational Leadership Council. For over 30 years he has taught The Sedona Method to individuals and corporations throughout the United States and the world.

Sedona Training Associates is an educational organization created to continue fulfilling Levenson's wish to share the practical and powerful methods he discovered for removing an individual's personal blocks to abundance, health, happiness and success. Hundreds of thousands of people from all walks of life worldwide have benefited from this work during the three-decade history of The Sedona Method® Course.

Sedona Training Associates currently offers seminars throughout the United States and the world. It also publishes books and audio programs that are distributed worldwide. www.sedona.com

Are You Ready For More?

You may also contact Sedona Training Associates for more information on our classes, corporate programs, books, and audio programs featuring The Sedona Method and other letting go processes. We offer a variety of programs and products designed to support you in your freedom and in having anything that your heart desires.

 Sedona
Training Associates

2000 Plymouth Road
Minnetonka, MN 55305-2335
Phone: (928) 282-3522
Toll-free: (888) 282-5656
Fax: (928) 203-0602
Web: www.Sedona.com and www.LettingGo.tv
E-mail: info@sedona.com

Visit www.SedonaMethodCommunity.com to find out how to access our amazing worldwide support network for people who love to release, as well as those who are dedicated to helping the planet.

- Participate in live online chats and regular releasing support teleconferences with Hale
- Connect with a vast support network of like-minded people in your geographical area—and all around the world

- Get one-on-one coaching for your particular issues
- Access all the latest releasing techniques and innovations through audio, video and Mp3 downloads
- Invite all your friends and family and help achieve Lester's dream of having 1% of the population releasing in order to bring about a radical global change in consciousness now

Find Lasting Happiness, Success, and Emotional Well-Being in just 1 hour and 8 minutes by watching the *Letting Go* movie!

What if you could . . . Let go of your fear . . . Let go of your anger . . . Let go of your sadness . . . What if you could leave all of your negative emotions and anxieties behind you forever? What if at the same time you could also create the happiness and success you have always desired? You can, by watching *Letting Go!*

Hale Dwoskin, Secret Teacher and New York Times best-selling author of The Sedona Method, has studied and mastered the art of Letting Go for over 35 years. In this inspiring, entertaining and thought-provoking movie, he reveals his wisdom – and proven, powerful and liberating techniques.

- Discover the happiness, prosperity and inner peace you deserve.
- Learn how to use these proven techniques to enrich your life.
- Learn how you can positively affect all those you care about.
- Uncover the exquisite joy and peace that is available to you now.
- Watch as individuals, just like you, come to grips with their deepest emotional burdens . . . and let them go.

Why suffer? Feel the Rejuvenating Freedom of *Letting Go!*

We tend to feel as if we have to suffer over our failures, losses or emotional stress from the past – not true!

We tend to bury troubling emotions so deep, that we don't even know they are there anymore . . . but they are waiting to explode and wreak havoc in our lives – and they hold us back from lasting success and radiant well-being.

Often, we don't realize that we feel this way . . . until we let go . . . and when we do – that's when this awe-inspiring realm of joy washes over us.

If you truly want to dissolve your emotional burdens once and for all – this movie will show you how.

At Last, You Can Finally Let Go of:
- Traumatic experiences from the past
- Limiting thoughts and beliefs
- Day-to-day anxieties
- Your inner fears
- Sadness from a lost love
- Deep-rooted anger
- Financial woes
- Frustration with your career
- Struggles with addiction

Experience the relief you feel by letting these burdens go. No matter how heavy, or light, your own personal burdens are – the *Letting Go* DVD helps you release all of the emotions that are holding you back from leading a happy life.

Plus, as you use the many tools and perspectives you have learned in this movie, the positive changes you experience in your life will cascade into the lives of all you hold dear – helping them wash their troubles away as well.

The Letting Go *Movie Shows You How to:*
- Achieve success
- Find a sense of inner peace
- Live your life the way it was meant to be
- Find longstanding happiness and joy

No longer do you have to dream about wanting all of these things – they can become a reality because your mind is clear . . . You are free of distraction and burden – and the world is yours to embrace.

The *Letting Go* Movie is an invitation for you to awaken from the dream of separation and limitation – and to live a life filled with love, happiness, abundance, joy and inner peace . . . yet this is just the beginning. Every time you watch the DVD you will continue to be amazed by your ever increasing insights and breakthroughs.

Get your *Letting Go* DVD today with some great bonuses including an immediate free view of the movie for just $19.97 + S&H!

Visit http://www.lettinggo.tv/SMBOOK to claim your special bonuses just because you have read this book.